Contents

Contents

The Sociology of the Health Service

Edited by

Jonathan Gabe,
Michael Calnan

and

Michael Bury

London and New York

First published in 1991
by Routledge
11 New Fetter Lane, London EC4P 4EE

Simultaneously published in the USA and Canada
by Routledge
a divsion of Routledge, Chapman and Hall Inc.
29 West 35th Street, New York, NY 10001

Typeset by LaserScript Limited, Mitcham, Surrey
Printed and bound in Great Britain by Mackays of Chatham PLC, Kent

British Library Cataloguing in Publication Data
The sociology of the health service.
 1. Great Britain. National health services – Sociological
perspectives
 I. Gabe, Jonathan II. Calnan, Michael, *1949-* III. Bury,
Michael, *1945-*
362.10420941

Library of Congress Cataloging in Publication Data
The Sociology of the health service/edited by Jonathan Gabe, Michael
Calnan, and Michael Bury.
 p. cm.
Includes bibliographical references and index.
 1. National Health Service (Great Britain) 2. Social medicine—
Great Britain. I. Gabe, Jonathan. II. Calnan, Michael.
III. Bury, Michael, 1945–
RA395.G6S64   1991
362.1'0941—dc20   90–38052
                                                            CIP

ISBN 0–415–03158–3
      0–415–03159–1 (pbk)

The Sociology of the Health Service

Why have health policy issues been so neglected by sociologists?

Despite health and health care having recently risen to the top of the political and policy agenda in Britain and elsewhere, little attention has been paid to health policy issues by sociologists researching health and illness.

The Sociology of the Health Service responds directly to the need to develop a sociological analysis of current health policy. Topics covered vary from privatization and health service management to health education and the politics of professional power. Also included is a historical review of sociology's contributions to health policy and proposals for an agenda for sociological health policy in the 1990s.

The Sociology of the Health Service will be of immediate interest to undergraduates and lecturers in medical sociology and social policy, also to policy analysts, health planners, medical sociologists, medical journalists and health service workers.

Jonathan Gabe lectures in medical sociology at Royal Holloway and Bedford New College, and University College and Middlesex Hospital Medical School, University of London; Michael Calnan is a Reader in Sociology of Health Studies at the University of Kent and Michael Bury is Senior Lecturer in Sociology at Royal Holloway and Bedford New College. All have published widely in the areas of medical sociology and health care.

Contributors

Alan Beattie Senior Research Fellow, Centre for Health Research, University of Lancaster.

Michael Bury Senior Lecturer, Department of Social Policy and Social Science, Royal Holloway and Bedford New College, University of London.

Michael Calnan Reader, Centre for Health Service Studies, University of Kent.

Angela Coulter Research Officer, Unit of Clinical Epidemiology, University of Oxford.

David Cox Professor, Department of Health Studies, Birmingham Polytechnic.

Mary Ann Elston Lecturer, Department of Social Policy and Social Science, Royal Holloway and Bedford New College/Department of Community Medicine, University College and Middlesex Hospital Medical School, University of London.

Jonathan Gabe Lecturer, Department of Social Policy and Social Science, Royal Holloway and Bedford New College, University College and Middlesex Hospital Medical School, University of London.

Margot Jefferys Emeritus Professor, Department of Social Policy and Social Science, Royal Holloway and Bedford New College, University of London.

Hilary Land Professor, Department of Social Policy and Social Science, Royal Holloway and Bedford New College, University of London.

John Mohan Lecturer, Department of Geography, Queen Mary and Westfield College, University of London.

Margaret Stacey Emeritus Professor, Department of Sociology, University of Warwick.

Preface

In recent years health and health care have come to occupy a central place in the cultures of industrialized societies. As part of this process people are regularly confronted with health-related information and problems. At the same time health and health care have risen to the top of the political and policy agenda both in Britain and elsewhere and now stand at the meeting point of a range of social conflicts. These in turn relate to profound changes in the social, economic and political map of Britain and other countries.

In our view the sociology of health and illness has only recently begun to inform explicitly the analysis of policy-related problems which these changes involve and its potential has yet to be fully realized. In order to facilitate the development of a sociological analysis of health policy, we have invited a number of sociologists and policy analysts to discuss a range of contemporary health policy issues and suggest areas for future research. All the contributors originally attended a seminar which we organized on the *Sociology of the Health Service* at the Kings Fund Centre in London in December 1988, with funding from the Economic and Social Research Council and the Medical Sociology Group of the British Sociological Association.

We believe that such a book should have an appeal for a number of reasons. First, while policy analysts have offered discussions of the British National Health Service (NHS) and its development (e.g. Allsop 1984; Ham 1982; Klein 1989), there has not been a major review of sociological approaches to British health policy since *The Sociology of the NHS*, edited by Margaret Stacey, over a decade ago. Our book is thus filling a gap in the literature.

Second, such a gap needs to be filled because of the widespread concern about the future of the NHS and the need for current debate about this subject to be informed by a sociological perspective. It is hoped that the book will appeal not only to medical sociologists, but also to a much wider audience, including health planners, policy analysts, medical journalists, health service workers and interested members of the public.

References

Allsop, J. (1984) *Health Policy and the National Health Service*, Harlow: Longman.

Ham, C. (1982) *Health Policy in Britain*, London: Macmillan.

Klein, R. (1989) *The Politics of the National Health Service*, 2nd edn, Harlow: Longman.

Stacey, M. (ed.) (1976) *The Sociology of the Health Service*, London: Routledge & Kegan Paul.

Introduction
Jonathan Gabe, Michael Calnan and Michael Bury

The essays which comprise this volume seek to highlight the contribution which sociologists and policy analysts with a sociological orientation can make to understanding a range of crucial issues currently facing the health service in Britain.

These issues are presently high on the political agenda and are a topic of media and popular concern. Yet, sociologists in recent years have given them relatively little attention. Why should this be so? In the following pages we seek to answer this question by documenting the development of medical sociology in Britain since 1945, both in relation to its parent discipline and the health policy context. In so doing we shall be providing a historical framework for the chapters which follow.

To facilitate this task we shall distinguish three broad phases of activity in British sociology. The first concerns the period from the end of the Second World War through to the early 1960s, during which sociology began to develop a distinctive disciplinary base in Britain. The second deals with the period of the late 1960s and 1970s which saw a number of new currents running through sociological enquiry. The third takes us from there until the present – the context of current activity and debate.

Sociology in post-war Britain

This first period followed hard on the establishment of the welfare state in Britain, including, of course, the founding of the National Health Service. Sociologists at this time were preoccupied with two basic sets of questions. On the one hand they were concerned with studies of poverty and community life, and of surveys of the impact of class-based inequalities which underpinned both of these. On the other hand, policy-oriented work was preoccupied with the equitable distribution and uptake of welfare and health services. Indeed, some influential figures such as David Glass at the London School of Economics linked the two with investigations of social mobility and a commitment to research

1

directed to policy ends (Bulmer 1989).

Challenges to this largely empirical tradition came during this period from more theoretically informed American sociologists, most notably Edward Shils and Talcott Parsons (Halsey 1982). Not only did these theorists point up the limits of an empiricist sociology, but they also challenged the substantive preoccupations of sociologists in Britain. Shils, for example, argued that some of the most popular institutions in British public life, such as the Royal Family, had never been taken seriously. Indeed, Edward Shils and Michael Young (1953) published a paper on the subject at the time of the coronation.

At this time medical sociology only existed in an embryonic form. Those sociologists concerned with health and health care worked largely within the Fabian tradition of social reform and occupied themselves with the task of consolidating the health service. They were thus concerned with how the service operated, what inhibitors there were to an equitable access to and distribution of the service and to increase understanding among participants in the service (Stacey and Homans 1978).

Many of the problems on which medical sociologists worked were defined directly by others, particularly public health specialists within the medical profession, or were set by the agenda of the medically dominated funding agencies (Illsley 1975). Not surprisingly, therefore, medical definitions of health and health-care problems were largely taken for granted. Moreover, sociologists who worked on health questions were not generally regarded as in the mainstream of the parent discipline and, isolated from departments of sociology (Johnson 1975), remained 'curiously incurious' about the assumptions on which medical care was based (Jefferys 1980).

In some ways the messages coming from American colleagues were themselves ambivalent on this point. Parsons (1951), for example, had used health and medical care as fruitful examples of the overall working of the social system. In this context health became sociologically defined as central to the value system of post-war American life, and doctoring to its pattern of social control. Other sociologists incorporated mental health and medicine as key social problem areas, but writers such as C. Wright Mills (1959) and Howard Becker (1963) specifically excluded physical ill health from their analyses of the sociological imagination and deviancy.

In this first period, then, medical sociology was struggling to find both its intellectual footing and an independent approach to both medical and policy issues. Health policy was very much under the control of those wedded to traditional (in Britain, Labour Party) loyalties, who saw little to question about the nature of medical knowledge or activity as such. The emphasis on increasing availability and access to services pulled in the opposite direction.

However, as British sociology came to take up the theoretical assaults of their American counterparts, and pay greater attention to fundamental issues such as conflict and power (e.g. Rex 1961), so medical sociology began to define its task in more consistently sociological terms.

The break with consensus

The second period we have marked out, namely that of the late 1960s and 1970s, saw the rapid development of a more 'critical' sociology and the growth of specialist areas such as medical sociology. During this period structuralist Marxist thought from France, the Frankfurt school of 'critical sociology' and phenomenology, in the guise of ethnomethodology and symbolic interactionism from the United States, came to challenge the dominance of structural functionalism and empiricism in British sociology (Halsey 1989). This process was aided by the student unrest and increasing economic and cultural power of youth in the late 1960s (Dennis 1989) and by the cold war, which denied explanations of social order in terms of Parsons' ultimate social values.

For many conservative-minded sociologists and social policy analysts, these developments confirmed their worst fears about the discipline. For others it gave the discipline a new injection of energy and broke its cosy relationship with the (Labour) establishment, and with so-called 'positivist' survey methods (Bulmer 1989). The resurgence of feminism and the growth of interest in such areas as deviancy attracted a widespread following among younger sociologists, providing them with a new territory on which to establish their own line of enquiry.

One consequence of this theoretical pluralism, however, was that sociological 'positivism' was transformed into 'one form or another of sociological "negativism" ' (Dennis 1989: 427) The assumption that society was basically benign, suffering from evils which were reformable, was replaced by an anti-authoritarianism which did not lend itself to sociologically informed policy-orientated research. Instead, those advocating these new theoretical approaches were primarily concerned with critique and the unmasking of a previously taken-for-granted benign social reality.

Medical sociology also developed rapidly in this period, with a new-found confidence that could challenge both the conservatism of Parsonian theory and the acceptance of medical definitions in the health field itself. Of the theoretical alternatives mentioned, phenomenology proved the most influential, with much work focusing on the patient's viewpoint and the nature of doctor–patient interaction (Gerhardt 1989). Indeed, a third of the papers in the two published volumes from the 1976 British Sociological Association Conference on the sociology of health and illness could be said to reflect these microsociological concerns (Stacey with Homans 1978).

At a macrolevel, a more critical perspective towards medical power was developed. In particular, Freidson's (1970) wide-ranging critique of medicine's monopoly over the definition and treatment of illness and different forms of Marxist analysis of medical power (e.g. Navarro 1976; Johnson 1977) encouraged medical sociologists in Britain to stop seeing the medical profession's claim to expertise and power as a legitimate and benign form of social control, as in the earlier period. Instead, it was seen as oppressive, being characterized as either a mask for unaccountable professional power (in the case of Freidson), or wider class interests (in the case of Marxists such as Navarro). From either standpoint the medical profession's dominance needed to be curtailed or made more accountable, and, if necessary, regulated by the state.

This view of the power of the medical profession as oppressive subsequently influenced those microsociologists employing both interactionist (e.g. Bloor 1976) and feminist (Barrett and Roberts 1978) perspectives and ironically led to the claim that medical sociology itself had become imperialistic: searching for, focusing on and exaggerating the negative aspects of medical practice for its own professional purposes (Strong 1979).

Equally significant, such 'negativism' and naive anti-authoritarianism encouraged medical sociologists to ignore policy-related questions, and this tendency was enhanced by the lack of any major public conflict over health care. For the majority of sociologists during this period, their 'critical' preoccupation with medical power seemed a potent enough issue, and one which could be tackled by means of structural analysis or ethnographic field work rather than by studying either policy development or policy enactment.

Retrenchment in adversity

Since the late 1970s, sociology in Britain has had to operate in a cold political climate and in the face of hostility from neoconservative politicians who look upon proponents of the discipline as 'folk devils' responsible for inducing moral panic (Halsey 1989). In such a climate it is hardly surprising that governmental support for sociological teaching and independent research has been meagre. Nor has the discipline's development been helped by the cuts in the ESRC's (Economic and Social Research Council) budget.

Faced with such uncertainty sociologists have looked to their laurels and have recovered their interest in the classic traditions in theory and method. As Bulmer (1989) has noted, there has been a proliferation of theoretical essays concerned with what has been said previously about a phenomenon (e.g. the nature of capitalism or anomie) or about a body of knowledge (such as the works of the classic theorists). At the same time, and with the encouragement of the ESRC (1987), there has been a resurgence of interest in quantitative methods and in secondary analysis in particular (e.g. Dale *et al.* 1987). And some of those associated with the anti-positivism of the 1970s have now rejected the quantitative/ qualitative distinction as a false polarity (Silverman 1985) or argued that ethnographers should be concerned with testing theories in the same way as quantitative sociologists (Hammersley 1985).

The sociology of health and illness has in many respects mirrored these developments. For instance, there have been a number of attempts to develop the subdiscipline's theoretical base by showing how the work of particular grand theorists illuminates the study of health, disease and medicine (Scambler 1987) and by establishing the different theoretical paradigms employed in explaining illness and their relationship to general sociological theory (Gerhardt 1989). These have recently been taken a step further under the impact of Foucault's writings and this has led to renewed theoretical debate about illness and its definitions (Armstrong 1983; Bury 1986). Likewise, quantitative methods have been making a comeback in, for example, secondary analyses of health-care data contained in the Office of Population Censuses and Surveys' (OPCS) General Household Survey (e.g. Arber and Gilbert 1989).

At the same time medical sociology, unlike its parent discipline, has been protected to some extent from the worst consequences of re-trenchment by its historical relationship with social medicine and epidemiology. This has been a mixed blessing, however. On the one hand, such an association has provided employment opportunities in an otherwise shrinking job market, as funding for medical sociology research units has been progressively withdrawn. On the other hand, those working as sociologists 'in medicine' (Straus 1957) have had to surrender much of the responsibility for selecting topics for investigation to physicians and to civil servants, as Illsley (1975) predicted. Moreover, as Scambler (1987) has argued, the combination of government cut-backs in research funding, together with its commitment to the more efficient allocation of health resources is resulting in an increasing number of medical sociologists doing research which is policy led and accepting of medical diagnostic categories. For example, the large-scale funding of research in AIDS, whilst providing new opportunities for medical sociology, illustrates the danger of a return to research being defined primarily by policy makers and clinicians.

Such a context provides few opportunities to develop a rigorous, reflexive sociological analysis of health policy issues. Yet, such an analysis is highly desirable, especially at a time when health and health policy have come to occupy a more central place in debates about the future of the welfare state and the impact of consumerism, and as the social consensus over the NHS is undergoing severe strain. The issues addressed in this volume relate to the emergence of a crisis over the development of health care in Britain. The chapters which follow attempt to discuss key aspects of this crisis, and in so doing provide an opportunity for rethinking the relevance of sociological propositions in the health field and thus for sociology to be more policy relevant.

The themes discussed in the book come out of current policy debates, although they also address issues of long-standing concern. Each contributor has been asked to analyse their subject in terms of the changes in the social context of health service provision since the mid-1970s. In this way it is hoped that the book will provide a useful update to Margaret Stacey's (1976) edited volume on *The Sociology of the NHS* which contained the last distinctively sociological analysis of British health policy.

In the first chapter, Margaret Stacey considers the development of medical sociology since the publication of her book and her state-of-the-art paper (written with Hilary Homans) 'The sociology of health and illness', published in *Sociology* in 1978. Using these as a bench mark, she surveys emerging themes in the subdiscipline by sampling books and articles in recent issues of *Sociology of Health and Illness, Social Science and Medicine* and *International Journal of Health Services*, and reported research in the research register, *Medical Sociology in Britain*. On the basis of these data, she argues that the knowledge base of sociology as applied to health care and health policy has been consolidated over the last decade, although much of this work has been done outside sociology departments. As a result of working closely with practitioners and researchers from other disciplines, however, she suggests that much of this work has been directed at health policy at the microlevel of professional patient contact and less at the macrolevel of the state, corporation and industry. Even so, it can be argued that interpretive sociology's concern with policy has been largely implicit in the sense that it has not directly addressed the public issues of health-care organization and politics. These more macro-issues, which are the focus of so much current public concern are addressed by the other contributors to this volume.

The next chapter by John Mohan considers privatization in the context of current policy and political debate in Britain. He examines the meaning of the term before considering some of the motivations for and explanations of privatization. In this regard he pays particular attention to the political and social forces that have brought this policy about. He then evaluates it in terms of its stated aims and actual impact as regards new forms of service delivery inside the NHS (e.g. income-generating activities) and new resources being generated for health care (e.g. a renewed emphasis on charitable activity). The chapter ends with a discussion about likely future developments and whether privatization is compatible with the maintenance of the National Health Service.

In the third chapter Mary Ann Elston analyses the politics of professional power, focusing on the possibility that medicine's professional dominance is beginning to wane. This is first explored theoretically by means of a critical review of proletarianisation and deprofessionalization – two theses which have been developed to explain the changes taking place in medical power and authority in the United States. These arguments are then related to two broad challenges facing the British medical profession: first a challenge to its freedom from managerial accountability to the state as buyer of medical services, which is significant according to the proletarianization thesis; and second a 'consumerist' challenge to its cultural authority and right to self-regulation, which advocates deprofessionalization stress. The medical profession's responses to these challenges is also discussed, including its attempts to defend existing arrangements in the name of 'clinical freedom' and its creation of new roles to enable it to exercise continued control over its members.

The next chapter by David Cox on health service management describes its recent history and its relationship to health administration. The reasons for management occupying a central place on the policy stage are considered before attention is focused on the Griffiths Report and the sociological and political factors which have influenced its appearance. The impact of the report on social relationships such as those between managers and health workers and on decision making within the NHS are then assessed. Finally, Cox outlines three key areas in health service management which could benefit from the application of a sociological perspective.

Recent proposals for changes in the health service, including the emphasis on management to control expenditure and improve quality, bring forward the thorny issues of the quality of care and its evaluation. In the fifth chapter Angela Coulter outlines the different levels and types of evaluation of health care and the main problems they involve, whether in terms of whole services or specific procedures. Following Donabedian, she examines the value of controlled trials in evaluating medical procedures, as well as their limits, especially where a variety of social factors influence or constitute outcomes. The chapter then focuses on one particular procedure – hysterectomy. Variations in rates of surgery are noted as is the tendency for research to touch on only one or other of a range of outcomes. In the final part of the chapter, Coulter goes on to outline an 'evaluation strategy' which could bring these various outcome measures together in a research programme, including sociological research.

The sixth chapter, by Michael Calnan and Jonathan Gabe, explores recent developments in general practice in terms of the sociological literature on medicine as a profession. Having outlined the current theoretical approaches to the medical profession (e.g. professional dominance, deprofessionalization and proletarianization) and their relationship to classic sociological theory, the authors explore the explanatory power of these approaches in relation to the changes which have taken place in primary care since the publication of the GP charter in 1965. Three main themes of relevance to occupational development are explored: general practitioners' relationship with hospital doctors and other health-related occupations, their relationship with the state and their relationship with their patients. This provides the basis for some critical comments about the various theoretical approaches and generates a series of questions about the likely impact on primary care of recent health policy concerning, for example, consumer sovereignty.

The next chapter, by Alan Beattie, seeks to clarify and review the disputes about the nature of health promotion in the light of social theory. He starts by developing a conceptual framework or 'structural map' for understanding the different forms of contemporary health promotion (health persuasion, legislative action, personal counselling and community development) and then uses this map to explore the tensions and conflicts found in policy and practice in this field. He then highlights some of the points at which debates about health promotion may benefit from rethinking within the terms of both middle- and longer-range social theory. Thus, attention is given to the relationship between policy debates about health promotion and the middle-range theoretical concerns of social administration and longer-range structuralist theory, following writers such as Bernstein and Foucault. He ends with some directions for further social enquiry.

In the eighth chapter Hilary Land tackles the longstanding yet urgent issue of community care. She first provides a historical sketch of the division of responsibilities between government departments for providing community care and its reinforcement, as a result of the recent government decision to separate the Departments of Health and Social Services. 'Community care' turns out to have a variety of meanings depending on the political and social circumstances of the day. Originally, she notes, it was developed in contrast to 'institutional' care. Now, however, rather than *providing* alternative forms of care in the community, local and national government agencies are being urged to *manage* such care. In her view, the renewed emphasis on the private sector means, at the informal level of care, a greater reliance on the family and carers, particularly women, without any provision for their needs. She concludes that these issues of shifting boundaries, at the formal and informal level, constitute the new agenda of 'community care' and need to be the focus of research if the term is to mean more than an ideological mask for cost cutting.

In the concluding chapter Margot Jefferys looks ahead and considers an agenda for sociological health-policy research in the 1990s. She starts by outlining the main changes which are likely to occur in the National Health Service over the remaining years of this century, with particular reference to hospitals, general practice and community care. The planned changes are seen as determining the research issues which will confront sociologists concerned with medicine and health care. She then considers the likely research interests of the Department of Health – the major client for health services research in Britain – and the contribution which sociologists might make. In her view, such socio-logists will be working in multi- or inter-disciplinary teams, which means that they are likely to be in a subordinate position, working on problems which are not of their choosing. However, she believes that this still provides sociologists with an important opportunity to con-tribute to a greater understanding of the processes and structure of health care. At the same time, she emphasizes the need for independently funded research on health policy which deals with the major concerns of classic sociological theory.

The future for sociologists of medicine and health care would thus seem to involve undertaking both policy-led and theoretically informed policy-relevant work. If so, it is hoped that the contributors to this volume have highlighted the value of the discipline in both these respects, while at the same time providing encouragement for medical sociologists to take a more proactive role in matters of health policy in the years ahead.

References

Armstrong, D. (1983) *Political Anatomy of the Body – Medical Knowledge in Britain in the Twentieth Century*, Cambridge: Cambridge University Press.

Arber, S. and Gilbert, N. (1989) 'Men: the forgotten carers', *Sociology* 23: 111–18.

Barrett, M. and Roberts, H. (1978) 'Doctors and their patients: the social control of women in general practice', in C. Smart and B. Smart (eds) *Women, Sexuality and Social Control*, London: Routledge & Kegan Paul.

Becker, H.S. (1963) *Outsiders: Studies in the Sociology of Deviance*, New York: Free Press.

Bloor, M. (1976) 'Professional autonomy and client exclusion: a study in ENT clinics', in M. Wadsworth and D. Robinson (eds) *Studies in Everyday Medical Life*, London: Martin Robertson.

Bulmer, M. (1989) 'Theory and method in recent British sociology: whither the empirical impulse', *British Journal of Sociology* 40: 393–417.

Bury, M. (1986) 'Social constructionism and the development of medical sociology', *Sociology of Health and Illness* 8: 137–69.

Dale, A., Arber, S. and Proctor, M. (1987) *Doing Secondary Analysis*, London: Allen & Unwin.

Dennis, N. (1989) 'Sociology and the spirit of sixty-eight', *British Journal of Sociology* 40: 418–41.

Economic and Social Research Council (ESRC) (1987) *Horizons and Opportunities in the Social Sciences*, London: ESRC.

Freidson, E. (1970) *The Profession of Medicine: A Study in the Sociology of Applied Knowledge*, New York: Dodd Mead.

Gerhardt, U. (1989) *Ideas About Illness*, Basingstoke: Macmillan.

Halsey, A.H. (1982) 'Provincials and professionals: the British post-war sociologists', *Archives of European Sociology* 23: 150–75.

—— (1989) 'A turning of the tide? The prospects for sociology in Britain', *British Journal of Sociology* 40: 353–73.

Hammersley, M. (1985) 'From ethnography to theory: a programme and paradigm in the sociology of education', *Sociology* 19: 244–59.

Illsley, R. (1975) 'Promotion to observer status', *Social Science and Medicine* 9: 63–7.

Jefferys, M. (1980) 'Doctors' orders. The past, present and future of medical sociology', paper to the British Sociological Association annual conference 'Practice and progress: British Sociology 1950–1980', Lancaster University.

Johnson, M.L. (1975) 'Medical sociology and sociological theory', *Social Science and Medicine* 9: 227–32.

Johnson, T.J. (1977) 'The professions in the class structure', in R. Scase (ed.) *Industrial Society: Class Cleavage and Control*, London: Allen & Unwin.

Mills, C.W. (1959) *The Sociological Imagination*, Oxford: Oxford University Press.

Navarro, V. (1976) *Medicine Under Capitalism*, New York: Prodist.

Parsons, T. (1951) *The Social System*, Glencoe: Free Press.

Rex, J. (1961) *Key Problems in Sociological Theory*, London: Routledge & Kegan Paul.

Scambler, G. (ed.) (1987) *Sociological Theory and Medical Sociology*, London: Tavistock Publications.

Shils, E. and Young, M. (1953) 'The meaning of the coronation', *Sociological Review* 1: 63–81.

Silverman, D. (1985) *Qualitative Methodology and Sociology*, Aldershot: Gower.

Stacey, M. with Homans, H. (1978) 'The sociology of health and illness: its present state, future prospects and potential for health research', *Sociology* 12: 281–307.

Straus, R. (1957) 'The nature and status of medical sociology', *American Sociological Review* 22: 200–4.

Strong, P.M. (1979) 'Sociological imperialism and the profession of medicine', *Social Science and Medicine* 13A: 613–9.

Chapter one

Medical sociology and health policy: an historical overview
Margaret Stacey

The sociology of medicine in the mid-1970s

My brief is to review the role which medical sociology has played in relation to health policy since the mid-1970s. It was in 1975 that Raymond Illsley declared that medical sociology had come of age (Illsley 1975). Sociology is now widely recognised in all the health-care professions and is treated as a basic science in the majority of curricula, although some struggles continue. Practising professionals continually turn to sociologists for elucidation of aspects of their work.

The world around us has changed a very great deal in the period under review. In 1975 the excitement of the radical democratic mood of the late 1960s was still about and influencing everyone whatever their view of those events may have been. The new feminist movement was in full swing. The ancillary workers' strike of 1973, a strike previously unthinkable, had had a lasting effect on inter-occupational relations in the health service, even though it may not have greatly altered the order of the division of health labour or the associated material differentials.

Policy to introduce organizational changes, such as the introduction of capitalist managerialism into the NHS, had already been initiated by government in the 1960s. Many had not even begun to understand the long-term implications of these changes, but its importance did not go unnoticed in medical sociology, where it was subjected to scrutiny in the mid-1970s (e.g. Carpenter 1977; Manson 1977). The extent to which the implications of these changes went in a contrary direction to the aspirations of the radical movements of 1968 had not yet been fully taken in. Furthermore, in 1975, none imagined that fifteen years hence a radically reforming right-wing government would have so profoundly challenged the basic assumptions of the NHS and of the professions: a challenge more successful and more fundamental than that of the ancillary workers.

11

The World Health Organization's Alma Alta declaration in 1978 called for policies to reorientate health services towards positive health and primary health care, rather than concentrating on disease treatment and high-technology medicine. In the 1970s, medical doctors still confidently talked of the defeat of all epidemic diseases, being particularly elated at the claimed eradication of smallpox. Now AIDS has ironically elevated consideration of health matters to Cabinet level. While the 'greying of the nation' and the need for policy to prepare for its impact was already in the mid-1970s recognized by some analysts, its implications for health and social services, as well as for the elderly themselves, was not so strongly felt as it has been since. Furthermore, in the 1980s unemployment levels have been higher than at any time since the 1930s, coinciding with extensive cuts in public expenditure. The health implications of these developments are only now beginning to be systematically counted.

All in all, the context in which the chapters in this volume have been written is radically different from that of the mid-1970s. This radical change has also had a profound impact on the opportunities for sociological research. The social sciences were early singled out as targets for cuts in public expenditure and sociology departments have been subject to contraction and closure over the past 15 years. In 1976 *Medical Sociology in Britain*, The British Sociological Association's register of research and teaching, included 151 personal entries, a number which rose to 215 by 1982 but fell to 186 in 1986. In 1976 41 of the 151 entrants were located in sociology departments, departments in which sociology was named in part of their title, or in medical sociology units. This had fallen to 36 out of 215 by 1982 and to 35 out of 186 by 1986. The proportion, however, but not the absolute numbers, had increased, showing the strength of the subdiscipline within sociology.

The expenditure cuts have directly affected research. Whereas there were three medical sociology units in 1976, there is now only one in Britain – in Scotland – and none in England or Wales. George Brown's Medical Research Council (MRC) team (a unit in all but name) specializing in social triggers to ill health has continued throughout the period under review. Taken with the cuts in sociology departments, the reduction in the numbers of more generalized medical sociology units means that most of the medical sociological research work is now taking place in interdisciplinary or multidisciplinary units or in medical or nursing schools. While 509 research projects were recorded in 1978, by 1982 there were 274 (Field and Clarke 1982: 79) and 220 in 1986.

How has medical sociology responded to the changes of the past fifteen years? What has been its contribution during this period to health policy?

Records of the state of the art in the mid-1970s

There are three bench marks which give an indication of the state of the art in medical sociology in the mid-1970s and what its contribution to health-care policy at that time was. The first is the Sociological Review Monograph, *The Sociology of the NHS*, which I edited (Stacey 1976a) and which included examples of sociological work relevant to the National Health Service. The second is the British Sociological Association conference of 1976 which was 'a far cry from that of 1953 reported by Marshall (1953) and discussed by Illsley (1975) and Reid (1975–76), when one-third of the sessions were devoted to health, but five of the seven papers were read by doctors' (Stacey with Homans 1978). Two volumes of papers emerged, both of which included articles relevant to health policy as well as others of a more fundamental nature (Dingwall *et al*. 1977; Stacey *et al*. 1977). The third marker is the 1977 report to the Social Science Research Council (SSRC) 'The contribution of the sociology of health and illness to health and health policy research' which I prepared with the help of Hilary Homans. This was designed as a guide to the SSRC for their future research-funding policy in the health area. Part of this was later published as a state-of-the-art paper (Stacey with Homans, 1978).

Sociology and health policy: some meanings and definitions

Before I proceed to summarize the contribution of sociology to health policy up to the mid-1970s and to review what it has been since, it would be well to define my terms. Sociology is what in medical education is understood as a basic science and in the humanities as a fundamental discipline. It constitutes a body of knowledge about societies and social relations within them and takes as its subject matter all areas of the social. Healing practices and their associated institutions are one such area. Analysis is not confined to biomedicine, nor to the activities of registered medical practitioners. The sociological analysis takes account of the historical development of medical knowledge, occupations and facilities as well as paying attention to comparative healing practices and institutions over time and space. Most sociologists take for granted the idea that healing knowledge and healing practices are socially constructed, although the level at which this construction can be taken to occur, and quite what the relationship between the biological base and medical knowledge and practice is, is in some dispute (Bury 1986, 1987; Nicolson and McLaughlin 1987, 1988).

This fundamental knowledge, these findings of the basic science, may be applied to assist the solution of problems in policy or practice.

In this chapter I am to discuss its application specifically to health policy. By health policy I understand those managerial, collective or aggregated individual decisions which affect the way in which health care is delivered. Health policy thus, includes the care and treatment policies developed by consultant clinicians, nurses, midwives and their teams, firms or divisions. It also includes the policies promulgated by general managers, health authorities, the Department of Health and those in charge of private health-care arrangements. It is important, I think, to recognise that policy decisions are taken at all levels from those of government, which have the most global effect, to those which directly impact on the treatment patients in a particular facility may receive. Mine may be a broader definition than that taken by some policy analysts, but it is of the nature of the division of health labour that health-care policy emerges from all these decision-making locales. Furthermore, sociology can be and is applied to policies at all these levels. If this is not recognized, an inadequate account of the socio-logical contribution results.

The second aspect which requires clarification is how sociology comes to be applied to health policy and the organizational contexts in which the relevant research is undertaken. There are four main ways in which the sociological contribution to the study of health policy may be made, some direct, others indirect. First, sociology as a basic science contributes to a number of other disciplines, for example, social policy, health studies. It also contributes to practice disciplines such as medicine and nursing, being used in initial training and as a research tool to help elucidate problems in treatment, care or management. Third, it may make a direct contribution to health-policy formation at the most general level through analyses of the social aspects of health and illness, of the social impact of existing health policies. Finally, it may contribute to specific developments in health policy. Its importance in under-standing and interpreting the social aspects of the HIV/AIDS syndrome may be cited as a currently important example.

These contributions may be made by sociologists working from their single-discipline base in university or polytechnic departments or by sociologists working as members of teams. In the latter circumstance, they may be working in a multidisciplinary manner developing an understanding of the sociological aspects of a common problem upon which members of other disciplines are also working. The teams may, on the other hand, be working in an interdisciplinary manner, in which case the sociological contribution will be one among others which will seek to establish a new integrated body of knowledge about the common topic. This last mode of working is the most difficult, in so far as it requires not only that each team member shall comprehend the con-ceptual foundation of the others, but that they should come to agreement about the conceptual foundation which they are using for their common enterprise. Probably many teams which set out to be interdisciplinary in practice turn out to be multidisciplinary. The Open University's course 'Health and Disease' (Black *et al.* 1984; U205a–h 1985) is an outstanding attempt at the undergraduate level to provide a course which makes such a common understanding possible across the natural and social sciences and lays the basis for movement towards interdisciplinary understanding. The course is itself predicated upon the knowledge developed by the basic sciences, social and natural, which compose it.

When set out like this, it becomes clear how frequently the sociological contribution to the analysis and establishment of health policy is an indirect one, the sociological knowledge feeding into a more general stream. Reference to *Index Medicus*, for example, shows that there is medical awareness of the importance of the social in many aspects of practice, but few specifically sociological papers. Sociologists must often wish the medical comprehension of the social was rather more disciplined. Finally, one should remember that with regard to health policy, as with any other policy area, much of the contribution of sociology comes through the way in which its researches lead to the reconceptualization of everyday thinking, so that the origins are obscured. This comes about because it is the task of sociology to lay bare the foundations of our society (as well as of other societies) and, from this, fundamental rethinking of values, attitudes and approaches may emerge. These contributions occur in health policy as elsewhere. The sociological in this case again joins with other sources of reappraisal. Necessarily, in the analysis which follows, the historic contribution of sociology to health policy will be focused on the more obvious, direct and visible contributions the discipline has made.

The state of the art in the mid-1970s

The 1978 state-of-the-art paper (Stacey with Homans, 1978: 281) showed how the origins of the sociology of medicine were rooted in practical concerns rather than deriving from sociological theory or general sociology. It pointed out that medical practitioners and researchers, health-care administrators, patients' movements and the feminist movement had all encouraged sociologists to turn their attention to health and illness issues. The then state of the subdiscipline was 'one of great activity, but little theoretical or methodological unity' (Stacey with Homans 1978: 281). For sociology, still influenced by the upheavals of the late 1960s, it was after all the time of 'the thousand flowers'.

The research contribution over the preceding five years had been to:

15

1. the social, including occupational, causes or consequences of particular illnesses, handicapping conditions and treatment;
2. health and illness aspects of particular stages of the life cycle; pregnancy, birth, development, family, old age, dying;
3. the division of labour in health care, notably:
   (a) work and occupation,
   (b) relationships between health-care professionals and patients,
   (c) the patient as a participant in health care;
4. the production and reproduction of knowledge about health, illness and treatment;
5. the organization of health care and associated processes;
6. the relationship to health and illness of major structural divisions, notably social class, sex and gender and race.

(Stacey with Homans 1978: 294–5)

One indication of the nature of the relationship of sociology with medicine at that time was that, as we noted (ibid: 295), so far as specific diseases were concerned, although a wide field was covered, there were many complaints which had not yet been examined sociologically, and much of the work as yet lacked depth. The diseases covered were mainly those where the practitioners felt some sense of limitation and were, therefore, willing to turn to social scientists for further insight. There was then no work connected with surgery. None of the six areas had yet been studied thoroughly enough for a coherent body of knowledge to have been developed. However, understanding in all of these areas could have implications for policy formation and implementation.

The 1976 monograph, focusing as it did on the NHS, included a number of contributions of direct policy relevance. There were papers on the 1974 reorganization of the NHS: about sociological aspects of that reorganization, particularly as it referred to community physicians, who had just been given new and enlarged roles (Gill 1976); about how nursing and junior medical staff viewed the structure of NHS hospitals (Davies and Francis 1976); about how the staff working in health centres saw them and the implications of this for the development of primary health-care teams or groups (Beales 1976); how the potential conflicts in the pro-natalist and anti-natalist policies of gynaecologists were avoided by structural and spatial features of health service provision (Macintyre 1976).

A number of the papers were concerned with aspects of the relationship between doctors and patients: general practitioners' written descriptions of the types of patient who cause the most and least trouble (Stimson 1976); how GPs tended to treat patients from different occupational classes differently (Cartwright and O'Brien 1976); how paediatricians perceive child patients in developmental assessment (Davis and

Strong 1976); how the NHS was leading patients to challenge the traditional authority of the general practitioner (Haug 1976); that the experiences of children in hospital can only be properly understood as an interactive experience and one more complicated than previously had been supposed (Hall *et al.* 1976); a study of the use of accident and emergency departments showed how remarkably well-informed patients were with regard to a variety of sudden illness and trauma, about how to get treatment and to get it most efficiently, even though their actions might not be the officially sanctioned ones (Holohan 1976).

The authors used a variety of methods, quantitative and qualitative, small and large scale. A methodological paper discussed how to extract data relating to children and general practice from the General Household Survey (Dajda and Mapes 1976) and in a theoretical note, I drew attention to the inappropriateness of the use of the concept of the 'consumer' for sociological analysis, since 'a patient can be said to be a producer as much as a consumer' (Stacey 1976b: 194). In all cases the articles had direct relevance for health policy or health care or for ways of analysing associated problems.

Developments since the mid-1970s

The evidence from books

Until the early 1970s, British medical sociologists were still largely relying on American work. Robinson's (1973) brief work *Patients, Practitioners and Medical Care*, written to introduce medical students, GPs and other health-care workers to medical sociology, appeared in 1973 followed by Cox and Mead (1975). In 1976, in addition to *The Sociology of the NHS* (Stacey 1976a), Dingwall's *Aspects of Illness* (1976) and Tuckett's *An Introduction to Medical Sociology* (1976), the first British collection for teachers of sociology to medical students, were published. The latter was followed two years later by the *Basic Readings* he edited with Kaufert (Tuckett and Kaufert 1978). Collections of essays in the sociology of health and illness continued to be published (for example, Davis and Horobin 1977; Davis 1978; Atkinson *et al.* 1979).

In 1980 Armstrong, himself a medical practitioner as well as a sociologist, produced his *An Outline of Sociology as Applied to Medicine*, from a less medically dominated or positivistic stance than Tuckett's. Armstrong's book was followed by Patrick and Scambler's (1982) collection from the London group of medical sociology teachers, also for medical students.

1980 was memorable as the year in which Raymond Illsley held the Rock Carling Fellowship, the first sociologist to do so. In his lecture he expounded the contribution which sociology could make to public health, pointing out among other things how the classical experimental mode was not appropriate to research into health policy, which necessarily was continually being revised throughout the research period (Illsley 1980). 1984 saw the publication, already mentioned, of the Open University series on health and disease with its accompanying reader (Black *et al.* 1984), written by a team which included community medicine, biology, sociology, social policy, history and health economics.

There were no British texts specifically for sociologists until 1985 when Hart's (1985) *The Sociology of Health and Medicine* in the Haralambos series for 'A' level students appeared and also Morgan *et al.*'s (1985) *Sociological Approaches to Health and Medicine* in Scase's *Social Analysis* series, a book developed from a University of Kent undergraduate course in the sociology of medicine. Scambler's (1987) collection specifically addressed the relationship of sociological theory to medical sociology. Latest in that line is my textbook *The Sociology of Health and Healing* (Stacey 1988). This aims, not only to reflect the important insights which have come to sociology from medical anthropology and from the social history of medicine, but to integrate feminist theory and research, hitherto developing in a separate stream, with the mainstream.

Many examples of monographs reporting empirical research, using a range of methodologies have been published during the fifteen years. Ann Cartwright's social science surveys of aspects of health care continued to appear with their expected high standard, providing valuable evidence for sociologists, practitioners and policy makers, e.g. on childbirth (Cartwright 1979) and general practice (Cartwright and Anderson 1981). Jefferys and Sachs (1983) and Heath (1986) have also written on the latter, but from very different points of view. Hall and Stacey (1979), Strong (1979), Blaxter (1981) and Davis (1982) reported on child health and the organization of child health care while Dingwall *et al.* (1983) wrote on child protection. These works showed the implications of current practice and suggested policy changes.

Some monographs addressed specific conditions and their meaning, e.g. Atkinson (1978) on suicide, Blaxter (1980) on disability, Stimson and Oppenheimer (1982) on heroin addiction. Empirical data on lay concepts of health, illness and health behaviour, important for issues associated with doctor–patient communication and for health education policies, are recorded by Blaxter and Patterson (1982), Cornwell (1984) and included in the major Cambridge life-style survey (Cox *et al.* 1987), while the acquisition of medical knowledge is examined in Atkinson (1981). Currer and Stacey (1986) gathered a range of readings on concepts of health, illness and disease together. The value and limitations of health surveys are discussed by Cartwright (1983). Larkin (1983) drew welcome attention to the development of health professions other than medicine. In terms of social structural issues, Townsend and Davidson's (1982) edition of the Black report should be mentioned, as should Wilkinson's (1986) *Class and Health*, although neither are strictly monographs.

Throughout the 1970s, and increasingly after the 1974 British Sociological Association conference on sex and gender divisions, there has been a strong and continuing interest in hitherto neglected areas of women's health, e.g. Oakley (1980) on childbirth, Graham (1984) on *Women and Health and the Family* and, from a historical point of view, Lewis (1980) on the politics of motherhood. Feminist sociologists have also contributed empirical work and theoretical analyses of the wider issues of reproduction, although this work has appeared more often in collections (e.g. Finch and Groves 1983; Homans 1985; Hutter and Williams 1981) than in monographs.

During the period it has become increasingly difficult to get monographs published. The publishers' definitions of a market for them is elusive, although the increasing price of books obviously plays its part. The number of excellent theses which languish unpublished or are cut up into numerous small articles, thus losing the impact of a monograph, is regrettable. Now this policy seems to have turned in favour of monographs and against collections.

Medical sociology did not originate from within the discipline of sociology itself, as was noted earlier. However, by the 1980s, extended theoretical work was beginning to be published. Sociological theorists as well as medical sociologists were becoming increasingly interested. Wright and Treacher's (1982) collection examined the social construction of medicine and included work from a range of historians and social scientists including sociologists. The following year, Armstrong published his Foucauldian, historically based critique of twentieth-century medicine *The Political Anatomy of the Body* (Armstrong 1983). Bryan Turner, hitherto perhaps most often thought of as a general sociological theorist, wrote on social aspects of the body (Turner 1984) and on *Medical Power and Social Knowledge* (Turner 1987), which he concluded by stressing the increasing importance of medicine and health and its inevitable and increasing politicization on the world scene. He encouraged sociology departments to pay the subject more attention than hitherto (Turner 1987: 226).

These books alone suggest that a considerable body of knowledge has been and is being built up. The increased interest in theory will help to direct empirical researches, the latter continuing to be in policy-relevant areas, particularly those relating to the effective delivery of health care.

The evidence from the journals

Other evidence comes from journals. I chose three journals and looked at what they had been publishing over the period. Then I sampled numbers around 1986–1988 to see what they published compared with the mid-1970s. The three I chose were *Sociology of Health and Illness, Social Science and Medicine* and the *International Journal of Health Services.*

Social Science and Medicine was founded in 1967 in the period when medicine was actively concerned to establish relations with the social sciences, including sociology. It is an international multidisciplinary journal, published by Pergamon, contributed to and read by both social scientists and health-care practitioners, especially medical practitioners such as community physicians and health policy-makers. *Sociology of Health and Illness*, house journal of the British Sociological Association Medical Sociology Group, first appeared in 1979. By now it is well established, never short of material from home and abroad and is published four times a year. Its very title confirms the move which sociologists have made during the period under review from narrow, medical professional interests to wider health issues. The *International Journal of Health Services*, American-based and first published in 1971, I chose because it represents a political-economy approach not found among British social science health journals, except to some extent in *Medicine and Society*, now succeeded by *Health Matters*.

In *Sociology of Health and Illness*, as one might expect, the articles are the most specifically sociological of the three journals. I took two years from the fourth number of 1986 to the third number of 1988: this yielded 33 articles in the eight numbers. Rather than forcing the articles into the categories I used in 1978 (Stacey with Homans 1978), I began by letting a classification emerge. However, it transpired that the 1978 categories could still be used, although a new category 7 – method and measurement – had to be added. There did not appear to have been any radical overall change of direction, but the categories were less discrete than they had been in the mid-1970s. Table 1.1 shows the allocation to the seven categories and Table 1.2 the major overlaps, which necessarily do not give a full impression of the interrelationships which exist: to do this would involve too many cells with very small numbers.

Three dominant impressions emerge: the first that sociologists, or rather those publishing in the journal, were still focusing particularly on issues of immediate relevance to practitioners; second, that few pay direct attention to policy issues at the global level; third, that a generalized body of knowledge relating to substantive data, theory and methods, not present in the mid-1970s, is emerging and informs most of the work.

Table 1.1: Sociology of Health and Illness: distribution of papers in
1986–88 by category

1	Specific illnesses, conditions and treatments	13
2	Life cycle	0
3	Division of labour	15
	(i) work and occupation	11
	(ii) professionals and patients	3
	(iii) patient as participant	1
4	Knowledge	13
5	Health-care organization	1
6	Structural divisions and health	5
7	Methods and measurement	3

Note: There were 34 articles; there are 50 entries in the table because 14 articles have been
attributed to two categories and one to three: see Table 1.2.

Table 1.2: Sociology of Health and Illness: cross-referencing of papers
among categories

	1	2	3	4	5	6	7	Total
1	9		1	2			1	13
2								0
3	1		5	8		1		15
4	2		8	2		1		13
5					1			1
6			1	1		2	1	5
7	1					1	1	3
Total	13	0	15	13	1	5	3	50

The evidence for the first point, the continuity of focus, derives from
the high proportion of articles in categories 1 (specific illness or
handicapping conditions and their treatment) and 3 (division of labour
in health care). Over a third of the articles (twelve) related to specific
illness conditions and even more (fifteen) in whole or in part to category
3, most of which (eleven) were about work and occupations (category
3(i)). My second impression arises partly because only one paper fell
overtly into category 5 (the organization of health care and associated
processes) and, although policy issues emerged in category 6 (the
relationship of major structural divisions to health and illness), there
were no more than five papers here. However, papers in category 1

about specific illness or conditions did also deal with service provision and in this sense could be said to make an important, if indirect, contribution to policy issues by increasing the general understanding of health-care professionals, managers and others. The third claim rests upon the much greater overlap between categories than appeared in the mid-1970s. Authors were calling upon understanding derived from other areas to explain their observations. Furthermore, three papers were specifically on methods and measurement (Bloor *et al.* 1987; Murphy and Pilotta 1987; Williams and Gabe 1987).

The thirteen papers which dealt with specific illnesses or conditions addressed a range of sociological problems: health and illness concepts – in relation to cancer (Pinell 1987; Taylor 1988), AIDS (Warwick *et al.* 1988) and Altzheimer's (Gubrium 1987); how lay concepts relate to illness adaptation (Radley and Green 1987); the effects of medical technology on patients (Locker and Kaufert 1988); mental health and mental handicap, including reference to service provision, treatment received and social control (Bloor 1986; Hughes *et al.* 1987; McKeganey and Bloor 1987); crowding and mental health (Gabe and Williams 1986); doctor/patient communication from the doctor's point of view (Taylor 1988); communicative usage (Gubrium 1987); the disabled as professionals (French 1988); evidence about the social construction of medical knowledge drawn from multiple sclerosis (Nicholson and McLaughlin 1988) and transsexualism (King 1987).

In *Sociology of Health and Illness* no papers dealt specifically with aspects of the life cycle, although there were two on gerontology (Askham 1988; Kart 1987) and one on mental handicap related specifically to teenagers (Hughes *et al.* 1987).

Of the fifteen articles wholly or partly on the division of health labour, eleven were about work and occupation: boundaries, establishing them, maintaining them, how they work out in practice (Birenbaum *et al.* 1987; Hughes 1988; Kart 1987; Nettleton 1988; Schepers 1988; Walker 1988); the part medical knowledge plays (Askham 1988; Kart 1987; Neff *et al.* 1987; Nettleton 1988; Thompson 1987). Three papers were about professional patient relations (Pill 1987; Taylor 1988) and one about patient participation (Carmel 1988). As well as the considerable overlap with health knowledge already noted, papers in this group also overlapped with those on specific diseases.

Thirteen papers discussed health knowledge, its production and reproduction. Among those on medical knowledge the most noticeable focus was around the issue of social constructionism, already mentioned, including two essentially theoretical papers (Nicolson and McLaughlin 1987; Bury 1987). The papers about lay concepts included discussion of lay ideas of illness causation (Pill 1987; Pinell 1987; Warwick *et al.* 1988).

The one paper on the organization of health care and associated policy issues analysed policy changes in the NHS (Davies 1987). However, the five papers on major structural divisions have macropolicy relevance: associations between unemployment and health (Bartley 1988); problems in the measurement of health inequalities (Bloor *et al.* 1987); doctor/patient relations and social class (Boulton *et al.* 1986); women and migration (Anderson, 1987); urban–rural differences (Williams and Gabe, 1987). The balance of the papers nevertheless fell outside the macropolicy area.

I looked at the 24 numbers of *Social Science and Medicine*, from the end of 1987 until November 1988. At one time this international journal had separate issues for the various contributory disciplines, such as sociology, anthropology, geography and health economics. It then moved to having discipline sections within each number. In volume 26, issue 2 (1988) the editor announced the abolition of the single disciplinary label because of the increasing difficulty of placing articles under a single head and because he had come to feel the practice was inconsistent with the logic of a multidisciplinary approach. The practice ceased at the end of 1987, although the first number of 1988 was a special issue devoted to medical geography. I thus picked up two numbers with the divisions and twenty-two without.

In some ways, examining these volumes told me more about what is happening in sociology as a discipline in the context of medicine than it did about what sociologists are contributing, although I learned something about this too. There was no clear evidence as to which papers were written by or with sociologists.

Over the year there were 266 articles published including editorials in special issues and research notes. Of these, I judged twenty-two to be clearly sociological while there was a sociological input into some eight others. In addition many were clearly sociologically informed. Of the twenty-four issues, eight were run as 'specials' with a guest editor. In only one of these did sociology feature at all significantly: this was an issue on worksite health problems where the editor was a sociologist (Conrad 1988), who saw the whole enterprise as an attempt to apply sociological theory and method to worksite health issues. The nine papers move from the macro- to the microlevel and from analyses of why corporations decide to become involved in workplace health promotion to what the employees think and how they, and their wives (*sic*), react.

For the rest, the sociological input in special issues was low. Where an issue is about the contribution of a particular discipline, one would not expect sociological articles to appear. None did, for example, in the issue on anthropology and diarrhoeal illness (1988: 27 (1)), although two in the medical geography issue already referred to (1988: 26 (1)), clearly had some sociological input. There were no sociological articles in the special issue on stress and coping in health and disease (1988: 3 (14)), nor in selective versus comprehensive health care (1988: 9 (12)). The issue on health, apartheid and the front-line states also included no sociology as such (1988: 27 (7)), but the issue on permanence and change in Asian health-care traditions did include one sociological contribution. There was, however, no sociology in the issue on social policy for pollution-related diseases. To some extent, these outcomes reflect the interests of those who volunteer to act as guest editors, but this itself may well be a comment, not so much on sociologists, as on their institutional situations.

Among the remaining sociological articles identified, Justice (1987) advocated that international health agencies use more social science knowledge to ensure the appropriate provision of services to rural communities. Bush and Ianotti (1988) and Calnan and Rutter (1988) looked at health beliefs, attitudes and health behaviour. Anson (1988) examined available adult support versus nurturant roles for women's health, while O'Reilly (1988) discussed methods of measuring social support and Macintyre (1988) advocated the value in measuring health status of height, weight, blood pressure and respiratory function against morbidity. Papers dealing with social structural issues included an analysis of statistics on types of violent death among Hispanic populations in the US (Shai and Rosenwaike 1988); the diminishment of class differentials in British youth as opposed to other age groups (West 1988); health-care organization and delivery (Calnan 1988a; Calnan and Butler 1988; Twaddle 1988); essays in medical knowledge compared biomedical and other medicines (McKee 1988; Fassin and Fassin 1988) and offered a framework for the evaluation of health knowledge (Calnan 1988b). British sociologists were quite well represented among the limited number of sociologists contributing.

Over the two years from November 1986 the *International Journal of Health Services* published eighty-four articles, to which 133 people contributed, twenty-six of whom were sociologists, who contributed to twenty articles. In this journal, a particular type of contribution which sociology can make to health policy may be clearly seen, for the journal itself has a more direct policy orientation than either of the others discussed. By the same token, it is less concerned with illness experience, caring, treatment or practice. Policy, here, is conceived much more at the macrolevel of state, corporation or industry. Many more articles fall into category 6 – structural divisions – but with an emphasis, hitherto not much found, upon the dominant mode of production of the societies studied or of health care, an approach informed in many cases by Marxism and sometimes by feminism, the latter rarely found in the journals so far surveyed. Table 1.3 shows the distribution of the twenty articles which sociologists wrote or to which they contributed.

Table 1.3: International Journal of Health Services: cross-referencing of papers among categories

	1	2	3	4	5	6	7	*Total*
1	2					1		3
2					2			2
3			4			2		6
4								0
5			2		1	2		5
6	1		2		2	7		12
7								0
Total	3	2	6	0	5	12	0	28

Note: there were 21 articles in all, of which 7 have been double counted.

Specific conditions discussed include women's health and housing (Gabe and Williams 1987), workers' health and asbestos (Myers *et al.* 1987), child abuse from a structural, feminist perspective (Stark and Flitcraft 1988). Health work and occupations include the effect of corporatization on doctors and doctoring (McKinlay and Stoeckle 1988); the development of Canadian nursing (Coburn 1988); deprofessionalization (Brown 1987); paid and unpaid women workers and the health-care 'cost crisis' (Glazer 1988); lay evaluation of medical practice (Calnan 1988c); the conceptualization of time in medical practice (Frankenberg 1988). Papers on the organization of health care all have overt policy implications: for the health care for the elderly (Binney and Estes 1988; Estes and Binney 1988); the role of hospitals in health-policy development (Labisch 1987); corporatism and health policy (Bergthold 1987); corporatism versus deprivatization in health care (Fried *et al.* 1987), the last two being structural analyses. A structural approach is also taken in relation to the causes of hazards to agricultural health and safety (Denis 1988); the right to refuse dangerous work (Renaud and St-Jacques 1988); the relationship between class and health (Schwalbe and Staples 1986); unemployment and health (Brenner 1987); socialism, capitalism and health (Ceresto and Waitzkin 1986; De Brun and Elling 1987); colonialism and health policy (Manderson 1987).

Margaret Stacey

Evidence from the research register

Medical Sociology in Britain, the register of research and teaching, records reported research according to substantive area. The research register probably gives the best available indication of activity at any one time, books reflecting research competed with articles coming in an intermediate position.

In the Preface to the research-projects section of the 1982 edition the editors (Field and Clarke 1982: 79) point out that while 509 research projects were recorded in 1978, there were now 274. They also note that within the overall decline, four areas increased their share: pregnancy and childbirth (from 4.5 per cent to 9.85 per cent of the total), nursing and related occupations (from 5.5 per cent to 9.8 per cent), while two new categories 'women and health' (4.7 per cent) and 'historical studies' (4.0 per cent) had had to be invented. At that time the most frequently researched areas were nursing and related occupations and pregnancy and childbirth (with 9.8 per cent each), general-practice-based studies and nursing and related occupations (8.3 per cent each).

In 1986, 220 research entries were made, a further but less dramatic fall. In that year research into disability, sustaining and slightly increasing its absolute numbers, shared first place with pregnancy and childbirth with 8.6 per cent each of the entries. A new category 'inequality and health including unemployment' came second with 7.7 per cent. One must note here that the entry 'social epidemiology' was dropped and no doubt some reclassification occurred. Work on women and health showed a slight absolute and some proportionate increase (fourteen entries, 6.4 per cent). Health-related beliefs and behaviour increased from eight to fourteen entries (that is to 6.4 per cent). GP-based studies declined from twenty-three to fourteen (i.e. from 8.3 per cent to 6.4 per cent). All other entries were less than 6 per cent.

One can see in these changes, small though the numbers are, some evidence of changing interests in applied medical sociology. Many general-practice studies were initiated when GPs were sorting out their professional role and when government was concerned with the services available. Work in general practice and with general practitioners is likely to continue, but with a new focus consequent upon the NHS review. Interest in women's health and allied matters continues, much of it with a feminist impetus. The renewed public interest in alternative medicine is reflected in the creation of a new category on this subject. Other new categories are community health care, drugs including alcohol, ethnicity and health. It is a reasonable guess to suppose that AIDS/HIV or STDs will constitute a category in the 1990 Register. Sociological work will undoubtedly remain of direct and indirect interest to health policy makers and practitioners.

Concluding comments

Taking all the evidence surveyed, a paradox emerges. As a body of knowledge the sociology of health and illness now has a clearer identity than it has ever had. At the same time most of the work is being done outside sociology departments and undoubtedly some good contributions to health care and health policy are being made as a result of working closely with practitioners and researchers from other disciplines. Perhaps for this reason, less work is directed to health policy at a macrolevel and much more to policy and practice at the level of professional patient contact or of interest to practitioners.

The continuance of this contribution, and indeed its extension to macro-policy areas when funding becomes more available, must depend on the continued strength of the parent discipline and of the sub-discipline within it. For example, if the sociology of health and healing were to be absorbed into a biopsychosocial medicine it would, as Armstrong (1987) has argued, cease to make its distinctive contribution, which is not only to medicine but to health more generally as the review just undertaken indicates.

Furthermore, the present position, of increasing strength in the discipline and increasing practical contributions, is based on researchers who were trained in a period when there was academic expansion and more postgraduate positions available than nowadays. The indications are that mainstream sociology is taking medical sociology more seriously than it did 15 years ago. However, there is a shortage of people in training as a consequence of the severe cuts which sociology, along with other social sciences, has suffered in the period under review. To ensure that the sociology of health will continue to make the optimum contribution on which health-care professionals and policy makers can draw for their applied understanding, scholars have to be well trained in sociology as a basic science before they move into team research in the applied field. Academic sociologists and some sociology departments are showing willingness to undertake these tasks. They will require support if we are to ensure that there is an adequate supply of well-trained researchers to build on the promising developments that I have been able to record.

References

Anderson, J. (1987) 'Migration and health: perspectives on immigrant women', *Sociology of Health and Illness* 9 (4): 410–38.
Anson, O. (1988) 'Living arrangements and women's health', *Social Science and Medicine* 26 (2): 201–8.
Armstrong, D. (1980) *An Outline of Sociology as Applied to Medicine*, Bristol: John Wright and Sons Ltd (2nd edn, 1983).

—— (1983) *Political Anatomy of the Body: Medical Knowledge in Britain in the Twentieth Century*, Cambridge: Cambridge University Press.

—— (1987) 'Theoretical tensions in biopsychosocial medicine', *Social Science and Medicine* 25 (11): 1213–18.

Askham, J. (1988) 'Review essay: the coming of age of gerontology', *Sociology of Health and Illness* 10 (3): 303–6.

Atkinson, J.M. (1978) *Discovering Suicide: Studies in the Social Organisation of Sudden Death*, London: Macmillan.

Atkinson, P. (1981) *The Clinical Experience: The Construction and Reconstruction of Medical Reality*, Farnborough, Hants: Gower.

Atkinson, P., Dingwall, R. and Murcott, A. (1979) *Prospects for the National Health*, London: Croom Helm.

Bartley, M. (1988) 'Unemployment and health: selection or causation – a false antithesis?' *Sociology of Health and Illness* 10 (1)): 41–67.

Beales, G. (1976) 'Practical sociological reasoning and the making of social relationships among health centre practitioners', in M. Stacey (ed.) *The Sociology of the NHS*, Sociological Review Monograph 22, Keele: The University of Keele.

Bergthold, L.A. (1987) 'Business and the pushcart vendors in an age of supermarkets', *International Journal of Health Services* 17 (1): 7–26.

Binney, E.A. and Estes, C. (1988) 'The retreat of the state and its transfer of responsibility: the intergenerational war', *International Journal of Health Services* 18 (1): 83–96.

Birenbaum, A., Bologh, R. and Lesieur, H. (1987) 'Reforms in pharmacy education and opportunities to practise clinical pharmacy', *Sociology of Health and Illness* 9 (3): 286–301.

Black, N., Boswell, D., Gray, A., Murphy, S. and Popay, J. (eds) (1984) *Health and Disease: A Reader*, Milton Keynes: Open University Press.

Blaxter, M. (1980) *The Meaning of Disability*, London: Heinemann.

—— (1981) *The Health of the Children*, London: Heinemann.

Blaxter, M. and Patterson, E. (1982) *Mothers and Daughters: A Three-Generational Study of Health Attitudes and Behaviour*, London: Heinemann.

Bloor, M.J. (1986) 'Social control in the therapeutic community: re-examination of a critical case', *Sociology of Health and Illness* 8 (4): 305–24.

Bloor, M., Samphier, M. and Prior, L. (1987) 'Artefact explanations of inequalities in health: an assessment of the evidence', *Sociology of Health and Illness* 9 (3): 321–64.

Boulton, M., Tuckett, D., Olson, C. and Williams, A. (1986) 'Social class and general practice consultation', *Sociology of Health and Illness* 8 (4): 325–50.

Brenner, M.H. (1987) 'Economic instability, unemployment rates, behavioral risks and mortality rates in Scotland 1952–1963', *International Journal of Health Services* 17 (3): 475–87.

Brown, J.V. (1987) 'The deprofessionalization of Soviet physicians: a reconsideration', *International Journal of Health Services* 17 (1): 65–76.

Bury, M.R. (1986) 'Social constructionism and the development of medical sociology', *Sociology of Health and Illness* 8 (2): 137–69.
—— (1987) 'Social constructionism and medical sociology: a rejoinder to Nicolson and McLaughlin', *Sociology of Health and Illness* 9 (4): 439–41.
Bush, P. and Iannotti, R.J. (1988) 'Origins and stability of children's health beliefs relative to medicine use', *Social Science and Medicine* 27 (4): 345–52.
Calnan, M. (1988a) 'Images of general practice: perceptions of the doctor', *Social Science and Medicine* 27 (6): 579–86.
—— (1988b) 'Towards a conceptual framework of lay evaluation of health care' *Social Science and Medicine* 27 (9): 927–33.
—— (1988c) 'Lay evaluation of medicine and medical practice: report of a pilot survey', *International Journal of Health Services* 18 (2): 311–22.
Calnan, M. and Butler, J.R. (1988) 'The economy of time in general practice: an assessment of the influence of list size', *Social Science and Medicine* 26 (4): 435–41.
Calnan, M. and Rutter, D.R. (1988) 'Do health beliefs predict health behaviour? A follow-up analysis of breast self-examination', *Social Science and Medicine* 26 (4): 463–5.
Carmel, S. (1988) 'Hospital patients' responses to dissatisfaction', *Sociology of Health and Illness* 10 (3): 262–81.
Carpenter, M. (1977) 'The new managerialism and professionalism in nursing', in M. Stacey, M. Reid, C. Heath and R. Dingwall (eds) (1977) *Health and the Division of Labour*, London: Croom Helm.
Cartwright, A. (1979) *The Dignity of Labour? A Study of Childbearing and Induction*, London: Tavistock.
—— (1983) *Health Surveys in Practice and Potential: A Critical Review of their Scope and Methods*, London: Kings Fund Publishing Office.
Cartwright, A. and Anderson, R. (1981) *General Practice Revisited: A Second Study of Patients and Their Doctors*, London: Tavistock.
Cartwright, A. and O'Brien, M. (1976) 'Social class variations in health care and in the nature of general practitioner consultations', in M. Stacey (ed.) *The Sociology of the NHS*, Sociological Review Monograph 22, Keele: The University of Keele.
Ceresto, S. and Waitzkin, H. (1986) 'Capitalism, socialism and the physical quality of life', *International Journal of Health Services* 16 (4): 643–58.
Coburn, D. (1988) 'The development of Canadian nursing: professionalization and proletarianization', *International Journal of Health Services* 18 (3): 437–56.
Conrad, P. (1988) 'Worksite health promotion', *Social Science and Medicine* 26 (5): 485–575.
Cornwell, J. (1984) *Hard-earned Lives: Accounts of Health and Illness in East London*, London: Tavistock.
Cox, B.D., Blaxter, M. *et al.* (1987) *The Health and Lifestyle Survey: Preliminary Report*, London: Profile Public Relations.
Cox, C. and Mead, A. (eds) (1975) *A Sociology of Medical Practice*, London: Collier-MacMillan.

Currer, C. and Stacey, M. (eds) (1986) *Concepts of Health, Illness and Disease*, Leamington Spa: Berg.

Dajda, R. and Mapes, R. (1976) 'The General Household Survey as a source of information', in M. Stacey (ed.) *The Sociology of the NHS*, Sociological Review Monograph 22, Keele: The University of Keele.

Davies, C. (1987) 'Viewpoint: things to come: the NHS in the next decade', *Sociology of Health and Illness* 9 (3): 3012–317.

Davies, C. and Francis, A. (1976) 'Perceptions of structure in National Health Service hospitals', in M. Stacey (ed.) *The Sociology of the NHS*, Sociological Review Monograph 22, Keele: The University of Keele.

Davis, A. (ed.) (1978) *Relationships Between Doctors and Patients*, Farnborough: Teakfield.

—— (1982) *Children in Clinics: A Sociological Analysis of Medical Work With Children*, London and New York: Tavistock.

Davis, A. and Horobin, G. (eds) (1977) *Medical Encounters: The Experience of Illness and Treatment*, London: Croom Helm.

Davis, A. and Strong, P. (1976) 'Aren't children wonderful? – a study of the allocation of identity in developmental assessment', in M. Stacey (ed.) *The Sociology of the NHS*, Sociological Review Monograph 22, Keele: The University of Keele.

De Brun, S. and Elling, R. (1987) 'Cuba and the Phillipines: contrasting cases in world-system analysis', *International Journal of Health Services* 17 (3): 681–701.

Denis, W.B. (1988) 'Causes of health and safety hazards in Canadian agriculture', *International Journal of Health Services* 18 (3): 419–36.

Dingwall, R. (1976) *Aspects of Illness*, London: Martin Robertson.

Dingwall, R., Eekelaar, J.M. and Murray, T. (1983) *The Protection of Children: State Intervention and Family Life*, Edinburgh: Churchill Livingstone.

Dingwall, R., Heath, C., Reid, M. and Stacey, M. (eds) (1977) *Health Care and Health Knowledge*, London: Croom Helm; New York: Prodist.

Estes, C. and Binney, E. (1988) 'Towards a transformation of health and aging policy', *International Journal of Health Services* 18 (1): 69–82.

Fassin, D. and Fassin, E. (1988) 'Traditional medicine and the stakes of legitimation in Senegal', *Social Science and Medicine* 27: 353–7.

Field, D. and Clarke, B.A. (1982) *Medical Sociology in Britain: A Register of Research and Teaching*, London: British Sociological Association Medical Sociology Group.

Finch, J. and Groves, D. (eds) (1983) *A Labour of Love: Women, Work and Caring*, London and Boston: Routledge & Kegan Paul.

Frankenberg, R. (1988) ' "Your time or mine?" an anthropological view of the tragic temporal contradictions of biomedical practice', *International Journal of Health Services* 18 (1): 11–34.

French, S. (1988) 'Experiences of disabled health professionals', *Sociology of Health and Illness* 10 (2): 170–88.

Fried, B.J., Deber, R.B. and Leath, P. (1987) 'Corporatization and deprivatization of health services in Canada', *International Journal of Health Services* 17 (3): 567–84.

Gabe, J. and Williams, P. (1986) 'Is space bad for your health? The relationship between crowding in the home and emotional distress in women', *Sociology of Health and Illness* 8 (4): 351–71.
—— (1987) 'Women, housing and mental health', *International Journal of Health Services* 17 (3): 667–79.
Gill, D. (1976) 'The reorganization of the National Health Service: some sociological aspects with special reference to the role of the community physician', in M. Stacey (ed.) *The Sociology of the NHS*, Sociological Review Monograph 22, Keele: The University of Keele.
Glazer, N.Y. (1988) 'Overlooked, overworked: women's unpaid and paid work in the health service "cost crisis"', *International Journal of Health Services* 18 (1): 119–37.
Graham, H. (1984) *Women, Health and the Family*, Brighton: Wheatsheaf.
Gubrium, J.F. (1987) 'Structuring and destructuring the course of illness: the Alzheimer's disease experience', *Sociology of Health and Illness* 9 (1): 1–14.
Hall, D., Pill, R. and Clough, F. (1976) 'Notes for a conceptual model of hospital experience as an interactive process', in M. Stacey (ed.) *The Sociology of the NHS*, Sociological Review Monograph 22, Keele: The University of Keele.
Hall, D. and Stacey, M. (eds) (1979) *Beyond Separation: Further Studies of Children in Hospital*, London: Routledge & Kegan Paul.
Hart, N. (1985) *The Sociology of Health and Medicine*, Ormskirk: Causeway Press.
Haug, M.R. (1976) 'Issues in general practitioner authority in the National Health Service', in M. Stacey (ed.) *The Sociology of the NHS*, Sociological Review Monograph 22, Keele: The University of Keele.
Heath, C. (1986) *Body Movement and Speech in Medical Interaction*, Cambridge: Cambridge University Press.
Holohan, A.M. (1976) 'Accident and Emergency Departments: illness and accident behaviour', in M. Stacey (ed.) *The Sociology of the NHS*, Sociological Review Monograph 22, Keele: The University of Keele.
Homans, H. (ed.) (1985) *The Sexual Politics of Reproduction*, Aldershot: Gower.
Hughes, D. (1988) 'When nurse knows best: some aspects of nurse/doctor interaction in a casualty department', *Sociology of Health and Illness* 10 (1): 1–22.
Hughes, D., May, D. and Harding, S. (1987) 'Growing up on ward twenty: the everyday life of teenagers in a mental handicap hospital', *Sociology of Health and Illness* 9 (4): 378–409.
Hutter, B. and Williams G. (eds) (1981) *Controlling Women: the Normal and the Deviant*, London: Croom Helm.
Illsley, R. (1975) 'Promotion to observer status', *Social Science and Medicine* 2: 415–53.
—— (1980) *Professional or Public Health? Sociology in Health and Medicine*, The Rock Carling Fellowship 1980, London: The Nuffield Provincial Hospitals Trust.

31

Jefferys, M. and Sachs, H. (1983) *Rethinking General Practice: Dilemmas in Primary Health Care*, London: Tavistock.

Justice, J. (1987) 'The bureaucratic context of international health: a social scientist's view', *Social Science and Medicine* 25 (12): 1301–6.

Kart, C.S. (1987) 'Review essay: the end of conventional gerontology?', *Sociology of Health and Illness* 9 (2): 76–87.

King, D. (1987) 'Social constructionism and medical knowledge: the case of transsexualism', *Sociology of Health and Illness* 9 (4): 351–77.

Labisch, A. (1987) 'The role of the hospital in the health policy of the German Social Democratic Movement before World War I', *International Journal of Health Services* 17 (2): 279–94.

Larkin, G.V. (1983) *Occupational Monopoly and Modern Medicine*, London: Tavistock.

Lewis, J. (1980) *The Politics of Motherhood*, London: Croom Helm.

Locker, D. and Kaufert, J. (1988) 'The breath of life: medical technology and the careers of people with post-respiratory poliomyelitis', *Sociology of Health and Illness* 10 (1): 24–40.

Macintyre, S. (1976) 'To have or have not – promotion and prevention of childbirth in gynaecological work', in M. Stacey (ed.) *The Sociology of the NHS*, Sociological Review Monograph 22, Keele: The University of Keele.

—— (1988) 'A review of the social patterning and significance of measures of height, weight, blood pressure and respiratory function', *Social Science and Medicine* 27 (4) 327–37.

McKee, J. (1988) 'Holistic health and the critique of western medicine', *Social Science and Medicine* 26 (8): 775–82.

McKeganey, N.P. and Bloor, M.J. (1987) 'Teamwork, information control and therapeutic effectiveness: a tale of two therapeutic communities', *Sociology of Health and Illness* 9 (2): 154–78.

McKinlay, J.B. and Stoeckle, J.D. (1988) 'Corporatization and the social control of doctoring', *International Journal of Health Services* 18 (2): 191–205.

Manderson, L. (1987) 'Health services and the legitimation of the colonial state: British Malaya 1786–1941', *International Journal of Health Services* 17 (1): 91–112.

Manson, T. (1977) 'Management, the professions and the unions', in M. Stacey, M. Reid, C. Health and R. Dingwall (eds) *Health and the Division of Labour*, London: Croom Helm.

Marshall, T.H. (1953) 'Conference of the British Sociological Association', *British Journal of Sociology* 4 (3): 201–9.

Morgan, M., Calnan, M. and Manning, M. (1985) *Sociological Approaches to Health and Medicine*, London: Croom Helm.

Murphy, J.W. and Pilotta, J.J. (1987) 'Research note: identifying "at risk" persons in community-based research', *Sociology of Health and Illness* 9 (2): 62–75.

Myers, J.E., Aron, J. and Macun, I.A. (1987) 'Asbestos and asbestos-related disease: the South African case', *International Journal of Health Services* 17 (3): 651–66.

Neff, J.A., McFall, S.L. and Cleaveland, T.D. (1987) 'Psychiatry and medicine in the US: interpreting trends in medical specialty choice', *Sociology of Health and Illness* 9 (2): 45–61.

Nettleton, S. (1988) 'Protecting a vulnerable margin: towards an analysis of how the mouth came to be separated from the body', *Sociology of Health and Illness* 10 (2): 156–69.

Nicolson, M. and McLaughlin, C. (1987) 'Social constructionism and medical sociology: a reply to M.R. Bury', *Sociology of Health and Illness* 9 (2): 107–26.

—— (1988) 'Social constructionism and medical sociology: a study of the vascular theory of multiple sclerosis', *Sociology of Health and Illness* 10 (3): 234–61.

Oakley, A. (1980) *Women Confined: Towards a Sociology of Childbirth*, Oxford: Martin Robertson.

O'Reilly, P. (1988) 'Methodological Issues in social support and social network research', *Social Science and Medicine* 26 (8): 863–73.

Patrick, D.L. and Scambler, G. (eds) (1982) *Sociology as Applied to Medicine*, London: Bailliere Tindall.

Pill, R. (1987) 'Models and management: the case of "cystitis" in women', *Sociology of Health and Illness* 9 (3): 265–85.

Pinell, P. (1987) 'How do cancer patients express their points of view?', *Sociology of Health and Illness* 9 (2): 25–44.

Radley, A. and Green, R. (1987) 'Illness as adjustment: a methodology and conceptual framework', *Sociology of Health and Illness* 9 (2): 179–207.

Reid, M. (1975–6) 'The development of medical sociology in Britain', discussion paper no. 13, Discussion Papers in Social Research, University of Glasgow, mimeo.

Renaud, M. and St-Jacques, C. (1988) 'The right to refuse in Quebec: five years evolution of a new mode of expressing risk', *International Journal of Health Services* 18 (3): 401–17.

Robinson, D. (1973) *Patients, Practitioners and Medical Care*, London: Heinemann Medical.

Scambler, G. (ed.) (1987) *Sociological Theory and Medical Sociology*, London and New York: Tavistock.

Schepers, R. (1988) 'Pharmacists and medical doctors in nineteenth-century Belgium', *Sociology of Health and Illness* 10 (1): 68–90.

Schwalbe, M.L. and Staples, C.L. (1986) 'Class position, work experience and health, *International Journal of Health Services* 18 (1): 583–602.

Shai, D. and Rosenwaike, I. (1988) 'Violent deaths among Mexican-, Puerto Rican- and Cuban-born migrants in the United States', *Social Science and Medicine* 26 (2): 269–76.

Stacey, M. (ed.) (1976a) *The Sociology of the NHS*, Sociological Review Monograph 22, Keele: The University of Keele.

—— (1976b) 'The health service consumer: a sociological misconception', in M. Stacey (ed.) *The Sociology of the NHS*, Sociological Review Monograph 22, Keele: The University of Keele.

—— (1988) *The Sociology of Health and Healing: A Textbook*, London: Unwin-Hyman.

Stacey, M. with Homans, H. (1978) 'The sociology of health and illness: its present state, future prospects and potential for health research', *Sociology* 12 (2): 281–307.

Stacey, M., Reid, M., Heath, C. and Dingwall, R. (1977) *Health and the Division of Labour*, London: Croom Helm, New York: Prodist.

Stark, E. and Flitcraft, A.H. 'Women and children at risk: a feminist perspective on child abuse', *International Journal of Health Services* 18 (1): 97–118.

Stimson, G.V. (1976) 'General practitioners, "trouble" and types of patients', in M. Stacey (ed.) *The Sociology of the NHS*, Sociological Review Monograph 22, Keele: The University of Keele.

Stimson, G.V. and Oppenheimer, E. (1982) *Heroin Addiction: Treatment and Control in Britain*, London and New York: Tavistock.

Strong, P.M. (1979) *The Ceremonial Order of the Clinic: Parents, Doctors and Medical Bureaucracies*, London: Routledge & Kegan Paul.

Taylor, K.M. (1988) ' "Telling bad news": physicians and the disclosure of undesirable information', *Sociology of Health and Illness* 10 (2): 109–32.

Thompson, D. (1987) 'Coalitions and conflicts in the national health service: some implications for general management', *Sociology of Health and Illness* 9 (2): 127–53.

Townsend, P. and Davidson, N. (eds) (1982) *Inequalities in Health: The Black Report*, Harmondsworth: Penguin.

Tuckett, D. (1976) *An Introduction to Medical Sociology*, London: Tavistock.

Tuckett, D. and Kaufert, J.M. (1978) *Basic Readings in Medical Sociology*, London: Tavistock.

Turner, B.S. (1984) *The Body and Society*, Oxford: Blackwell.

—— (1987) *Medical Power and Social Knowledge*, London: Sage.

Twaddle, A.C. (1988) 'Swedish physicians' perspectives on work and the medical care system – III: private practitioners on the public system', *Social Science and Medicine* 26 (7): 761–8.

U 205 Course Team (1985a) *Studying Health and Disease*, Milton Keynes: Open University Press.

—— (1985b) *Medical Knowledge: Doubt and Certainty*, Milton Keynes: Open University Press.

—— (1985c) *The Health of Nations*, Milton Keynes: Open University Press.

—— (1985d) *The Biology of Health and Disease*, Milton Keynes: Open University Press.

—— (1985e) *Birth to Old Age: Health in Transition*, Milton Keynes: Open University Press.

—— (1985f) *Experiencing and Explaining Disease*, Milton Keynes: Open University Press.

—— (1985g) *Caring for Health: History and Diversity*, Milton Keynes: Open University Press.

—— (1985h) *Caring for Health: Dilemmas and Prospects*, Milton Keynes: Open University Press.

Walker, M. (1988) 'Training the trainers: socialisation and change in general practice', *Sociology of Health and Illness* 10 (3): 282–302.

Warwick, I., Aggleton, P. and Homans, H. (1988) 'Constructing commonsense – young people's beliefs about AIDS', *Sociology of Health and Illness* 10 (3): 213–33.
West, P. (1988) 'Inequalities? Social class differentials in British youth', *Social Science and Medicine* 27 (4): 291–6.
Wilkinson, R.G. (ed.) (1986) *Class and Health: Research and Longitudinal Data*, London: Tavistock.
Williams, P. and Gabe, J. (1987) 'Research note: urban–rural prescribing: a critique of the "minimalist" position', *Sociology of Health and Illness* 9 (3): 318–24.
Wright, P. and Treacher, A. (eds) (1982) *The Problem of Medical Knowledge: Examining the Social Construction of Medicine*, Edinburgh: Edinburgh University Press.

Chapter two

Privatization in the British health sector: a challenge to the NHS?

John Mohan

Introduction

One of the rising ideologues of the New Right, John Redwood, recently argued that privatization had become the 'biggest international political phenomenon of the 1980s' (Redwood 1988, 71). This seems an exaggerated conclusion in the light of the recent experience of the British health sector. The predictions made by some advocates of the private health sector some ten years ago now seem wildly optimistic: no-one would be likely to claim, as Gerald Vaughan did in 1980, that 25 per cent of the British population would ultimately be covered against the cost of private medical treatment. Following the announcement of the NHS review, a fearsome arsenal of apparently radical options were brandished by various right-wing policy institutes, but within months most had been rejected by the Social Services Committee, which concluded that the case had not been made for radical change to the NHS. Even the NHS White Paper in 1989 ostensibly departed little from the original objectives of the service, at least in terms of comprehensiveness, public funding and absence of charges at the point of use, although it did in terms of the organization and management of the service.

Nevertheless, privatization has still had an important impact on the delivery of health care in Britain. The purpose of this chapter is consequently threefold: to analyse the explanations put forward for privatization, to consider the material and ideological impact of privatization and to discuss likely future developments, especially in the aftermath of the White Paper. In doing so I draw on analyses of the political economy of the welfare state, which seek to explain policy developments, not simply in terms of secular trends, party competition or pluralist negotiation and bargaining, but in terms of the wider economic and political pressures on the capitalist state. Thus Gough (1979: 138) identified several ways in which the welfare state could be 'restructured', against a background of economic recession and political pressures to reduce public expenditure. Gough's analysis, written before the 1979 election, was merely pointing to tendencies and options; the precise way in which these work out in individual states is a contingent matter. In addition to a consideration of wider political and economic changes affecting the welfare state, a full explanation of privatization would also have to focus on the political strategies pursued by the Conservatives, the reasons for their adoption, the interests served by them and their intended and actual impacts. Thus, the chapter rejects explanations which stress the role of the free play of market forces, as well as those emphasizing the role of the New Right, and instead relies on interpretations of 'Thatcherism' as a political phenomenon.

First, though, exactly what is meant by privatization? Health services can be provided in a number of ways by various agents and agencies, and so simple oppositions between 'state' and 'market' are inadequate. For example, privatization is not simply synonymous with *commercialization*. Although a key feature of recent years has been the growing significance of profit-making organizations, especially in acute hospital care, many other private agencies are involved. Nor do recent developments mark a *decollectivization*, a retreat by the state from its acceptance of responsibility for health-care provision. Despite the serious and continuing underfunding of the service, there has been no *national* renunciation of a commitment to the availability of comprehensive health care. Instead, there has been a questioning of the legitimate scope of state activities. A climate of opinion is being created in which individual and community initiative and effort are seen as supplementing the state's finite resources. This could even be regarded as a *reprivatization* of services, for it draws inspiration from what some regard as a rich tradition of community effort (Green 1985), which was established before the NHS, and which reminds us that privatization must be put in its historical context.

Le Grand and Robinson (1984) have attempted to clarify some of these definitional issues by arguing that just as the state can intervene in welfare provision in three ways – provision, subsidy and regulation – so privatization involves a reduction in state activity in one of these methods of intervention. I would qualify this, since one aim of government policy has ostensibly been to mobilize private provision in order to supplement, not supplant, state provision. This definition also ignores reforms of NHS management, notably the Griffiths Report (DHSS 1983a), which have introduced private-sector management styles and methods into the NHS; these may have more far-reaching implications for the character of health-care delivery (Haywood and Ranade 1989). Furthermore, privatization has been happening independently of political decisions on the welfare state. Expenditures on private health care were rising steadily in the 1970s, private nursing homes were established well before the NHS and several health authorities and hospitals have used private contractors for many years. However much of the recent impetus has come from three successive Conservative governments, which have deliberately sought to create a climate favourable to privatization.

Aside from these definitional questions, some issues of wider political significance arise from a consideration of privatization. Of these the most important is whether privatization has genuinely provided a challenge to the NHS, or whether it has simply had the ideological effect of shaking producers and consumers out of their complacency with the state's monopoly of service provision. Related to this is whether the steps the government have taken are best thought of as a long-term strategy to dismantle the NHS or as an ideological project aimed at recasting public attitudes to welfare. The proposals contained in the White Paper are, of course, highly relevant here; they may prefigure a new mode of service provision in which communities take on much more of the responsibility for developing services, while the central state provides a basic minimum.

In analysing privatization, I first consider possible explanations for it, paying particular attention to the political and social forces that have brought about privatization. From there I shall analyse its impacts, in two main areas: outside the NHS I look at the continued expansion of the private sector; within the NHS, I consider new resources being generated for health care. I will ignore, largely for reasons of space, questions concerning the introduction and impact of new forms of work organization in health care (e.g. competitive tendering, the Griffiths Report (DHSS 1983a)), as well as the 'care in the community' initiative (see Audit Commission 1986; Public Accounts Committee 1988; and also Land, Chapter 8, this volume), though these are certainly relevant to a fuller consideration of privatization. I also ignore the debate about the relative efficiency of the public and private sectors (see Judge and Knapp 1985). I then discuss the implications of the NHS White Paper. Finally, I speculate on likely future developments, and propose that despite the apparently diverse character of the developments discussed here, a common thread can be discerned: a new model of health-care delivery in which a wide range of resources are brought to bear on providing health services and in which the balance between 'state, market and community' (Papadakis and Taylor-Gooby 1988) varies considerably from place to place.

Explanations: privatization and the politics of Thatcherism

The several possible explanations of privatization include: the free play of market forces; the impact of the New Right's social and economic doctrines; the direct influence of government concessions to the private sector; the indirect effect of expenditure policies on the NHS and the wider economic and political strategies pursued by the Conservatives. I concede that the first of these is important, but I place greater emphasis on the impact of the direct and indirect steps taken by the Conservatives.

One interpretation of privatization would see it as being solely the result of the free play of market forces – as the result of individuals exercising free choice in the market place. There is considerable truth, but not the whole truth, in such a claim; rising standards of living undoubtedly do lead individuals to take out private health insurance. However, individuals making this choice do not do so without consideration of whether the NHS can provide for them. Hence, growth of the private sector is not independent of the condition of the NHS. Moreover, the main growth in private insurance has been in insurance schemes paid for wholly or in part by employers, and not individual policies. The NHS's near-monopoly of health-care provision is such that it is naive to explain private-sector growth in isolation from developments in the NHS.

While New-Right commentators have offered a vigorous defence of the potential role of market-based solutions to the problems of the NHS, they have yet to make a significant impact on the legislative agenda. The New Right is not a homogeneous, united movement, but its liberal and conservative strands both reject the social democratic state's notion of citizenship and the rights attached to it. For New-Right thinkers, citizenship becomes defined 'in terms of the opportunities available to individuals in markets and no longer in terms of entitlements' (Gamble 1989: 11). In health-policy terms, the New Right's views have found expression through 'think tanks' such as the Adam Smith Institute and the Centre for Policy Studies, who have put forward a number of ideas which have had the effect of keeping the right on the offensive in the ideological debate. Furthermore, because these organizations operate at arm's length from government, though with access to it at the highest level, it has been possible for radical proposals to obtain an airing without criticism being directed at the government. However, the political costs of change have limited the government's scope for manoeuvre. The famous Prime Ministerial pledge that 'the NHS is safe with us' was extracted in response to a leak that the government were considering alternative sources of funds for the service, though according to the Bow Group (1983), the 1983 election 'could, and should, have been won without that pledge'. Even the small charges proposed in the 1987 Health and Medicines Bill nearly resulted in a Commons defeat for the government. Hence, there have been very limited concessions to private-sector demands. The NHS White Paper blurs the boundaries between public and private sectors, but – for the moment – it doesn't depart from the basic concept of the NHS.

So if the New Right isn't wholly to blame, how should we account for privatization? I interpret privatization largely in relation to government political strategies, and suggest that three sets of reasons – economic, political and ideological – account for the attractiveness of privatization to the government. The economic motivations for privatization stem from monetarist-inspired demands for reductions in the public-sector borrowing requirement, and a related desire to 'roll back the state', exposing more of the economy to the dictates of competitive market forces. Private provision also supplements the state's limited resources: individuals or businesses choosing to 'go private' are reducing the demands placed upon the public sector. Privatization can also be seen as contributing to the government's aims of stimulating small-business formation and entrepreneurial initiative, both of which are seen as central to the promotion of economic recovery.

Privatization can also serve wider political goals. One of the most convincing interpretations of the Conservatives' political strategies has been as a 'two-nation' politics of inequality (see Jessop *et al.* 1984, 1987; Krieger 1987; Gamble 1988). Broadly, the government's policies have prioritized the 'productive', who produce goods and services that can be profitably marketed, and marginalized the 'parasitic', who are either dependent on state benefits or whose economic activities are deemed 'unprofitable' in narrowly conceived terms. The 'productive' are to be rewarded through the market for their contribution to production, while the 'parasitic' suffer for their failure to contribute adequately to the market. This suggests encouragement of private forms of service provision and tax structures which prioritize the interests of the 'productive', while at the same time seeking deliberately to limit, as far as possible, state support for and provision of welfare services. For instance, it can be claimed that NHS resources have been maintained at or around the level at which the government can claim that growth has occurred, but not to the point where significant improvements have taken place. Encouragement of private provision in its various forms therefore contributes to this politics of inequality as the gap between private prosperity and public decline increases.

Privatization is also notable for its ideological effect in stressing the limits to state action and the necessity and desirability of individual and community effort. In this regard, privatization's most important role may be that of preparing the ground for far-reaching change. In fact, the government have attempted to turn the recent 'crises' in the NHS to their advantage by claiming that, despite the additional funds made available to the NHS, the problems the service faces are ultimately insoluble, and that Britain is unique in Western Europe, at least, in the low proportion of expenditure on *private* health care. The extent to which it has become possible, in the last two years, for apparently radical options to be widely publicized and discussed, is an indication of how far the climate of opinion has changed since the famous leak of the Think Tank's report in 1982.

Thus, privatization fits in neatly with the government's wider strategies, and so they have taken several direct and indirect steps to encourage it. As far as direct steps are concerned, private nursing-home expansion has been stimulated by changes in DHSS benefit regulations, and various minor legislative changes, such as relaxations in controls on private hospital developments or permitting consultants to undertake additional private practice, have undoubtedly facilitated private acute-sector growth. Other decisions, for example, directives on competitive tendering for ancillary services, are also relevant here. But the government's hand has been stayed by considerations of political expediency; they have not gone as far as some private-sector representatives would have liked.

The indirect steps may be of greater significance, especially with regard to the government's record on NHS expenditure. It seems generally agreed that the NHS has, at best, merely kept its head above water when one considers the growing pressures on it (House of Commons Social Services Committee 1986, 1988). This, plus the impact of RAWP (Resource Allocation Working Party) on the distribution of funds to health authorities, has provoked the 'crisis' in the acute sector, with lengthening waiting lists to the point where some DHAs (District Health Authorities) are finding it almost impossible to admit for elective surgery. Related to this is the impact of the government's internal reforms of NHS management, which have had the effect of promoting a competitive, individualistic and entrepreneurial culture in the service (Haywood and Ranade 1989). The emphasis on self-help and on managerial initiative has been strong and it is not surprising, therefore, that some DHAs have responded eagerly to calls for greater collaboration with the private sector and to proposals for income generation and for tapping other sources of funds. Thus, the government may not have satisfied the ideologues of the New Right in their concessions to the private sector, but their policies on the NHS have undoubtedly created a climate in which the private sector can flourish. Simply, they have blurred the boundaries between the two sectors, and increased the attractiveness of a more competitive approach to service delivery in the NHS.

In summary, while one should not discount the importance of market forces and individual choices, the expansion of the private sector is hardly attributable solely to market forces, while within the NHS, privatization reflects the impact of numerous government decisions. Until the 1989 White Paper, the far-reaching critiques of the New Right had very limited impact on the NHS, due to the likely political costs of change. The key influence on privatization in recent years has been the wider economic and political strategies of the Conservative governments, and they have taken a number of steps which, directly or indirectly, have expanded the scope for privatization.

Impacts of privatization

I look here at two important areas of privatization and then go on to consider the implications of the NHS White Paper. I first discuss continued growth and change in the private nursing-home and acute sector, and then describe various developments which promise to break down some of the barriers between the NHS and private provision, including income generation, collaborative developments, etc. In this context, finally, I argue that the White Paper's proposals are to be seen as a logical extension of other initiatives already going on within the NHS.

Private provision of health care

The acute-hospital sector

The main dimensions of this are well known: over 10 per cent of the population are now insured for private treatment; locally, the proportions probably rise to around 30 per cent in the Outer Metropolitan Area; for the professional and managerial socioeconomic groups, coverage is over 30 per cent; and there are now over 200 private acute hospitals, providing some 10,000 beds (see OPCS 1988; Griffith *et al.* 1987).

Important factors in this growth were two policies introduced by the 1974–79 Labour government: restrictive incomes policies and attempts to abolish pay beds. These helped stimulate rapid expansion in insurance cover (insurance was one of a range of perks offered to circumvent incomes policies) and private-hospital construction (to anticipate the day when private practice would no longer be permitted in NHS facilities). Such occupational welfare schemes are still the driving force behind continued growth in the insured population, which raises the question of whether this growth really reflects free choice in the market place by individuals. Company-paid insurance will probably continue to rise as tight labour-market conditions, especially for highly qualified and skilled workers in the South-East, make it necessary for employers to raise the stakes in competing for a limited pool of labour. This could widen the regional variations in insurance cover in what, to paraphrase Titmuss (1962), is an emerging *spatial* division of welfare.

Public perceptions of the state of the NHS, especially after the 1978–79 'winter of discontent' have been skilfully exploited by private-sector advertising, which emphasized the deficiencies of the NHS from a consumer standpoint (see Griffith *et al.* 1987). But the actual steps taken to stimulate private care have been indirect and have not gone as far as representatives of the private sector would like. The ideological message has been consistent – that individuals should relieve the state of the burden of caring for them, because the state's funds are perforce limited – but the material concessions have not matched this (Mohan 1986), at least prior to the NHS White Paper.

Private-sector growth has not been without problems; in the early 1980s there was speculation that the private-insurance boom had burst (Laurance 1983) and numerous reports suggest low hospital occupancy levels in the private acute sector (Forman and Saldana 1988). Consequently, there has been a rationalization of capacity, associated with greater commercialization and internationalization. A crucial stimulus to such changes has been the involvement of multinationals, mainly from the USA, whose involvement in Britain was informed by their perception of the ailing NHS. They have rapidly established a position of market leadership, if not dominance (Rayner 1987; Berliner and Regan 1987). Whether there is genuine *competition* in large areas remains doubtful: outside London and the South-East, there are not many places with more than one private hospital within easy reach, and the multinational corporations and the British hospital chains tend to target distinct subgroups of the potential market. On the whole, though, overoptimistic estimates of insurance growth have produced excess hospital capacity.

In the mid-1980s these heightened competitive pressures stimulated calls for additional government support and regulation. The private sector has lobbied for tax relief on insurance premiums, called for additional controls on new private-hospital developments and requested that NHS pay-bed charges should be more accurately costed so as to permit competition on a fair basis with the private sector. (Some of these proposals were incorporated into the White Paper.) These calls serve as a reminder that the state effectively sets the parameters within which the private sector operates – that markets do not operate in a vacuum. More recently, there has been evidence of growing confidence within the private sector, with several companies proposing joint deals with the NHS on hospital development, and others, such as American Medical International (AMI), diversifying into new fields.

In evaluating these developments, we should note that the private sector was estimated in 1986 to be carrying out at least 30 per cent of elective surgery in some localities (Nicholl *et al.* 1989). Given its numerical size and the extent of insurance coverage, it is easy to see why speculation has developed about the existence of a two-tier health system. Private health care is, however, less significant for its material impact than for its effect on attitudes to welfare; those with private health insurance simply do not require the NHS, except in emergencies, and may therefore be more inclined to campaign for better private services than to defend public facilities (Crouch 1985; see also Taylor-Gooby 1989). This could be especially significant in terms of the geography of support for the government. Reductions in NHS services have been most severe in inner-city areas, notably Greater London, where almost all DHAs lost between 10 and 30 per cent of their acute beds between 1983 and 1986; the inner-city areas of London have relatively low levels of private health insurance, and are not known for returning Conservative MPs. Conversely, Conservative members in the Outer Metropolitan Area could be insulated from constituency complaints about the NHS, simply because so many of their constituents now possess private insurance.

Private nursing homes

This form of service provision has been largely state-funded with changes in the provisions for the payment of Supplementary Benefit permitting the costs of accommodating the elderly to be met from the non-cash limited funds of the DSS, in cases where no suitable public-sector accommodation is available. It has been estimated that some £1,000 million annually is now spent on accommodating people in these homes (the *Independent*, 22 November 1988), and this has funded a massive boom in the industry. In total there were 57,000 beds in private nursing homes for the elderly in 1988; in other words, provision had more than trebled from the 1982 figure of 17,728. In several DHAs there are now more beds available in the private sector than in the NHS. The ostensible rationale for this policy was to increase choice, by ensuring that individuals were not debarred from receiving private care by virtue of their inability to pay for treatment. It was also assumed, implicitly, that provision in the public sector would not be expanded, which reflects the government's ideological predisposition in favour of small-business formation.

One justification for this policy was a consumerist one – to increase choice for the elderly – but it is debatable whether choice has actually increased. For the proprietors of such homes, it is sensible to admit patients who are easy to manage: as Andrews (1984: 1520) recognized, patients could be admitted on grounds of their ability rather than dis-ability. A study of local-authority and private homes in Devon concluded that that choice was not in fact increased, and that the range of services available had not expanded. The authors argued that 'the inequalities with which individuals approach the market affect their abilities successfully to manipulate the market in their own best interests' (Vincent *et al.* 1987: 459). This suggests that the consumerist

approach taken by the government to this issue has very real deficiencies: the vast funds devoted to it have not produced any demonstrable
increase in choice, nor is there evidence that expenditure is targeted in
any meaningful way to those most requiring it (Public Accounts
Committee 1988).

A second, and wider, implication of these developments is the
question of control and regulation. It is not clear whether the necessary
regulatory mechanisms are in place. Anecdotal evidence suggests that
standards of provision in private nursing homes leave much to be
desired (e.g. Holmes and Johnson 1988; West Midlands County Council
1986). Such practice is not confined to private homes but this points to
the need for strict regulation of *all* providers of long-term care for the
elderly. This poses an ·ideological dilemma for the Conservatives.
Private nursing homes are in some ways the archetypal small business
which the Conservatives see as one way to economic regeneration and
the government have sought to remove restrictions on small businesses,
as far as possible. Furthermore, the consumerism evident in the expansion of private nursing homes would imply that private institutions
which offered low-quality services would be driven out of business via
market forces. However, accountability demands regulation, and this
would implicitly compromise the independence of these small
businesses (Phillips and Vincent 1986). Although privatization has
meant that the state has in one sense been rolled back, then, the demands
of regulation may require that it is rolled forward in another direction
(Day and Klein 1987), in order to protect the vulnerable.

*New resources for health care? Commercialization and privatization
within the NHS*

A key point in government statements on the NHS has been the stress on
the finite public purse. A notable feature of recent policy debate has
therefore been the insistent calls for additional private-sector resources,
with the government claiming that Britain's health expenditures are low
by European standards because of low expenditure on private health
care. The corollary, as in the public sector generally, has been the call
for greater efficiency, more determined management and an entrepreneurial approach, on the grounds that the problems of the NHS are
not ones of resources but of management and local political interference
in the running of the service. The most interesting innovations, in terms
of the future development of the NHS, are the calls for greater
collaboration between the NHS and the private sector, for income
generation by health authorities and charitable support for the NHS.
Their political significance is disproportionate to their impact on the
NHS's financial position.

Blurring the boundaries: collaboration between the public and private sectors

There has always been collaboration between public and private providers of health care. When the NHS was founded, some 270 hospitals remained in private hands. These often treated NHS patients on a contractual basis, which helped the NHS considerably in cases where new hospitals could not be built due to public-expenditure restraint in the early post-war years. More recently, government policy has stressed that health authorities should take into account the existing and planned distribution of facilities in the private sector (DHSS 1981); DHSS guidance issued in 1983 emphasized that the 'benefits of partnership with the private sector were disproportionate to its size' (quoted by Griffith *et al.* 1987: 49); and within months of the 1987 election, John Moore, the then Secretary of State for Social Services, extolled the benefits of collaboration with the private sector in an introduction to a directory of private health services produced by BUPA. Health authorities have explored, among others, the following options:

1. proposals to keep hospitals open as *charitable trusts*, relying on donations, legacies and other fund-raising activities to bridge the gap left by the withdrawal of NHS finance. The best-known example is Tadworth Court (a branch of Great Ormond Street Children's Hospital), but several other DHAs have at least investigated this option (see Mohan 1986);
2. proposals for *commercial involvement* in the management and finance of NHS facilities. Examples include various proposals for commercial management of private wings in NHS hospitals, for sharing skilled staff with nearby NHS facilities and for jointly funded capital developments (see Mohan 1989);
3. proposals by DHAs either to contract-out patient care to private hospitals, to set up community facilities as independent trusts whereby patients can claim rent from the DHSS or even to rely on the private sector entirely for long-stay provision (see West Midlands Health Watch 1988).

For the DHAs involved, these no doubt represent rational responses to adverse financial circumstances. The interest in such ideas may well come from Thatcherite health authority chairs and/or innovative managers, keen to demonstrate their authority and managerial talent (and to reap the rewards, in the form of performance-related pay) by implementing novel forms of service delivery or work organization. For commercial organizations, these developments offer an opportunity to demonstrate their readiness and willingness to play a much larger part in managing health services and this could prefigure proposals to hand over the management of health services to private organizations, which right-wing commentators have urged upon the government. These developments might also serve as useful demonstrations of the possibilities for removing inflexibilities in the NHS, such as nationally agreed wage rates. One consequence of transferring Tadworth Court to charitable ownership, for instance, was that wage rates were to depend on the resources available to the Trust and that NHS unions were not recognized.

Income-generation schemes

In most health authorities these schemes are of recent origin. They can, however, be bracketed with the proposals outlined in the DHSS's guidance to DHAs issued for the 1982 reorganization, and with the emphasis on cost improvements and land sales (DHSS 1983b), as measures designed to encourage health authorities to take a more entrepreneurial approach to raising resources. Various DHAs had engaged in experiments along these lines before a national initiative was introduced in the 1987 Health and Medicines Bill. On one level, the logic is impeccable: health authorities have considerable assets which are not always fully utilized, and large numbers of people (staff, patients and visitors) use NHS premises. Bring the two together and there are large potential marketing opportunities. Furthermore, who can object to the laudable aim of raising money for the NHS?

The reality may be rather different. The sums raised are minimal – it is estimated that after three years the result will be some £70 million pounds, or some 0.3 per cent of total expenditure on the service. As Ken Grant (general manager of City and Hackney DHA) observed, 'in terms of what the NHS needs, the money we are raising (through income generation) is peanuts. *It's just that at the moment, peanuts are bloody useful*' (evidence to the House of Commons Social Services Committee 1988 – emphasis added). But critics have argued that services will be geared towards generating income rather than meeting local health needs and that funding will often be temporary so that planning and provision of services will be short-term and piecemeal. Finally, health authorities would be most likely to make money by doing what they are best at – namely, clinical activity. They would probably concentrate on short-stay, high-return surgery, or on screening, both of which could easily be sold, at a profit, to the private sector. The implication is that such schemes could lead away from the basic aims of the NHS (GLACHC 1987). The small sums raised so far (see National Association of Health Authorities 1988) raise the suspicion that income generation is simply a method for general managers to demonstrate flair rather than to address real health problems. Quantitative targets, in terms of sums raised, are more easily demonstrable than specific targets for health standards.

Charities: back to the thirties?

Charitable donations fit neatly with the new ideological doctrines of 'active citizenship' being promulgated by Conservative ministers. The argument is essentially that those who have participated in the fruits of economic recovery have a moral duty to those who are less fortunate. The sort of active participation the government would like to see is evident from John Patten's statement that individuals should accept that 'I produce, therefore I have a moral duty to care and provide' (writing in the *Guardian*, 28 September 1988: 23). In the case of the NHS, charitable support has usually taken the form of appeals for expensive pieces of equipment such as whole-body scanners, or high-profile national campaigns for specific hospitals. The most famous examples have been the 'Wishing Well' appeal to provide funds to redevelop the Great Ormond Street Children's Hospital, and Jimmy Saville's efforts to raise £10 million for Stoke Mandeville spinal injuries hospital. Several hospitals have reopened under charitable trusts, and there are instances of appeals for funds to keep hospitals open 'from Alnwick to Penzance', as one Opposition MP put it in a recent debate.

It is easy to criticize these developments. They distort planning; they are inherently unreliable and uncertain sources of funds. Access to charitable sources self-evidently varies greatly. National appeals, properly orchestrated and with central-government backing, can raise enormous sums, but the funds available to health authorities and hospitals from charitable sources are typically small, making a limited contribution to the purchase of equipment, provision of patient recreational facilities, etc. There are major variations between and within regions, and it is obvious that hospitals in different areas will have different access to funds and be capable of mobilizing different resources for raising them. The more serious political question to be answered about the role of charity, however, is where the boundary should be drawn between state and charitable provision. The Great Ormond Street appeal could be regarded as a one-off demonstration project but the national prominence of this hospital would almost guarantee success; the scope to replicate Wishing Well elsewhere may be strictly limited. Furthermore, increased charitable activity of this kind would encourage a *localism* in service provision in which people and communities defend their own services (there has, for instance, also been evidence of competition between national appeals such as Wishing Well, and local campaigns for less-well-known hospitals (*Guardian*, 14 September 1988: 21) while ignoring the wider political context in which that charitable giving takes place.

The White Paper: a change of pace, not direction?

The significance of the White Paper is not that it marks a radical break with the concept underlying the NHS, for the service will continue, as now, to be free at the point of use and financed largely from direct taxation. Nor does it mark a departure even within the context of the last ten years: many of its central themes – competition, welfare pluralism, managerial efficiency – were well established some years ago. In discussing the White Paper's implications for privatization, I first look at the continuities and discontinuities with previous policy before noting the likely impact of specific proposals such as those for 'self-governing hospital trusts' and finally, evaluating the likely effects of the White Paper on privatization of services.

The White Paper (Secretary of State for Health 1989) emphasizes the importance of localism and local management in the provision of services. Rather than impose centrally determined solutions, the argument runs, management should be free to react locally to whatever difficulties arise in their district or hospital. Since 1979, there has been unprecedented growth in the service, a vast increase in activity, achieved through a combination of the government's generosity and improved efficiency. Despite this, a 'wide variation in performance' still exists. The solution is better management, in order to 'raise the performance of all hospitals and GPs to that of the best'. It is argued that 'experience in both the public service and the private sector has shown that the best-run organizations are those in which local staff are given responsibility for responding to local need'. Therefore the vision for the future is one in which local managers are freed, as far as possible, to make their own decisions. The paper also stresses that this freedom will bring great benefits – local managers will be able to draw on the resources available in the local community to provide a wide range of services; these resources might include charitable and commercial facilities, sponsorship and so on.

There are several important continuities with previous practice. There are proposals for greater flexibility from constraints such as national wage rates and, for DHAs and hospitals, greater freedom from supervision by RHAs (Regional Health Authorities) and the Department of Health. Hospitals and health authorities will have the scope to determine whether they wish to continue to provide all their support services 'in-house' or to subcontract them to the private sector. This could lead to the widespread introduction, into the health service, of methods more usually associated with the much-vaunted 'flexible firm' (Atkinson and Meager 1986): concentration on 'core' functions and on a 'core' workforce, while buying in as many functions as possible from outside (note, for instance, the reports of DHAs and RHAs considering

49

establishing their management and information-services divisions as separate entities). Nor is the entrepreneurial approach implicit in the White Paper anything new, though it is strengthened by proposals for commercialization, such as those for capital charging. By forcing health authorities to take a commercial approach to valuation of their assets, the policy is designed to maximize throughput and turnover; health authorities will have an incentive to treat as many patients as possible, as quickly as possible. Similarly, under the proposals for the 'internal market', health authorities will compete to ensure they attract patients with low-cost packages while shopping around for the best possible deal for their own patients. It is proposals like these that support the *British Medical Journal*'s editorial comment that the White Paper 'subjects the NHS to a full dose of the enterprise culture that has characterised the Thatcher years' (Warden 1989).

While the general thrust of the White Paper is towards continuity rather than change, one proposal for greater privatization marks a radical departure: the tax concessions for insurance premiums for those aged over 65. This was the sole proposal in the Paper which involved spending additional public money, and was apparently included at the insistence of the Prime Minister against the advice of the Chancellor of the Exchequer and the Minister of Health. There are echoes of the introduction of Medicare (for the elderly) in the USA, in the sense that the elderly are generally seen as a 'deserving' group worthy of support, but arguably, this proposal can be regarded as the harbinger of greater concessions to the private sector in due course. It also directly prioritizes one of the Conservatives' key groups of supporters – the middle-aged and elderly in the south.

One of the most novel proposals is that for the establishment of 'self-governing hospital trusts'. It is examined here since the ability of hospitals to secede from the NHS is perhaps one of the most significant developments in the White Paper. It is a novel form of privatization which will, in some senses, recreate the pre-NHS 'voluntary hospital'. The rationale is to 'encourage a stronger sense of *local* (my emphasis) ownership and pride, building on the enormous fund of goodwill that exists in local communities . . . it will encourage local initiative and greater competition'. NHS Hospital Trusts will have the ability to depart from nationally agreed wage rates and to borrow on capital markets, to have autonomy in acquiring and disposing of assets, and they will be permitted to generate surpluses.

The most likely hospitals to opt out will be those with a high regional (if not national) profile, capable of attracting patients over a wide area, and likely to attract substantial charitable or commercial support. There will be several effects on the way these hospitals run their business. First, capital funds raised from commercial sources will require a rate-of-return on assets and this will mean that hospitals will be forced to generate profits on their trading account. Moreover, there is the danger that only certain hospitals will have access to such funds. The experience of the USA suggests that access to Wall Street finance in effect determines whether or not hospitals can be built; those likely to serve large numbers of the poor – and therefore possibly unprofitable – are most unlikely to attract financial backing for capital investment (Berliner 1987). Second, self-governing hospitals will be competing for funds to give them an edge over their rivals. There is ample historical evidence of the problems to which this can lead: duplication of facilities was typical, with many small and (ultimately) uneconomic specialist hospitals being established, especially in London, to gain a niche in the market (Nuffield Provincial Hospitals Trust 1946). Inevitably capital equipment – scanners, lithotripters, etc. – will be duplicated. The experience of the USA is, again, instructive. Califano (1986) has commented on the difficulties of persuading hospitals that there really is no need for additional diagnostic equipment and that their money could be more usefully spent elsewhere.

Third, there are going to be problems of planning. Hospital Trusts, especially in the acute sector, are going to be primarily concerned with throughput and quick post-operative discharge. It is essential, therefore, that adequate community care is provided to enable this to happen if self-government and the internal market are not to represent an implicit form of privatization, namely the transfer of responsibility for care of convalescents to families (see also Land, Chapter 8, this volume). There are certain to be serious problems of co-ordinating the activities of Hospital Trusts with those of the health authorities from which they are drawing their patients: there may, indeed, be problems actually persuading such hospitals to treat 'costly' categories of patient. The contract mechanism for funding will, it is true, force hospitals to compete for patients and give them an incentive to treat greater numbers; but contracts will have to be drawn up in a way which ensures that *all* patients receive equal treatment; costs will need to be specified very precisely, otherwise there is a risk of high-cost patients receiving inadequate treatment. (Note, in this context, Le Grand's (1989) proposal for education vouchers tailored towards working-class children, thus giving schools an incentive to attract them; the NHS proposals, in contrast, are a modified capitation system, which pay little attention to relative needs.) More generally, the thrust of the Paper is towards identifying those parts of the service which can, in principle, be made 'profitable' and then fragmenting the service accordingly; with individual hospitals operating as *de facto* separate units, the possibilities of cross-subsidization, which are inherent in the NHS in its present form, will be lost.

51

This example suggests that the White Paper is likely to lead to fragmentation within the NHS and towards a two-tier service. It is ironic that this is so in a document which so heavily emphasizes *consumerism*; for there is an implicit conflict with the principal financial proposals of the Paper. We can applaud much of the stress on consumer rights – indeed, attempting to redress the balance between producers and consumers is long overdue – but the question of *choice* will come down to where the patient's GP or DHA can obtain the best deal. Choices are likely to be heavily constrained anyway, by the extent to which patients are willing and able to travel, and by the GP's knowledge not just of the cost of hospital treatment but also of the quality of care in several institutions, but it is hard, at this stage, to disagree with Robin Cook's criticism that 'this is not money following patients, it is patients following money' (*Hansard*, 31 January 1989, vol. 146, col. 171). In a sense the plans to expand GPs' freedom of referral simply convert the costs saved by cheaper treatment into a price for the consumer in the form of greater travel costs.

In summary, the White Paper does indeed represent a change of pace, with processes of commercialization and privatization *within* the service being given a further boost. This tendency will be strengthened by the managerial reforms of the service which will further weaken local representation by removing local-authority and trade-union nominees and replacing DHAs by boards composed of individuals appointed for the contribution they can make as individuals, not as representatives of interest groups. The interests prioritized are medical and managerial rather than those of consumers and communities; to echo Alford's (1975) analysis, the interests of the majority of users of services are 'repressed'. Greater scope is given to managers to demonstrate their flair and initiative, but the scope for communities to articulate their views – and have them acted upon – seems highly restricted. The impacts on service quality and availability remain to be seen; the enormous gaps that exist in, say, the USA's health-care system seem unlikely to develop, but the scope is certainly there for fragmentation.

Conclusion

I have argued that these diverse forms of privatization have to be understood as parts of a wider political strategy towards the welfare state, and not as the results of the independent operations of market forces. I therefore attempted to show how a number of direct and indirect steps have been taken, which in many respects represent a blueprint for a future health service. I then looked at the existing and likely future impacts of privatization, both in the independent sector and within the NHS. In assessing the wider political and social significance of these developments, I focus first, on likely future directions for privatization. I then consider whether these developments constitute a coherent strategy and a challenge to the NHS. I follow Davies (1987) in arguing that a form of welfare pluralism is emerging, and see the significance of privatization less in direct material terms than in its effects on the way the NHS delivers its services and on public attitudes to welfare.

The preceding analysis of the White Paper has suggested that the NHS is moving in the direction of greater commercialization and privatization, with an emphasis on entrepreneurial activity by managers, authorities and doctors at all levels. This trend is likely to be coupled to two others, which will indirectly constitute privatization by transferring more of the costs of health care either to individual consumers or by subsidies to specific groups of taxpayers in the form of tax concessions. In respect of the former, the government's view seems to be that the beneficiaries of recent economic growth would be willing to pay more towards the cost of NHS services, but they have argued this in a way which makes it appear that growth in the NHS is *conditional* on people paying more. Margaret Thatcher expressed this view in Parliament recently, saying that many people would 'feel that it was quite wrong if they were not allowed to pay the small sums [for eye tests], *which they can well afford* to enable substantial developments in the NHS to take place' (*Hansard*, 1 November 1988, vol. 139, c.819, my emphasis). Could this prefigure, at last, an attempt to introduce on a large scale, charges at the point of use (such as 'hotel charges', favoured by many Conservatives)? Second, it is unlikely that having established the principle of tax relief in the White Paper, no attempt will be made to extend this subsidy to others.

Do the apparently disparate developments described here represent a coherent strategy or blueprint for the future? The Thatcher governments do appear to have consistently encouraged a range of commercial, individual and community initiatives in the provision and financing of health care, as well as promoting privatization within the service by their own managerial reforms. In this vision, individuals, the market and the 'community' play a much greater role in financing and providing health care; DHAs will assume a more co-ordinating role in health service delivery, seeking to draw upon public and private, formal and informal sources of health care; and the role of managers will be to 'deliver' within finite budgets and to explore options for expanding those budgets. The danger in these proposals is that the availability of resources will come to depend more and more on unplanned sources – volunteers, charitable donations, corporate sponsorship, commercial decisions taken in the private health sector – to the point where, although the NHS provides a bedrock of services, communities will differ greatly in the other resources at their command. This will not be planning according to need, and local control could be lost as management of services will depend on a multiplicity of agencies. The net effect is likely to strengthen the hand of managers against community claims for additional funds, and to decentralize blame (for poor service quality or for service reductions) from government to local management. A key area for future research is the continued uneven impact of privatization and also the likely future effects on work organization and attitudes within the NHS.

Has privatization in fact provided a 'challenge to the NHS'? The private health sector has not challenged the near-monopoly of the NHS, and the other forms of privatization reviewed here have had limited impact to date. Management styles and assumptions have also been challenged, although it is arguable whether the 'new managerialism' is appropriate to the NHS (Petchey 1986). In the long term, perhaps the key challenge may prove to be in the area of public attitudes to welfare. There remains considerable public support for the NHS, and recent opinion polls suggest considerable disquiet about the government's proposed reforms. However, there is also endorsement, even among Labour supporters, of private health care. Now while the vast majority of the population have an interest in the availability of a national health service, placing them in the position of individual consumers (which will be one effect of the White Paper), may erode collective solidarity in this regard (Taylor-Gooby 1989). The rhetoric of choice – for instance of where to be treated, or of paying extra for additional 'hotel' services – could be seductive. The possibility exists of many more people exiting to the private sector, especially if tempted by an extension of tax relief. Against this, Taylor-Gooby points out that exit does not preclude voicing of complaints about the state of the NHS, so it does not automatically follow that collective support for the NHS will be eroded. In this respect it would be useful if more were known about the attitudes of those using the private sector towards the NHS. Also relevant here is the growing trend of 'exit' from the NHS in the form of alternative therapies and medicines and self-help groups; this is perhaps a more genuinely consumerist movement than the private acute sector and it may be that those opting for it have somewhat different attitudes towards the NHS than the beneficiaries of private insurance policies. The extent to which privatization succeeds in breaking up what is still a fairly coherent bloc of consumer and employee support for NHS will determine whether the White Paper is the end of the line for the present government's policies, or merely the first step along the road towards a wholesale privatization and breakup of the NHS.

Acknowledgement

I should like to acknowledge the financial support of an ESRC Post-doctoral Research Fellowship, grant no A23320036.

I should also like to thank Peter Taylor-Gooby for his comments on this chapter.

References

Alford, R. (1975) *Health Care Politics: Ideological and Interest-Group Barriers to Reform*, Chicago: University of Chicago Press.

Andrews, K. (1984) 'Private rest homes in the care of the elderly', *British Medical Journal* 288: 1518–20.

Atkinson, J. and Meager, N. (1986) *New Forms of Work Organisation* (IMS Report no 121), Brighton: Institute for Manpower Studies.

Audit Commission (1986) *Making a Reality of Community Care*, London: HMSO.

Berliner, H. and Regan, C. (1987) 'Multinational operations of US for-profit hospital chains: trends and implications', *American Journal of Public Health* 77: 1280–4.

Bow Group (1983) *Beveridge and the Bow Group Generation*, London: Bow Group.

Califano, J. (1986) *America's Health Care Revolution*, New York: Random House.

Crouch, C. (1985) 'Can socialism achieve street credibility?' *The Guardian* 14 February 1985, p. 9.

DHSS (Department of Health and Social Security) (1981) *Contractual Arrangements with Independent Hospitals and Nursing Homes*, London: DHSS.

—— (1983a) *NHS Management Inquiry Report (Griffiths Report)*, London: DHSS.

—— (1983b) *Under-used and Surplus Property in the NHS*, London: HMSO.

Davies, C. (1987) 'Things to come: the NHS in the next decade', *Sociology of Health and Illness* 9: 302–17.

Day, P. and Klein, R. (1987) 'The business of welfare', *New Society* 80 (1277): 11–13.

Forman, R. and Saldana, N. (1988) 'The role of private insurance in health care cost containment', in Institute of Economic Affairs Health Unit, *Keeping the Lid on Costs?* London: Institute of Economic Affairs, pp. 11–22.

Gamble, A. (1988) *The Free Economy and the Strong State*, London: Macmillan.

—— (1989) 'Thatcherism and the new politics', in J. Mohan (ed.) *The Political Geography of Contemporary Britain*, London: Macmillan, pp. 1–16.

Gough, I. (1979) *The Political Economy of the Welfare State*, London: Macmillan.

GLACHC (Greater London Association of CHCs) (1987) *Dismantling the NHS? A Report on Income Generation Schemes in City and Hackney*, London: GLACHC.

Green, D. (1985) *Working-class Patients and the Medical Establishment: Self-help in Britain from the Mid-nineteenth Century to 1948*, Aldershot: Gower.

Griffith, B. Iliffe, S. and Rayner, G. (1987) *Banking on Sickness: Commercial Medicine in Britain and the USA*, London: Lawrence & Wishart.

Haywood, S. and Ranade, W. (1989) 'Privatizing from within: the NHS under Thatcher', *Local Government Studies* 15: 19–34.

Holmes, B. and Johnson, A. (1988) *Cold Comfort: The Scandal of Private Rest Homes*, London: Souvenir Press.

House of Commons Social Services Committee (1986) *Fourth Report from the Social Services Committee, Session 1985–6: Public Expenditure on the Social Services*, London: HMSO.

—— (1988) *Sixth Report, Session 1987–88: Public Expenditure on the Social Services*, London: HMSO.

Jessop, B., Bonnett, K., Bromley, S. and Ling, T. (1984) 'Authoritarian populism, two nations, and Thatcherism', *New Left Review* 147: 32–60.

—— (1987) 'Popular capitalism, flexible accumulation and left strategy', *New Left Review* 165: 104–22.

Judge, K. and Knapp, M. (1985) 'Efficiency in the production of welfare: the public and private sectors compared', in R. Klein and M. O'Higgins (eds) *The Future of Welfare*, Oxford: Blackwell, pp. 131–49.

Krieger, J. (1987) 'Social policy in the age of Reagan and Thatcher', *Socialist Register* 23: 177–98.

Laurance, J. (1983) 'Collapse of the BUPA boom', *New Society* 25 February, pp. 295–6.

Le Grand, J. and Estrin, S. (eds) (1989) *Market Socialism*, London: Unwin Hyman.

Le Grand, J. and Robinson, R. (eds) (1984) *Privatization and The Welfare State*, London: Allen & Unwin.

Mohan, J. (1986) 'Private medical care and the British Conservative government', *Journal of Social Policy* 15: 339–60.

—— (1989) 'Rolling back the state? Privatization of health services under the Thatcher governments', in J. Scarpaci (ed.) *Privatisation of Health Services: An International Survey*, Rutgers: Rutgers University Press, pp. 112–29.

National Association of Health Authorities (1988) *Income Generation Schemes in the NHS: A Directory*, Birmingham: NAHA.

Nicholl, J.P., Beeby, N.R. and Williams, B.T. (1989) 'Role of the private sector in elective surgery in England and Wales, 1986', *British Medical Journal* 298: 243–6.

Nuffield Provincial Hospitals Trust (1946) *The Hospital Surveys: the Domesday Book of the Hospital Service*, London: Nuffield Provincial Hospitals Trust.

OPCS (1988) *Social Trends*, London: Office of Population Censuses and Surveys.

Papadakis, E. and Taylor-Gooby, P. (1988) *The Private Provision of Public Welfare: State, Market and Community*, Brighton: Wheatsheaf.

Petchey, R. (1986) 'The Griffiths reorganisation of the NHS: Fowlerism by stealth?' *Critical Social Policy* 17: 87–101.

Phillips, D.R. and Vincent, J.A. (1986) 'Petit bourgeois care: private residential care for the elderly', *Policy and Politics* 14 (2): 189–208.

Public Accounts Committee (1988) *Twenty-Sixth Report, Session 1987–88: Community Care Developments*, London: HMSO.

Rayner, G. (1986) 'Health care as a business: the emergence of a commercial hospital sector in Britain', *Policy and Politics* 14: 439–59.

—— (1987) 'Lessons from America? Commercialisation and growth of private medicine in Britain', *International Journal of Health Services* 17: 197–216.

Redwood, J. (1988) *Popular Capitalism*, London: Routledge.

Secretary of State for Health (1989) *Working for Patients*, London: HMSO, Cm 555.

Taylor-Gooby, P. (1989) 'Disquiet and welfare: clinging to nanny' *International Journal of Urban and Regional Research* 13: 201–16.

Titmuss, R.M. (1962) 'The social division of welfare', in R.M. Titmuss *Essays on the Welfare State*, London: Unwin University Books.

Vincent, J. Tibbenham, A. and Phillips, D. (1987) 'Choice in residential care: myths and realities', *Journal of Social Policy* 16 (4): 435–60.

Warden, J. (1989) 'NHS Review', *British Medical Journal* 298: 275.

West Midlands County Council (1986) *The Realities of Home Life*, Birmingham: NUPE/West Midlands CC.

West Midlands Health Watch (1988) 'Another geriatric hospital to be privatised', *West Midlands Health Watch* Jan/Feb.: 19.

Chapter three

The politics of professional power: medicine in a changing health service

Mary Ann Elston

Introduction

During the 1960s and 1970s, one theme recurred in British and American writing in medical sociology and health policy: that medical power was an entrenched feature of modern systems of health care. In sociological terms, medicine, with law, was the paradigmatic profession, a publicly mandated and state-backed monopolistic supplier of a valued service, exercising autonomy in the workplace and collegiate control over recruitment, training and the regulation of members' conduct (Freidson 1970; Johnson 1972). Moreover, in the eyes of some sociologists, this dominant profession was imperialistic, apparently ruthlessly intent on enlarging its sphere of influence through the medicalizing of society (e.g. Zola 1972) as well as subordinating other occupations in the health division of labour (Freidson 1970).

Studies of health policy-making during the same period generally emphasized the monopoly of legitimacy enjoyed by the medical profession, relative to other health workers, in the development of health policy and the profession's unique ability to block change at national or local levels (e.g. Klein 1974; Ham 1981; Haywood and Alaszewski 1980). Thus, the medical profession was repeatedly portrayed as the dominant structural interest in health-care policy, consistently able to defeat the attempts of third parties to control them (Alford 1975).

Beneath this consensus on medical power there was considerable disagreement among social scientists as to its basis. Did it stem from organizational characteristics of the profession or from its control of valued expertise; from societal trust of the profession, its success in achieving market closure or from its function in reproducing capitalism's labour force (e.g. Klein 1974; Freidson 1970; Larson 1977; Navarro 1976)? Few writers in the 1970s suggested that medical authority and dominance might be or become threatened (examples included Haug 1973; Armstrong 1976; Elston 1977a) or cautioned against hyperbole in sociological conceptions of medical imperialism (Strong 1979).

As we enter the 1990s, we can see significant changes in the academic literature over the past decade. In the 1960s and 1970s, scant attention was paid to the non-medical participants in the health division of labour. For example, nursing, if it appeared at all, typically appeared as a failed profession or, at best, as a member of that 'stunted occupational subspecies', the 'semi-professions' (Salvage 1988: 517). But since then, the work and organization of other health-care occupations have been increasingly scrutinized in their own right and in relation to medicine (e.g. Larkin 1983; Ovreteit 1985; Homans 1987). Nursing-policy studies is a growing field (e.g. White 1985; Robinson and Strong 1987). Stacey and her colleagues at Warwick have demonstrated the value of a shift from the analysis of discrete professions towards the analysis of the overall division of labour and negotiation of occupational boundaries in particular sectors of health care (Stacey and Davies 1983). Indeed, in Britain over the past decade there have been few studies of the contemporary medical profession and its institutions.

Among the many factors behind these shifts in academic attention are the influence of feminism and awareness of the increasing complexity of the health division of labour. There has also been the strong influence of more historically informed accounts of the development of health-care occupations, as evidenced by the flourishing 'new nursing history' and several studies of the professionalization of medicine. This latter process is now generally seen as contingent on nineteenth-century social and economic developments rather than as the unproblematic evolution of an occupational 'natural history' (although the various historical accounts differ over the precise timing and causes of successful professionalization (Peterson 1978; Larson 1977; Waddington 1984)). This shift in the way the development of medical power is conceptualized has perhaps made it easier to contemplate the possibility of its decline in changed social circumstances.

And it is this last possibility that is the new recurrent theme of literature on the American medical profession in the 1980s. Take, for example, the titles of some recent publications discussing the latest stage in the *The Social Transformation of American Medicine* (Starr 1982): 'Towards the Proletarianization of Physicians' (McKinlay and Arches 1985); *From Physician Shortage to Patient Shortage: The Uncertain Future of Medical Practice* (Ginzberg 1986); *The Physician as Captain of the Ship: A Critical Re-Appraisal* (King *et al.* 1988). In these accounts, increasing state and corporate involvement in American medical care and education, with its associated bureaucratization of work organization, decreasing public confidence in doctors and changes in their market position, e.g. through oversupply, are seen as gradually bringing about diminution of doctors' autonomy and influence over policy-making or even their relegation to the ranks of 'wage-slaves'. American medicine is seen by some writers as undergoing a process of 'deprofessionalization' or 'proletarianization' (e.g. Haug 1976; Starr 1982; McKinlay and Stoeckle 1988). Even those who are critical of what they perceive as exaggerated reports of the death of medical dominance do not dispute that major changes are taking place in the American health-care system and in medical power and authority (Stevens 1986; Freidson 1985; 1986; Rosenthal 1987).

In Britain, as yet, this theme is muted in the academic literature. But, in the context of furious political debate about the future of our current health-care system and the possibility of radical change taking place, questions about it are increasingly heard in the profession's own journals and in the mass media. It is timely, therefore, to consider whether we are on the threshold of a decline in medical dominance and in the professional autonomy of medicine in Britain.

In this paper I tentatively explore this question and the validity of claims of incipient proletarianization or professionalization of medicine in the British context. My comments are necessarily somewhat speculative as any question about the waning of professional sovereignty in Britain resists a definitive answer at present for several reasons. First, the impact of new challenges on the medical profession is hard to assess on the evidence available now. In some cases, we are talking of policy proposals, which promise radical change, at least according to some interpretations, but which may be very different in their eventual implementation (e.g. the enactment of the White Papers on Primary Care (DHSS 1987) and on NHS reform, *Working for Patients* (DH 1989)). In other cases, there is little or no systematic information about the implications of changes that are already occurring.

Second, the inherent difficulty of assessing changes in the distribution of that elusive and multidimensional quality, power, (Lukes 1974) remains an obstacle to assessing the validity of claims of deprofessionalization or proletarianization of medicine. Few would dispute that overt questioning of medical autonomy and expertise has increased markedly in the past decade in Britain or that this has intensified in the past two years as the debate over the future of the NHS has gathered momentum. 'Doctor-bashing' and calls for reform have become major sports in the mass media. Indeed, the British Medical Association has felt obliged to publicly protest at this, for example, accusing the Secretary of State for Health of complicity in 'what appears to be a deliberate attempt ... to denigrate the work of doctors and undermine their standing in the public's eyes' (*BMJ* 1988, 297: 1132). Increase in overt challenges and the provocation of organized response may in themselves signify some shift in power relationships, indicating that the dominant are no longer able to keep some issues unarticulated and off political agendas. But the expression of desire for radical change should not be mistaken for that change.

Third, and relatedly, there is the persistent problem of inadequate conceptualization of professional autonomy and medical dominance in empirical research. Too often, different theories about the present and future status of medicine seize on one aspect of change and draw general conclusions about overall rise or fall, ignoring other, countervailing tendencies. Accounts of the development and extent of professional power in the United States have sometimes been applied to Britain with little consideration of their validity. Without clearer initial bench marks and specification of the dimensions of professional power, assessment of change is likely to remain a contentious business. The following points should help to clarify my subsequent discussion.

In discussion of medical power, the concepts of autonomy and dominance are often used interchangeably. They are clearly closely related but an analytic distinction can be made. 'Medical dominance' I take to refer to medicine's authority over others. This authority can, following Starr (1982: 13) be subdivided into social authority (akin to Weber's *Herrschaft*), i.e. medicine's control over the actions of others through the giving of commands, and cultural authority, i.e. the probability that medical definitions of reality and medical judgements will be accepted as valid and true (Starr 1982: 13).

Professional autonomy refers to the legitimated control that an occupation exercises over the organization and terms of its work. Autonomy is not an absolute property. Professionalized medicine in Britain has never been completely free of external constraint nor free to impose its will on government in all circumstances. Nor are all other health-care occupations wholly lacking some degree of autonomy in their work. The question is how much control medicine possesses over different aspects of its work and how this is changing, for different dimensions of professional autonomy need to be distinguished. For example, we should separate autonomy as a property of individuals by virtue of their membership of a profession from autonomy that is vested in a profession as a corporate body and identify the different levels at which occupational self-control might be exercised (national, local, individual).

Various classifications have been put forward of the different aspects of work activity over which professional autonomy might be exercised (Freidson 1970; Ovretveit 1985; Schulz and Harrison 1986). Three main categories recur: economic autonomy, the right of doctors to determine their remuneration; political autonomy, the right of doctors to make policy decisions as the legitimate experts on health matters; and clinical or technical autonomy, the right of the profession to set its own standards and control clinical performance, exercised, for example, through clinical freedom at the bedside, professional control over re-cruitment and training or collegial control over discipline and mal-practice. It is an empirical question how far a change in one type of control has implications for autonomy over other aspects or at other levels. Moreover, a decline in some types of medical autonomy does not necessarily affect medicine's standing relative to other occupations if, for example, those other occupations' autonomy is also declining. Finally, differences in interests, status and autonomy between segments of the medical profession (and changes in these differences) should not be ignored (Elston 1977a).

These points suggest that simple answers to question about changes in medical power are unlikely to be forthcoming: hardly a surprising conclusion given the complexity and variety of health-care practice and policy in modern societies. Claims made about the incipient proletarianization or deprofessionalization of medicine, whether in the United States or Great Britain should therefore be subjected to critical analysis.

The proletarianization and deprofessionalization theses examined

There is much common ground between those sociologists who claim that the American medical profession's loss of power is tantamount to their becoming members of the proletariat and those who prefer to speak of deprofessionalization. First, both are claims that medicine is finally falling victim to general social trends affecting all occupations who claimed privileged status on the basis of technical expertise in late twentieth-century societies. Thus, there are prior questions to be asked about the validity of these two views as general accounts as well as about their applicability to medicine. Second, both claim only that these changes are developing, not that the process is complete. So there is much scope for argument about the interpretation of data trends and time scales. Third, both are claims about the significance of changes in American medical practice over the past two decades: the trend away from independent, free-for-service-based, solo practice towards salaried practice carried out within complex bureaucratic organizations. That this trend has been occurring cannot be disputed (although the trans-formation is far from complete) but its sociological implications are less clear[1].

The proletarianization thesis is particularly associated with Oppenheimer (1973) and McKinlay (McKinlay and Arches 1985; McKinlay and Stoeckle 1988). These Marxist writers argue that the logic of capitalist development is such that medicine is now undergoing a transformation of its labour process equivalent to that described by Marx as affecting independent artisans in the Industrial Revolution i.e.

their incorporation into a factory-like production system, with progressive loss of autonomy and skills. The term 'proletarianization' is used to 'denote *the process by which an occupational category is divested of control over certain prerogatives relating to the location, content and essentiality of its task activities and is thereby subordinated to the broader requirements of production under advanced capitalism*' (McKinlay and Arches 1985: 161, emphasis in the original).

Seven specific professional prerogatives are identified as diminishing for physicians (ibid: 161–2): control over (1) criteria for entrance, (2) content of training, (3) terms and content of work, (4) objects of labour (e.g. clients served), (5) tools of labour (equipment, drugs, etc.), (6) the means of labour (premises, etc.), (7) amount and rate of remuneration. Manifestations of changes in physicians' formerly privileged position include the deskilling allegedly inherent in the increasing specialization and technological approach of medicine, ceding of control over decision making within the complex organization that constitutes the modern hospital to managers, increasing physician unionization and increasing challenge to doctors' social and cultural authority from the lay public.

Thus American physicians allegedly face increasing economic, organizational and technical alienation from their labour (cf. Larson 1977). This alienation, and associated loss of autonomy and dominance, is attributed to the bureaucratization of the American health-care system, a process occurring through increasing state control of the financing of health care and increasing corporate provision of health care for profit. Although it is the 'corporatization' of medicine that is emphasized, increased state intervention is regarded as part of the same process, the state being regarded in this Marxist theory as functioning to support capitalist accumulation (McKinlay and Arches 1985: 176–91).

Extensive criticisms of these arguments in relation to developments in the United States have been put forward by, among others, Freidson (1985; 1986), Stevens (1986), Rosenthal (1987), Roemer (1986) and will not be repeated in full here. Among the general criticisms that can be made of the proletarianization of medicine thesis are that its acceptance presupposes the validity of the general account of progressive proletarianization of virtually the entire labour force in advanced capitalist societies and the identification of this process with Weber's ideas about bureaucratization: claims which are highly contentious within Marxist writing, let alone within the wider body of sociological theory. For example, theoretical debates about the development of a 'service class' or the significance of educational credentials for class formation (Giddens 1973) are ignored by McKinlay and his co-authors. The evidence presented is generally weak or ambiguous, particularly concerning physician behaviour in these bureaucratic organizations. The same observations sometimes appear as both cause and effect of the proletarianization process. In sum, there are *prima facie* grounds for accepting Freidson's conclusion that 'proletarianization' itself remains unarticulated as a concept, making its applicability to the medical profession unclear. It is perhaps best regarded as 'a slogan' rather than an analytic concept (Freidson, 1986: 15; 21).

The deprofessionalization thesis is mainly associated with Haug (1973; 1975; Haug and Lavin 1983) and, to some extent, Starr in his detailed history of the waxing and alleged waning of the professional sovereignty of American medicine since the nineteenth century (Starr 1982). Although concerned with the sociological significance of the same general developments as the advocates of proletarianization, proponents of deprofessionalization identify different factors as the key changes. Whereas the proletarianization thesis places most emphasis on the changing work conditions of doctors, especially the growth of salaried practice and the alleged subordination to managerial control, writers like Haug and Starr stress changes in the relationship between doctors and their patients. Increased rationalization of medical practice and knowledge, e.g. through computerization and increased lay knowledge about health have, Haug suggests, led to a decline in the cultural authority of medicine and in the extent of its monopoly over health-related knowledge.

Unlike the proletarianization thesis, arguments for deprofessionalization do not explicitly draw on a general theory of social change. But the changes in medicine are seen as part of more general social trends of rationalization and codification of expert knowledge and the development of more critical public attitudes to professional experts' paternalism. The main limitations of the deprofessionalization thesis are similar to that of proletarianization: i.e. the lack of specificity makes it hard to test. The evidence proffered is limited, often leaving the significance of changes to be inferred rather than demonstrating it. For example, no direct evidence is presented on whether increased use of computers in medicine actually does bring about a demystification and routinization of medical procedures, rendering them more amenable to lay scrutiny. Yet it is not self-evident (to me at least) that the potential impacts on professional autonomy of greater computer use in, for example, analysing information about operation costs, simulating pharmacological and toxicological processes to replace *in vivo* experiments, or magnetic resonance imaging, e.g. reducing the need for invasive exploratory neurosurgery, are necessarily identical. To suggest that they are is to adopt an extreme technological determinist position. When claims of deprofessionalization are made, it is not always clear exactly what the end point of the process would be. Does it refer to a radical democratization of knowledge and skills leading towards the elimination of a separate skilled cadre of healers as envisaged by Illich (1977), or to a diminution in collegiate control over medical work in favour of greater mediation by third parties or consumer patronage (cf. Johnson 1972) or to the elimination of medicine's privileged position within the health division of labour?

Thus, as presently formulated, neither of these two alternative accounts of diminishing medical power can be regarded as satisfactorily developed theories amenable to rigorous testing. Their value in the American context has been to stimulate debate and empirical research, by drawing attention to the possible significance of changes in the organization of American medicine for doctors and identifying different factors as the possible keys to understanding these changes. In the rest of this Chapter I shall use them in a similar way in the hope of stimulating debate in Britain about the effect of the current changes and challenges facing the British medical profession. After a brief consideration of some of the differences between the American and British medical profession's past and present position, I shall focus on two of the challenges currently being made to the British medical profession's influence and occupational self-control. These are, first, a challenge to medicine's freedom from managerial accountability to the state as buyer of medical services; i.e. a challenge that is significant according to the proletarianization thesis. Second, I consider the extent and significance of the 'consumerist' challenge to medicine's cultural authority and right to self-regulation; a development similar to that emphasized by the American proponents of the deprofessionalization thesis.

The power of the medical profession in the United States and Great Britain

Sociological analysis of the medical profession in Britain has often drawn heavily on the American literature, implicitly accepting Freidson's view that the autonomous professional as described in this sociological tradition is an Anglo-American phenomenon (Freidson 1977). Yet in his seminal text published in 1970, Freidson clearly recognized that there were differences in the work situation of doctors in the two societies. He argued that British doctors had a high technical and political autonomy in common with their American peers. What they lacked, given that the National Health Service (NHS) was the *de facto* monopoly buyer of health services, was economic autonomy. For Freidson, as for many spokesmen for the profession on both sides of the Atlantic, the American medical profession in the early 1970s came closer to the ideal type of the autonomous professional because of the absence of state intervention in health care (Freidson 1970).

Indeed, taking the key professional prerogatives identified as indications of proletarianization by McKinlay and Arches (1985), the British medical profession would appear to have been pushed considerably further down this road than their American counterparts many years ago. Thus, one might argue that they began to lose control over criteria for entrance in 1939 when government quotas for medical school places were first introduced, a process apparently reinforced by subsequent developments such as the acceptance of the 1944 Goodenough Report's recommendation that state financing of medical schools should be conditional on all schools becoming co-educational, and the state-sponsored expansion in medical school places following the Royal Commission on Medical Education in 1968 (Elston 1977b). Analogously, control over the content of undergraduate training might be said to have been gradually decreasing since 1908 when the first medical schools sought state financial support, culminating in the present situation whereby the ability of medical schools to change curricula is constrained by the limits of state finance. The coming of the NHS completed the removal of ownership of the tools and means of labour from doctors who worked in hospitals as well as removing their control over the remuneration of labour. By these criteria, only two of McKinlay's and Arches' (1985) key professional prerogatives, autonomy over the terms and content of work and the convention under which patients 'belong' to individual doctors, survived after 1948.

But rather than demonstrating that proletarianization of the British medical profession was virtually accomplished forty years ago, these points indicate the weakness of the proletarianization argument as currently formulated and the importance of disaggregating components of autonomy in analysis. As indicated earlier, detailed studies of the history of the NHS suggest a very different picture from medicine in the USA. Forty years testing within the NHS suggests that, whatever professional rhetoric may have claimed at times, salaried status and state intervention are not incompatible with a high level of some aspects of professional autonomy and dominance.

Undoubtedly, the inception of the NHS did limit professional freedom to directly determine its own levels of remuneration from patients. The long history of disputes over pay since 1948 suggests that doctors have not always been able to dictate their financial terms of service to the state, although their degree of organization has given them considerable financial muscle in pay negotiations compared to other public-sector workers. But then a direct 'fee-for-service' payment system does not itself guarantee freedom to set high charges or to obtain a satisfactory income. This requires a sufficient supply of consumers able

and willing to pay well for medical services. The lack of such a supply has been a major factor in the development of third-party mediation (whether state or private) in medical care financing throughout the developed world in the second half of the twentieth century.
The coming of the NHS provided a substantial shelter from economic uncertainty for the medical profession as a whole. More generally, in 1948 an 'underlying concordat' between the state and the profession was established with respect to resource allocation. The state determined the level of overall resources devoted to medical care, leaving the profession largely free to determine the use of these resources, under the rubric of 'clinical autonomy' (Klein 1983: 57). This freedom extended to include a considerable level of representation as of right on policy-making bodies at all levels as well as freedom from managerial supervision over patient care. In many respects, the NHS enhanced professional control over the organization and terms of its medical work by, among other things, removing some of the economic constraints on clinical practice. Depending on commentators' political views, this form of state intervention has been variously seen as a progressive emancipation from ill-informed external control (e.g. Honigsbaum 1979) or as a regrettable consolidation of the medical profession's monopolistic powers leading to an inefficient health-care system (Green 1985a, 1985b).

Thus, in contrast to the implications of the proletarianization argument, 'it is not impossible to find evidence that consultants in the "socialized (i.e. bureaucratized) NHS" have more clinical autonomy to diagnose and treat within available resources than their American counterparts' (Schulz and Harrison 1986: 352). Schulz and Harrison go on to suggest that there have been long-standing differences in the extent of peer surveillance of doctors' work between the two countries such that US physicians have accepted restrictions on their clinical autonomy, which would be unthinkable to British doctors but at the same time have had economic autonomy to maximize their earnings (Harrison and Schulz 1989: 205). What they suggest may now be happening is a convergence in patterns of professional autonomy as greater third-party control over both global health-care budgets and clinical decisions develops in both countries. They suggest that, in Alford's terms, the 'corporate rationalizers' seem to be in the ascendant on both sides of the Atlantic (ibid: 209).

The rest of the chapter is concerned with examining the extent and significance of challenge to the British medical profession's autonomy and dominance from corporate rationalizers in the form of the state and its bureaucratic agents and from 'consumers'.

67

A changing relationship between the state, management and medicine

The concordat between the state and the medical profession described previously did not appear to be significantly brought into question during the first thirty years of the NHS, not even when, in the mid-1970s, concern over continuously escalating costs led to marked financial constraints and proposals for rational resource allocation between regions and for national priorities (Elston 1977a). (After all, insufficiency of overall resources (in the profession's eyes) was not itself new). But this concern over apparently inexorably increasing costs in all western health-care systems coincided with the end of an 'era of optimism' (Dollery 1978) about the contribution high-technology scientific medicine was making to health. Evidence of diminishing returns in terms of reducing adult mortality, the iconoclastic epidemiology of McKeown (1976) and Cochrane (1972) and the more dramatic claims of epidemic iatrogenesis of Illich (1977) created a climate in which questioning of the efficiency and effectiveness of medicine's use of resources could become a more legitimate activity for politicians. We may now be seeing the effect of the percolation of these academic ideas to a receptive political audience.

Klein (1984) argued that the election, in 1979, of a government with a strong commitment to reducing public expenditure and to breaking the post-war consensus about state welfare did not immediately change the established pattern of relationships between medicine and the state as buyer of medical services. For the first few years of the Conservative administration, ideological commitments appeared to be repeatedly dashed on the rock of medical power (Klein 1984). But then signs of a possible change began to appear. Increased demands for professionals' financial and managerial accountability accompanied greater financial constraints (in the hospital and community sectors of the NHS). And these demands for accountability have increasingly included reference to outcomes of treatment as well as of service inputs and outputs. Doctors have become progressively typecast in the role of careless users of resources (Davies 1987: p. 315).

The swift introduction, following the Griffiths Report in 1983 (DHSS 1983), of general managers charged with responsibility for the efficient use of resources, apparently cut a swathe across established lines of professional responsibility and clinical freedom. These 'managers' were intended to have a much more directive role than the old-style health service 'administrator'. The unequivocal assessment of these proposals by Trevor Clay, Secretary to the Royal College of Nurses, was not unique: 'The Griffiths Inquiry . . . signalled the demise of professional power in the NHS. The doctors were deemed important only in so far as they could be nudged into management. . . . The nurses were deemed monumentally unimportant' (Clay 1987: 57).

By 1985, it was possible to identify 'a series of (government) moves which arguably at least are beginning to amount to a confrontation with the medical profession' (Davies 1987: 312). The style and content of the announcement of plans to impose a 'limited list' for NHS prescriptions for some categories of drugs in general practice was widely condemned as 'not a method by which a skilled and dedicated group of workers would expect to be controlled'. (Newton and Burt 1985: 17). Ministers and the mass media attacked NHS consultants' alleged misuse of opportunities to increase private practice through the new contracts so recently given them by the Conservative government (e.g. *Independent* 19 December 1987; Davies 1987; 312). Calls for ending consultants' contracts for life and professional control over the allocation of distinction awards, thus exposing the major disposers of NHS resources to managerial and financial discipline, began to be heard (Maynard 1988). Demands for greater 'value for money' have spawned a plethora of techniques for managerial evaluation and control of clinical activity. The new acronyms, QA, PIs, DRGs, QALYs, promise a new era in which doctors' clinical freedom of action within the NHS might be progressively circumscribed through bureaucratic assessment.[2]

The self-employed status of general medical practitioners has not exempted them from scrutiny. Indeed, such scrutiny has focused on the difficulty of imposing cash limits and managerial discipline on independent contractors who are the gatekeepers to the hospital sector. An enquiry into workload in general practice was accompanied by reform of the Family Practitioner Committees (FPCs) giving them new managerial responsibilities. A similar emphasis on the need for increased managerial supervision of general practitioners by FPCs was contained in subsequent Green and White Papers on primary health care proposing a new contract for GPs (Day and Klein 1986; DHSS, 1987). One form of central direction being introduced is the imposition of a compulsory retirement age for general practitioners. Originally put forward as a means of improving inner London's primary health care in the Acheson Report in 1981, this was then strongly resisted by the BMA as a breach of GP autonomy. Put forward as a nation-wide measure to modernize care and eliminate an alleged misuse of public resources through 24-hour retirement, in the context of growing professional concern about surplus doctors, it appears to be being less strongly resisted. Other changes, such as incentive payments for achieving targets for some preventive health procedures in place of fees per procedure have been more vigorously opposed in the name of patient welfare.

Developing alongside managerialism in the NHS has been renewed debate about the appropriate balance of public and private provision of health care, against a backcloth of apparent crisis of NHS resources and morale. At the beginning of 1988, a 'no-holds-barred review' of the NHS was publicly announced. (*Independent* 27 January 1988.) In line with the government's general approach, this was set up to be a swift and searching scrutiny carried out behind closed doors by those whose commitment to radical change was assured in advance: a far cry from the expert-dominated, protracted, public proceedings of a Royal Commission. Throughout this process, the voice of the medical profession has been raised in defence of the status quo: raised, but not necessarily listened to. Far from being at the centre of events, its senior members and collective organizations have appeared to be on the outside, trying to get in. For example, when the Presidents of the Royal Colleges declared the NHS to be near breakdown and demanded a fundamental review of NHS funding, they were instantly rebuffed (*Sunday Times* 13 December 1987). They had no formal part in the state's review when it was established.

Since its publication, the British Medical Association has campaigned unceasingly against many of the specific proposals of the NHS review, *Working for Patients* (DH 1989) and ensuing legislation, and against the manner in which reform is being approached (e.g. *BMJ* 1989, 298: 676–9. 'What do you call a man who refuses to listen to doctor's advice?' demands one of the BMA's advertising slogans. 'Healthy' was the robust response of the Secretary of State, Kenneth Clarke (Speech to Conservative Party Conference, 10 October 1989, BBC Radio News)', concisely conveying the sceptism towards the BMA's claims to professional disinterestedness and the rejection of their claim to a central place in policy making that has characterized his term of office. The failure to include the government's own Chief Medical Officer as an *ex officio* member of the newly created NHS policy board symbolizes for some the displacement of the profession from the centre of health policy-making (*Independent* 15 May 1989).

Space does not permit detailed discussion of all the proposals for NHS reform (e.g. DH 1989). But it is certainly possible to see many of them as *prima facie* examples of further attempts to extend managerial control over professional behaviour with the object of securing better value for money. The emphasis on information technology's potential to provide data on cost and outcome of medical procedures, the proposals for management involvement in consultant appointments and distinction award procedures and for increased use of formal medical audit procedures could all work to circumscribe clinical autonomy. The increased managerial responsibilities and reduced professional input to FPCs (renamed Family Practitioner Authorities (FPAs)) proposed in the White Paper suggests a reduction in professionals' freedom is intended but how much detailed control FPCs could exercise over GPs in practice remains open to doubt.

The proposal that health authorities become contractors for non-core services for their residents from designated providers has the potential to limit clinicians' traditional freedom of referral throughout the service. Moreover, the drawing up of contracts would presumably involve detailed specification of the clinical services to be provided. The introduction of indicative drug budgets for general practitioners could introduce significant economic constraints on prescribing autonomy. This aspect has given rise to considerable public acrimony between ministers and the profession, exacerbated by the simultaneous disagreements over the implementation of a new contract for general practitioners (see, for example, *BMJ* 1989, 298: 884–5, 1276, 1317–23; *Independent* 29 September, 2 October 1989).

Many aspects of the future direction of the NHS remain uncertain at the time of writing. We are still largely at the level of grand political gestures (at least in public) rather than detailed negotiation over the specific reforms. But it is probable that the fifth decade of the NHS will be very different from its first four. Time will tell whether the challenges just described will bring about a major shift in the relationship between the state and the medical profession and the replacement of managerial control for professionalism. In the meantime I offer some cautions against making too sweeping predictions.

First, the breakdown of consensus about the welfare state and the shift to a confrontationist style of government is not necessarily the direct outcome nor the cause of a decline in medical power. These developments have, I suggest, exposed constraints on medicine's political autonomy in relation to the state that have existed throughout the history of the NHS, but which remained largely latent in the era of political consensus. Klein argues that the history of the NHS suggests that 'the power of the medical profession is in inverse relationship to the size of the stage on which a specific health care issue is played out' (Klein 1983: 55–6). We are now on a very large stage indeed. Furthermore, much of the profession's power is negative in character, frustrating rather than initiating change. Even if it could impose positive policies on the state, the profession's ability to formulate these through its collective organizations has always been constrained by internal divisions (ibid: 28).

Since the 1970s, the British Medical Association appears to have reversed a relative decline in membership and has engaged in vigorous defence of its members' terms and conditions of service through defending the status quo, a process reinforced by the degree of unity engendered by opposition to *Working for patients* (*BMJ* 1989, 298: 1661–2). But for it to develop positive solutions to what have become defined as political questions is much more problematic, a point that the

Secretary of State has not been slow to seize on (*BMJ* 1989, 298: 1405–6). The history of the new general practitioners' contract clearly demonstrated that the gap between the profession's leaders and its rank-and-file members that was so evident in the 1940s can easily open up again. Their negotiators' acceptance of a contract after many hours of bargaining with the Department of Health was rejected by the majority of the country's general practitioners (e.g. *Observer* 14th May 1989).

The Royal Colleges and Faculties may be less deeply segmented, but they lack the BMA's legitimate role in 'trade union' matters and are less certain of their role in this now unfamiliar situation of exclusion from the centre. Nowhere are the difficulties of adjusting to the breakdown of consensus more apparent than in current internal debates about the role of the Royal College of General Practitioners (RCGP). Since its foundation in the 1950s, partly as an antithesis to the BMA's approach to raising the status of general practitioners, there has always been tension between the College's academic and political role. But this has intensified as its positive proposals for reform have been partially incorporated into government proposals. The College has been accused of ineptly abetting the onset of managerialism by some GPs and of failing to enter the political arena in defence of the NHS by others (e.g. *Journal of the Royal College of General Practitioners* 1988: 30, 126–8). These divisions were also manifest in the College's response to the 1989 White Paper when there were indications that the leadership's inclination to accept at least some degree of reform were overridden by a more militant membership (*Independent* 18 April 1989).

Closer examination of the introduction of the 'limited list' into general practice in 1984–85 (see Calnan and Gabe, Chapter 6, this volume) shows some of the same processes at work. The idea of encouraging rational prescribing through substituting generics for branded versions and reducing the provision of allegedly irrational and ineffective drugs was neither new nor rejected in many sectors of the profession. Indeed, by 1984, agreed restricted pharmacopoeias and cash limits had meant individual doctors in many hospitals were subject to much greater restriction in their prescribing habits than was ever proposed by the government. In individual hospitals or district health authorities, mechanisms existed through which agreements between consultants and pharmacists could be negotiated. Such local mechanisms are, at present, largely absent in general practice. As a policy issue, this was, perforce, a national issue but not one which either the BMA or the RCGP were likely to take a lead on, given the symbolic importance of prescribing freedom. With hindsight, it seems unsurprising that a government anxious to limit general practice expenditure took the lead nor that, in the ensuing row, concessions to the profession were made.

In 1984, this style of policy making was new, but the implications for clinical autonomy of the actual measures introduced were perhaps not very significant in the long run. After all, there was no overt attempt to circumscribe the profession's autonomy to prescribe those drugs which a government-sponsored committee, composed predominantly of professional experts, deems safe to market .[3] It was only the patient's right to have the cost of certain prescriptions subsidized by the state that was curtailed. Sir Raymond Hoffenberg, the then President of the Royal College of Physicians, has commented that 'the profession in this instance chose a weak issue on which to defend its rights' (Hoffenberg 1987:15). In doing so, the BMA's campaign perhaps hardened politicians' belief in the intransigence of general practitioners. Whether the NHS reform's proposal for indicative drug budgets for GPs will prove to be a more dramatic managerial encroachment on professional prerogatives or an extension of professionally led prescribing audit remains to be seen. The government imposed a new contract on NHS GPs following failure to win acceptance from the profession at large, not only illustrating the relative lack of economic autonomy enjoyed even by independent practitioners, but also exemplifying the same pattern of policy-making as the 'limited list' issue. In the face of professional divisions, the centre can and will act in those areas where professional autonomy is weak.

The introduction of general managers from 1983 has brought some tension and overt conflict with doctors, most recently, for example, over the question of hospitals opting for self-governing status under the reform proposals. The 'Griffiths' reforms', reinforced by the implementation of *Working For Patients* (DH 1989), may turn out to be more than just another in a long list of failed attempts to incorporate doctors into NHS management, other than as individuals competing against each other for limited resources. Its significance is discussed in detail in Cox's contribution to this volume (see Chapter 4). I shall make only two comments.

First, the main strategies general managers envisage for incorporating doctors, as identified by Scrivens, are to *increase* clinicians' participation in resource-use decisions in committees or to devolve budgets to clinicians. The latter has the potential to enhance collective clinical control over resource use, even if encroaching on the technical autonomy of some individual doctors. Clinicians' commitment to health authority goals would still have to be achieved, through traditional means, such as encouraging participation in decision-making or by more radical changes to create a health service 'based upon the entrepreneurship and the motivations of clinicians' (Scrivens 1988: 33): not so much the subordination of clinicians to managers as the emergence of clinician-managers with very different responsibilities from those of the medical administrators once found in many large psychiatric hospitals or community physicians. For example, at Guy's Hospital in London, clinical directorates have been created, in effect mini-hospitals for each major area of work run by a consultant with a nurse and business manager (*Independent* 2 November 1988). If this or medically qualified general managers became widespread, it would be one way of harnessing clinical entrepreneurship and managerial commitment within the NHS. The idea of the clinician as manager was a prominent theme in *Working For Patients* (DH 1989). Recognized managerial ability is envisaged as part of the good consultant's skills. Evidence of clinicians' involvement in management will be a prerequisite for a hospital's being granted self-governing status (although what this evidence would be remains unspecified). General practitioners holding their own practice budgets will be responsible for a much broader range of decisions concerning resource management. There is no suggestion of conceding such responsibility to managers within the practice, even though one can predict an increase in the numbers of so-called general practice managers.

Advocates of the proletarianization thesis are unequivocal about the implications of the growth of medically qualified managers in the United States, claiming that their loyalties lie with their corporate sponsors not their clinical colleagues (McKinlay and Arches 1985; McKinlay and Stoeckle 1988). Freidson disagrees, arguing that, for example, the widespread adoption of new techniques for monitoring the efficiency of performance and resource allocation does not in itself constitute diminished professional autonomy. What is crucial is whose criteria for evaluation and appraisal are adopted and who controls any action that ensues. Most of the 'production standards' that are emerging in the new corporate medicine in the United States are both set and supervised by physicians, potentially reinforcing stratification within the profession between supervisors and supervised. Supervisory doctors' behaviour within the modern medical organization does not conform to that of the purely bureaucratic functionary of the proletarianization thesis. They retain the values of and commitment to their profession but, at the same time, collegial relations are being altered. Thus, the identification of some clinicians as having entrepreneurial or managerial responsibility and not others is, he suggests, driving a wedge into the principle of collegiality, of a community of autonomous peers at the local level. Institutionalized professional autonomy is being retained through continued medical control over the supervision and management of medical care even though some individual doctors' technical autonomy in the work place may be being eroded (Freidson 1985, 1986).

Although it is too early to be sure, I suggest that the kind of changes proposed for managing clinical activity within a reformed NHS will provide for the retention of institutionalized technical autonomy along the lines indicated by Freidson. Ham and Hunter (1988) have emphasized the importance of gaining clinicians' co-operation in any attempts to raise professional standards and involve doctors in management. They suggest that experience in other countries (by which they mean mainly the United States) indicates that external control is of limited effectiveness in changing physician behaviour. There are many signs that the profession, or sections of it, are increasingly engaged in developing their own procedures of medical audit and appraisal (e.g. Buck *et al.* 1987; Royal College of Surgeons 1988; Hoffenberg 1987) as well as seeking and promoting courses in management for clinicians. One of the few proposals in *Working for Patients* (DH 1989) to command widespread professional assent is for increased attention to and resources for medical audit, so long, that is, as it is *medical*, not managerial audit.

My second point about the new managerialism concerns medicine's status *vis a vis* other health-care occupations. Within the medical profession, the impact of general managers has been greatest so far on those for whom clinical autonomy is not directly applicable, community physicians (Harvey and Judge 1988). But as Trevor Clay's understandably bitter comment (quoted p. 68) indicated, while doctors were regarded as potentially 'natural managers' in the Griffiths report, nurses, paramedical occupations and other groups stood to lose much of their self-management. Similarly, in the proposals for reforming primary health care, general medical practitioners are treated very differently from other occupations under FPC administration (DHSS 1987). If what is underway is a reformulation of professionalism as a means of occupational control in the NHS, then, so far, it has affected the doctors less than other groups. Doctors' authority over these others is not directly reduced. In this sense, medical dominance in the health division of labour clearly persists although its extent should not be exaggerated (Larkin 1983).

In summary, then, the breakdown of consensus about the role of the state in health care has led to an apparent diminution of the profession's privileged status in health-policy decisions at the centre. But perhaps this is because the very breakdown means that the major issues in health-care politics now lie in an arena in which the profession's power has always been limited. As the detailed negotiations proceed, the profession's organization may come in from the cold to negotiate a modified concordat, although the experience of negotiations over the new GPs' contract suggests that internal professional divisions will be an important influence on the ease with which such a concordat can be reached. Continuing pressure from the centre for financial and managerial accountability looks set to lead to further constraints on individual clinicians' freedom to use resources as they wish. But it is conceivable that these may be invoked primarily through new forms of institutionalized professional control over members rather than through managerial fiat. It may turn out that it is the 'corporate rationalizers' *within* the profession who are in the ascendant in Britain.

My discussion on the impact of managerialism on medical power has focused entirely on the relationship between the state and the profession, as the dominant form of 'bureaucratized' medical care in Britain. As yet the implications of the expansion and changing form of private hospital care in Britain for clinicians' autonomy over the terms and content of their work remain largely uninvestigated by sociologists.

Since the 1940s and the negotiations over the establishment of the National Health Service, the right to do private practice has had a strong symbolic function for the profession. It represented a theoretically available 'exit' from state employment, in which the terms and conditions of practice approximated to those set out in the classic image of the autonomous professional: solo practice, with payments on a fee-for-service basis, to highly individualized clients with little or no external control over clinical decision-making.[4] Yet, as Mohan (Chapter 2, this volume) has documented, private medical care in Britain has been changing in ideology and in form. Its advocates now stress its merits in providing competition and breaking professional monopoly rather than the opportunities it provides for clinical freedom (e.g. Green 1988). Provision has become increasingly the concern of large corporations, including profit-making concerns, over the last decade.

Those committed to the proletarianization thesis might predict, on the basis of analogy with the putative shifts in the United States (Derber 1984; McKinlay and Stoeckle, 1988), that pressures for managerial rationality in corporate health care will progressively constrain the autonomy of doctors working in this sector. This is certainly what right-wing critics of professional power would like to see (e.g. Green 1986). On the other hand, the comparatively weak market situation of many investor-owned hospitals in Britain at present means that they need to attract doctors who can attract patients. This might be easier if they offer such doctors comparative freedom from the perceived financial and managerial constraints of the NHS. Only detailed empirical research will resolve which, if either, of these alternatives will occur.

The changes discussed so far relate to the possible erosion of some types of medical autonomy over the terms and conditions and content of work, through the subordination of physicians to the state and its bureaucratic agents or to medical corporations. These are the kind of changes identified as significant by those who claim 'proletarianization' of doctors is imminent in the United States (McKinlay and Arches 1985). I have argued for caution in accepting too readily that strengthening of management is tantamount to an imminent erosion of all aspects of medical autonomy and dominance within the British health-care system.

Claims of 'deprofessionalization' in contrast, place more emphasis on changes in the relationship between doctors and their patients and in the public mandate for collegiate control over members' conduct.

The challenge to medicine from the articulate 'consumer'?

According to many commentators, the past decade has witnessed not only the end of an era of optimism about scientific medicine, but also, and not unconnectedly, the 'end of the era of the passive patient' and the beginning of an era of active 'consumerism' (Stevens 1986: p.76). At its simplest, it is argued that increased lay knowledge about medicine, declining deference to experts in society at large, changing attitudes of doctors and changing patterns of morbidity are modifying social expectations about doctor–patient relationships in the direction of mutual participation (Szasz and Hollander 1956). For example, a greater sense of personal responsibility for health promoted by health education is seen as supplanting obedience to doctor's orders. Some suggest that a more radical rupture of societal trust in medical expertise is taking place, with a consequent marked decline in medical dominance over clients and clients' faith in professional self-discipline. Several overlapping but analytically distinct elements can be identified in such claims. I shall discuss three.

The first, chronologically, was the corollary of the medical imperialism thesis, the cultural critique of the quality of the emperor's wardrobe. Claims of interventionist medicine's ineffectiveness, of epidemic iatrogenesis, of medicine's sapping of personal autonomy and, most potently, the women's health movement's attacks on medicine as sustaining patriarchy, all overtly challenged the profession's claims to be trusted with sole charge of the public's health (Illich 1977: Kennedy 1981; Ehrenreich 1978; Ehrenreich and English 1974). Historians of medical professionalization, such as Larson (1977) and Starr (1982), have argued that medicine's identification with the values of science was a key element in medicine's achievement of near-monopoly over the market for health care by the early twentieth century. Proponents of a cultural crisis in medicine challenge the beneficence of medical science and, by implication, the claims to legitimate authority of those who apply it.

For example, the image of 'the magic bullet' from the pharmaceutical revolutions of the 1950s and 1960s has been under sustained attack since the thalidomide catastrophe of the 1960s ushered in an era punctuated by episodic pharmacological disasters. Grave charges are laid against the drug industry and against those who prescribe its allegedly ineffective and unnecessary or even harmful and anti-social products; for example, the current media attacks on GPs' prescription of tranquillisers (Gabe and Bury 1988). Anti-vivisectionist attacks on the morality of methods for obtaining much biomedical knowledge have gained in visibility in the past decade. And such attacks have increasingly incorporated the arguments of the cultural critique (e.g. Sharpe 1988). Feminist critiques of the new reproductive technologies have accused medical scientists of experimenting on women for their own benefit rather than women's (e.g. Arditti *et al.* 1984). Associated with these challenges to medical and scientific paternalism are calls for the development of new forms of health care. On the one hand, there are calls for a new 'public health', social measures for preventing ill-health, arguably replacing medical imperialism with intervention into far more areas of life in the name of health (Strong 1979). On the other, there are demands for lay reskilling and lay responsibility for health and for greater recognition of the patient as a person rather than a collection of cells.

The emphasis on holism, patient participation and collective provision should not, however, obscure the strongly individualistic element implicit in much of the cultural critique (e.g. Illich 1977). This element has been extended in the 1980s into the second of the three strands, a vigorous neo-liberal challenge to professional monopoly as inhibiting informed consumer choice. Elements of this challenge relate to the relationship between the state and the profession by attacking state-legitimated licensed monopoly. Radical proposals to curtail restrictive practices in the name of consumer power have emanated from right-wing think tanks (e.g. Green 1988) and statutory agencies (Monopolies and Mergers Commission 1989). Collegial controls over individuals on behalf of the collective interest, such as advertising bans, are loudly condemned. Others have argued for exposing to the discipline of competition the panoply of state-sponsored activities which provide professionals with a substantial market-shelter. For example, the former Director of the Centre for Policy Studies claims:

> Medicine is not a homogeneous profession. The Harley Street and nursing-home segment, which draws much of its income from foreign patients, is highly competitive. It is the NHS which operates union closed shops like other nationalized industries, though even here the professions are far less culpable than the manuals. Were the NHS quasi-monopoly dismantled, many monopolistic practices would be curtailed.
>
> (Sherman 1988)

This emphasis on the discipline of the market and consumer power is echoed in the current reforms of the NHS, particularly general practice: for example, increasing the sensitivity of general practitioners' pay to patient workload and providing information to enable patients to make a more informed choice of general practitioner (DHSS 1987; DH 1989) Increasing patient choice was one of the two explicit aims of *Working For Patients* (DH 1989) in accord with the present government's pro-market ideology.

Declining trust in medical expertise, suspicion of collegial control and the growth of individualism come together into a third strand, challenge from the dissatisfied patient: growing public concern about the profession's claim to effective self-discipline and over medical malpractice (in the widest sense). The past decade appears to have seen a marked increase in overtly expressed complaints about the quality of medical care: for example, through the NHS complaints machinery or increased numbers of civil actions for compensation. Here, ever-larger settlements led to steep rises in medical defence premiums and the beginnings of differential assessment of risk between specialties (*Independent* 15 November 1988). As a result of this and professional concern about its implications, the Department of Health has proposed that crown indemnity should be extended to include doctors as for other health workers, a proposal that was strongly resisted when the NHS was first established on the grounds of infringement of clinical autonomy (*BMJ* 1988, 297: 1356). Public (or media) concern with the inadequacies of institutionalized systems of victim compensation through the courts and GMC disciplinary procedures has intensified, with the creation of pressure groups such as Action of Victims of Medical Accidents and a self-proclaimed specialist cadre of solicitors willing to act in such cases. Apparently in response, the channels through which patients may express complaints have increased, for example, the establishment of the Health Service Commissoner. But complaints about the adequacy of these channels, particularly in dealing with questions concerning clinical competence, have also proliferated (Rosenthal 1987).

In the late 1980s, two dramatic episodes exposed the operation of professional self-regulation and collegiate control to public scrutiny in Britain. The first was the Wendy Savage affair (Savage 1986). The unprecedented step of holding an enquiry into the competence of an NHS consultant in public revealed the limitations of internal professional mechanisms for resolving either a 'personality clash' or profound differences in approach to obstetrics between two colleagues. Furthermore, in the eyes of some, it showed the enquiry procedure itself to be 'a blunt and expensive instrument' (*BMJ* 1987, 294: 52) and the medical profession at large as behaving in the manner of 'an Edwardian gentleman's club, concerned to close ranks against anyone with non-conformist tendencies and taking on faith the integrity of "clubbable" individuals' (*BMJ* 1986, 293: 285.) Second was the explosion of public controversy in Cleveland in 1987–88 over a marked increase in cases of alleged child sexual abuse which culminated in a judicial inquiry (Butler-Sloss 1988). In these events, differences in clinical judgement, the seemingly arbitrary power of consultant moral entrepreneurs, doctors' resort to informal professional boycott as the means of managing disagreements and the lack of professional discipline following the judicial inquiry were important subthemes in a larger media debate about the limits to state and expert control over the intimate world of the family.

The intensity of controversy over these two cases partly reflected the particular areas of medical practice concerned; the one an area where medical and lay control is heavily contested, the other an area of profoundly 'dirty work' (Strong 1980). That the two doctors centrally involved were women clearly shaped the course of events and media coverage (e.g. Campbell 1988). But such glaring controversy appeared to reflect as well as fuel debate about professional self-regulation in general.

Whether this growing public discussion about professional regulation of competence reflects a real change in either societal expectations or in people's experience of medical care is hard to establish on present evidence. Any rise in the number of overt complaints has to be set against the rising level of medical contacts and the overall expansion in 'the malpractice system' for receiving complaints (Rosenthal 1987). Moreover, just because of the unresponsive structure of the malpractice system, the court and GMC cases currently being reported in the media are concerned with incidents that happened some time ago. The increased media coverage may be contributing to more organized responses by dissatisfied patients, but it also reflects the vigorous claims-making activity of would-be reformers, both lay and, increasingly, medical.

There are, then, signs of three interrelated *social problems* emerging onto both public and professional agendas: careless, sick and undisciplined doctors (cf. Stimson 1985; Richards 1989), the inadequately compensated victim (e.g. Ham *et al.* 1988) and the implications for medical practice of increasing litigation (e.g. *BMJ* 1986; 293: 461–2). As social problems they warrant sociological analysis of their development. Dingwall and colleagues have recently argued that the perception of a major malpractice crisis in the United States should not be seen in isolation from the changing conditions of medical practice there. They suggest that it is premature to talk in such terms in Britain although they note that even unfounded concern over litigation may affect practice (Quam, Dingwall and Fenn 1987; Quam, Fenn and Dingwall 1987).

There are signs of response within the system of professional self-regulation to this growth in public concern over and scrutiny of doctors' activities. For example, Rosenthal's (1987) account of the British malpractice system catalogues changes in the GMC, the main institution for professional self-regulation since 1978. Although some of these changes stemmed from the need to resolve internal divisions, they have been broadly in the direction of increased lay involvement and increased concern with clinical competence as well as with professional conduct in the traditional sense. Mechanisms for the medical management of certain aspects of physician deviance, especially addiction, have been instituted. Disciplinary procedures for consultants have been reviewed by a joint working party of the profession and the Department of Health and a more streamlined procedure suggested (*BMJ* 1987; 294: 789; *Independent* 25 October 1988).

Further growth in medical litigation, in demands for clinical appraisal and accountability and in media exposées of incompetence may well subject increasing numbers of individual doctors to external scrutiny. But this might also create new niches for professional arbiters of clinical standards. Once again, retention of institutionalized professional control may accompany a diminution in individual members' autonomy from clinical accountability. Stimson (1985) suggested that the external challenge facing American medicine has led to a shift towards active intervention in members' activities. Here, there are small signs of this, for example, the proposal of the Central Committee for Hospital Medical Services and the Royal Colleges of a consultant body in each district to 'investigate and reprimand colleagues who persistently fail to honour contractual commitments' suggests some movement. But it was made clear that 'such groups, however, would act only after "receiving allegations"' (*BMJ* 1989, 294: 789).

To date, the modifications of professional self-regulation appear as a series of incremental adjustments to contain criticism rather than substantial diminution of collegiate control. The widespread criticisms have certainly generated a considerable level of internal scrutiny and professional self-consciousness (see, for example, Smith's recent series of articles on the GMC, and the response to them (*BMJ* 1989, 298: 1241–4, 1297–300, 1372–5, 1441–4, 1502–5, 1569–71, 1632–4, 1695–8, 299: 40–3, 109–12, 137–8)). But once again this is an area which warrants much more empirical research, to extend and complement Stacey's current study of the GMC (Stacey 1989).

The advocates of informed consumer power also appear to have had limited impact so far. The language of the market and of meeting customer desires is manifestly replacing the language of planning and patient need in debates about the NHS (Owen 1988: 22). It seems virtually certain that one of the symbols of collegiate control, the ban on individual advertising, will be modified at least for general practice (*BMJ* 1989, 298: 774). The recently published *Good Doctor Guide* (Page 1989) came out to a flurry of media interest and some professional hostility (but contains little information about the 500 selected doctors that was not previously available to the public).

Most advocates of informed consumer power in competitive medical markets concede that there is limited scope for applying the rule of *caveat emptor* without the mediation of a professional agent. The lay public may have become more knowledgeable about many health and medical matters than they used to be. But the knowledge gap between them and doctors is not necessarily closing as a result, particularly in high-technology specialties, nor are patients any less vulnerable when seriously ill. Nor is it clear how compatible demands for increased choice are with either increased managerial accountability or greater personal *responsibility* for health; two other goals of health service reformers. The choosing *consumer* might not want to be treated according to managerially rational protocols or to absolve their paid adviser from responsibility (see Stacey 1976; Klein 1983: 182–94). The tension between promoting 'consumer choice' and increasing efficiency by managerialism is readily apparent in *Working for Patients* (DH 1989).

Returning to the first of the three claims for incipient deprofessionalization there is little hard evidence to support a new and wholesale rejection of medical science and medicine's cultural authority. The growth of the women's self-help health movement and holistic well-woman centres and the apparently increasing use of alternative practitioners suggests some of the disillusioned are exiting from the system, but only partially and on a small scale. There is little baseline data against which changes in the level of public confidence in and valuation of medicine can be tested. Just as those who put forward claims of increasing 'medicalization' in the 1970s had little or no direct evidence to support their claims, so those who claim the converse in the 1980s have to rely largely on circumstantial pointers. Two recent small-scale studies suggest that scepticism about the value of medical science and technology, particularly drugs, is not necessarily incompatible with using and valuing the advice of doctors (Calnan 1988: Gabe and Calnan 1989). As a circumstantial pointer in the same direction, it is perhaps worth noting that if the British public had very little confidence in their doctors, the Secretary of State for Health might not have been led to admit that surveys of public opinion about the NHS reforms suggested that the doctors were winning the battle (*Independent* 5 July 1989).

It is true that in Britain, as in the United States, patient and public voice has been most critical of medical science and practice in specific areas. These are where 'consumers' are not ill, as in the management of reproduction; where patients have experiential expertise or curative medical science has little to offer, as in disability, chronic illness and terminal care; and in areas of experimental treatment or where rapid scientific developments arouse fundamental societal concerns, e.g. transplant surgery or pre-natal screening. Freidson sees this as a sign of the limited social base of the 'consumer' movement and of its incapacity 'to change drastically the position of the medical profession in the health care system' (Freidson 1985: p. 18). This may be true. But the health-care system is itself changing because of the growing significance of these very areas, with an ageing population, increased prevalence of disability and growing applications of the new genetics and molecular biology.

The burgeoning field of philosophical medical ethics is also pre-occupied with these same aspects of medical work. Judging from the demand for medical ethics teaching in medical schools and the prolifer-ation of textbooks these are growing professional preoccupations. There are other signs, such as the considerable recent activity of the BMA's Scientific and Ethics division, producing major revisions to the latest edition of the BMA *Handbook of Medical Ethics* (BMA 1988), pro-posing a national ethics committee (*Guardian* 3 August 1988) and steering its members to recognition of the right for informed consent for the most routine of medical procedures, taking blood, as a result of the AIDS epidemic. If we regard 'ethical codes as guidelines for internal control and cohesion of members [and] as instruments of socialization to acceptable behaviour' (Rosenthal 1987: 237), then perhaps we should note the shift in content of this symbolic mode of collegiate control. The shift is in the direction of increased concession to, even welcoming, of patient and societal involvement in difficult moral decisions. Perhaps the medical profession is facing an uncomfortable period of adjustment induced by the changing content of its work as much as from ideological onslaughts from outside. But to describe this adjustment as deprofessionalization is premature.

Conclusion

I have outlined two of the current challenges to medicine's institution-alized freedom from external accountability and sketched some of the professional responses to these challenges. I have suggested that it is inappropriate to describe these challenges as bringing about either pro-letarianization or deprofessionalization of medicine at present. Much of the response from the profession's organizations undoubtedly takes the form of defending existing arrangements in the name of 'clinical free-dom'. But this partly reflects the difficulties such organizations face in developing positive policies. There are also many signs of change within professional institutions. Some of these promise acceptance of new limits to the area covered by the term 'clinical autonomy' and new roles within the profession in exercising continued control over its members. As yet, such changes that have occurred look more like uncomfortable adjustments than a major waning of either the medical profession's institutionalized technical autonomy or of their social and cultural authority. But this judgement may prove premature and is partly based on the view that British medical sociologists overestimated medical power in the 1960s and 1970s.

In preparing this paper, I have been forcibly reminded of the paucity of recent detailed empirical studies by medical sociologists of the major institutions of British medicine. Research into the professional organizations and the institutions of medical education and collegiate control have been conspicuous by their absence in recent years. As we seem certain to be facing a period of continued public and internal scrutiny of doctors' power and performance, such research is needed more than ever now.

Acknowledgements

I should like to thank all the participants in the original conference for their helpful comments in revising this paper, particularly, Phil Strong, my discussant, Jon Gabe and Mike Bury.

Notes

1. A special issue of *The Millbank Quarterly* (1988, 66, Supplement 2) was published too late to be considered in this paper. Two essays are particularly relevant to my own arguments. Haug (1988) reconsiders her earlier writing on deprofessionalization. Larkin (1988) shares my reservations about imposing an essentially American account of professional power on the British situation.
2. These acronyms stand for, Quality Assurance, Performance Indicators, Diagnostic Related Groups and Quality-Adjusted Life Years.
3. The Committee on Safety of Medicines, established under the 1968 Medicines Act advises the Department of Health on the issuing of product licences for new drugs and is responsible for post-marketing surveillance.
4. Bjorkman suggests that the possibility of emigration to the alleged 'freedom of the States' fulfilled a similar function for British doctors until recently, a factor which inhibited state attempts to control technical practice lest doctors leave. Recent constriction of this exit option has, he argues, both decreased this inhibition and increased the tendency of British doctors to give voice when faced with attempts to control their technical autonomy (Bjorkman 1989: 73).

References

Alford, R. (1975) *Health Care Politics,* Chicago: University of Chicago.

Arditti, R., Klein, R.D. and Minden, S. (eds) (1984) *Test-Tube Women: What Future for Motherhood,* London: Pandora.

Armstrong, D. (1976) 'The decline of the medical hegemony: a review of government reports during the NHS'. *Social Science and Medicine* 10: 157-63.

Bjorkman, J.W. (1989) 'Politicizing medicine and medicalizing politics: Physician power in the United States', in G. Freddi and J.W. Bjorkman (eds) *Controlling Medical Professionals: The Comparative Politics of Health Governance,* London: Sage, pp. 28-73.

BMA (British Medical Association) (1988) *Handbood of Medical Ethics,* London: BMA Publications.

Buck, N., Devlin, H.B. and Lunn, J.V. (1987) *Report of Confidential Enquiry into Peri-Operative Deaths,* London: Nuffield Provincial Hospitals Trust.

Butler-Sloss, Rt. Hon. Lord Justice (1988) *Report of the Inquiry into Child Abuse in Cleveland, 1987,* London: HMSO.

Calnan, M. (1988) 'Lay evaluation of medical practice: report of a pilot study', *International Journal of Health Services* 18: 311-22.

Campbell, B. (1988) *Unofficial Secrets: Child Sexual Abuse – The Cleveland Case,* London: Virago.

Clay, T. (1987) *Nurses: Power and Politics,* London: Heinemann.

Cochrane, A. (1972) *Effectiveness and Efficiency: Random Reflections on Health Services,* London: Nuffield Provincial Hospitals Trust.

Davies, C. (1987) 'Viewpoint: things to come; the NHS in the next decade', *Sociology of Health and Illness* 9: 302–17.

Day, P. and Klein, R. (1986) 'Controlling the gatekeepers', *Journal of Royal College of General Practitioners* 36: 129–30.

Derber, C. (1984) 'Physicians and their sponsors: the new medical relations of production' in J. McKinlay (ed.) *Issues in the Political Economy of Health Care,* New York: Tavistock, pp. 217–56.

DH (Department of Health) (1989) *Working for Patients,* London: HMSO, Cmnd 555.

DHSS (Department of Health and Social Security) (1983) *NHS Management Enquiry, London: HMSO* (Griffiths Report).

——(1986) *Primary Health Care: An Agenda for Discussion,* London: HMSO, Cmnd 9771.

——(1987) *Promoting Better Health: The Government's Programme for Improving Primary Health Care,* London: HMSO, Cm 249.

Dollery, C. (1978) *The End of an Age of Optimism,* London: Nuffield Provincial Hospitals Trust.

Ehrenreich, B. and English, D. (1974) *Complaints and Disorders: The Sexual Politics of Sickness,* Westbury, New York: Glass Mountain Pamphlet no. 2.

Ehrenreich, J. (ed.) (1978) *The Cultural Crisis of Modern Medicine,* New York: Monthly Press.

Elston, M.A. (1977a) 'Medical autonomy: challenge and response', in K. Barnard and K. Lee (eds) *Conflicts in the National Health Service,* London: Croom Helm, pp. 26–51.

——(1977b) 'Women in the medical profession: whose problem?' in M. Stacey, M. Reid, C. Heath and R. Dingwall (eds) *Health and the Division of Labour,* London: Croom Helm. pp. 115–40.

Freidson, E. (1970) *Profession of Medicine,* New York: Dodd, Mead.

——(1977) 'The futures of professionalization' in M. Stacey, M. Reid, C. Heath and R. Dingwall (eds) *Health and the Division of Labour,* London: Croom Helm. pp. 14–38.

——(1985) 'The reorganization of the medical profession', *Medical Care Review* 42: 11–35.

——(1986) 'The medical profession in transition', in L.H. Aiken and D. Mechanic (eds) *Applications of Social Science to Clinical Medicine and Health Policy*, New Brunswick: Rutgers University Press. pp. 63–79.

Gabe, J. and Bury, M. (1988) 'Tranquillisers as a social problem', *The Sociological Review* 26: 321–51.

Gabe, J. and Calnan, M. (1989) 'The limits of medicine: women's perception of medical technology', *Social Science and Medicine* 28: 223–31.

Giddens, A. (1973) *The Class Structure of Advanced Societies*, London: Hutchinson.

Ginzberg, E. (ed.) (1986) *From Physician Shortage to Patient Shortage: The Uncertain Future of Medical Practice*, Boulder: Westview.

Green, D.G. (1985a) *Which Doctor?*, London: Institute of Economic Affairs, Research Monograph 40.

——(1985b) *Working-class Patients and the Medical Establishment*, London: Temple Smith/Gower.

——(1986) *Challenge to the NHS: A Study of Competition in American Health Care and the Lessons for Britain*, London: Institute of Economic Affairs, Hobart paperback 23.

——(1988) *Everyone a Private Patient*, London: Institute of Economic Affairs Health Unit.

Ham, C.J. (1981) *Policy-making in the National Health Service*, London: Macmillan.

Ham, C.J. and Hunter, D. (1988) *Managing Clinical Activity in the NHS*, London: King's Fund Institute, Briefing Paper no. 8.

Ham, C.J., Dingwall, R., Fenn, P. and Harris, D. (1988) *Medical Negligence: Compensation and Accountability*, London: King's Fund Institute, Briefing Paper no. 6.

Harrison, S. and Schulz, R. (1989) 'Clinical autonomy in the United Kingdom and the United States: contrasts and convergence', in G. Freddi and J.W. Bjorkman (eds) *Controlling Health Professionals: The Comparative Politics of Health Governance*, London: Sage.

Harvey, S. and Judge, K. (1988) *Community Physicians and Community Medicine*, London: King's Fund Institute, Research Report no.1.

Haug, M. (1973) 'Deprofessionalization: an alternative hypothesis for the future', *Sociological Review Monograph* 20: 195–211.

——(1975) 'The deprofessionalization of everyone?', *Sociological Focus* 3: 197–213.

——(1976) 'The erosion of professional authority: a cross-cultural inquiry in the case of the physician', *Millbank Memorial Fund Quarterly* 54: 83–106.

—— (1988) 'A re-examination of the hypothesis of deprofessionalization', *The Millbank Quarterly* 66, Supplement 2: 48–56.

Haug, M and Lavin, B. (1983) *Consumerism in Medicine: Challenging Physician Authority*, Beverly Hills, Ca.: Sage.

Haywood, S. and Alaszweski, A. (1980) *Crisis in the Health Service*, London: Croom Helm.

Hoffenberg, R. (1987) *Clinical Freedom*, London: Nuffield Provincial Hospitals Trust.

Homans, H. (1987) 'Man-made myths: the reality of being a woman scientist in the NHS', in A. Spencer and D. Podmore (eds) *In a Man's World: Women in Male-Dominated Professions*, London: Tavistock, pp. 87–112.

Honigsbaum, F. (1979) *The Division in British Medicine*, London: Kogan Page.

Illich, I. (1977) *The Limits to Medicine*, London: Penguin.
Johnson, T.J. (1972) *Professions and Power*, London: Macmillan.
Kennedy, I. (1981) *The Unmasking of Medicine*, London: Allen & Unwin. ✓
King, N.M.P., Churchill, L.R. and Cross, A.W. (eds) (1988) *The Physician as Captain of the Ship: A Critical Reappraisal*, Dordrecht: D. Reidel.
Klein, R. (1974) 'Policy problems and policy perceptions in the National Health Service', *Policy and Politics* 2: 217–34.
——(1983) *The Politics of the NHS*, London: Longman.
——(1984) 'The politics of ideology versus the reality of politics: the case of Britain's NHS in the 1980s', *Millbank Memorial Fund Quarterly* 62: 82–108.
Larkin, G. (1983) *Occupational Monopoly and Modern Medicine*, London: Tavistock.
—— (1988) 'Medical dominance in Britain: Image and historical reality', *The Millbank Quarterly* 66, Supplement 2: 117–31.
Larson, M. S. (1977) *The Rise of Professionalism*, Berkeley: University of California.
Lukes, S. (1974) *Power: A Radical View*, London: Macmillan.
McKeown, T. (1976) *The Role of Medicine*, London: Nuffield Provinicial Hospitals Trust.
McKinlay, J. and Arches, J. (1985) 'Towards the proletarianization of physicians', *International Journal of Health Services* 15: 161–95.
McKinlay, J. and Stoeckle, J. (1988) 'Corporatization and the social transformation of doctoring', *International Journal of Health Services* 18: 191–205.
Maynard, A. (1988) 'Go easy on the doctor bashing', *Health Service Journal*, 15 September.
Monopolies and Mergers Commission (1989) *Services of Medical Practitioners*, London: HMSO, Cmnd 583.
Navarro, V. (1976) *Medicine Under Capitalism*, London: Croom Helm.
Newton, J.M. and Burt, B.W. (1985) 'Prescribed or proscribed . . .' *Times Higher Education Supplement* 15 March, p.17.
Oppenheimer, M. (1973) 'The proletarianization of the professional', *Sociological Review Monograph* 20: 213–237.
Ovreteit, J. (1985) 'Medical dominance and the development of professional autonomy in physiotherapy', *Sociology of Health and Illness* 7: 76–93.
Owen, D. (1988) *Our NHS*, London: Pan. ✓
Page, M. (1989) *The Good Doctor Guide: A Unique Directory of Recommended Specialists*, London: Sphere.
Peterson, M.J. (1978) *The Medical Profession in Mid-Victorian London*, Berkeley: University of California Press.
Quam, L., Dingwall, R. and Fenn, P. (1987) 'Medical practice in perspective: I: the American experience', *British Medical Journal* 294: 1529–31.
Quam, L., Fenn, P. and Dingwall, R. (1987) 'Medical malpractice in perspective: II: the implications for Britain', *British Medical Journal* 294: 1597–9.
Richards, C. (1989) *The Health of Doctors*, London: King's Fund, Project Paper no. 78.
Robinson, J. and Strong, P. (1987) *Professional Nursing Advice after Griffiths: An Interim Report*, Nursing Policy Studies Centre, University of Warwick.

Roemer, M. (1986) 'Proletarianization of physicians or organisation of health services?', *International Journal of Health Services* 16: 469–71.

Rosenthal, M.M. (1987) *Dealing with Medical Malpractice: The British and Swedish Experience*, London: Tavistock.

Royal College of Surgeons (1988) *Report of the Working Party on the Composition of a Surgical Team*, London: Royal College of Surgeons.

Salvage, J. (1988) 'Professionalization – or struggle for survival? A consideration of current proposals for the reform of nursing in the United Kingdom', *Journal of Advanced Nursing* 13: 515–19.

Savage, W. (1986) *A Savage Enquiry*, London: Virago.

Schulz, R. and Harrison, S. (1986) 'Physician autonomy in the Federal Republic of Germany, Great Britain and the United States,' *International Journal of Health Planning and Management* 2: 335–55.

Scrivens, E. (1988) 'The management of clinicians in the National Health Service', *Social Policy and Administration* 22: 22–34.

Sharpe, R. (1988) *The Cruel Deception: The Use of Animals in Medical Research*, London: Thorsons.

Sherman, A. (1988) 'How government is the mainspring of monopoly power', *Independent* 11 March.

Stacey, M. (1976) 'The health service consumer: a sociological misconception', *Sociological Review Monographs* 22, Keele: University of Keele.

——(1989) 'The General Medical Council and professional accountability', *Public Policy and Administration* 4: 12–27

Stacey, M. and Davies, C. (1983) *Division of Labour in Child Health Care: Final Report for the SSRC*, Coventry: University of Warwick, Mimeo.

Starr, P. (1982) *The Social Transformtion of American Medicine*, New York: Basic Books.

Stevens, R. (1986) 'The future of the medical profession' in E. Ginsberg (ed.) *From Physician Shortage to Patient Shortage: The Uncertain Future of Medical Practice*, Boulder: Westview, pp. 75–93.

Stimson, G. (1985) 'Recent developments in physician control: the impaired physician movement in the USA', *Sociology of Health and Illness* 7: 141–66.

Strong, P.M. (1979) 'Sociological imperialism and the profession of medicine: a critical examination of the thesis of medical imperialism', *Social Science and Medicine* 13A, 2: 199–215.

——(1980) 'Doctors and dirty work', *Sociology of Health and Illness* 2: 24–47.

Szasz, T. and Hollander, M.H. (1956) 'A contribution to the philosophy of medicine: the basic models of the doctor–patient relationship', *Archives of Internal Medicine* 97: 585–92.

Waddington, I. (1984) *The Medical Profession in the Industrial Revolution*, London: Gill & Macmillan.

White, R. (ed.) (1985) *Political Issues in Nursing*, I, Chichester: John Wiley.

Zola, I.K. (1972) 'Medicine as an institution of social control: the medicalising of society', *The Sociological Review* 20: 487–504.

Chapter four

Health service management – a sociological view: Griffiths and the non-negotiated order of the hospital

David Cox

Introduction

The British National Health Service was founded in 1948 as part of a broad programme of post-war social reconstruction. While continuing to be widely popular, the service has invariably suffered from under-funding and regional and sector disparities in resources. Over the last twenty years, health-service organization has become a major focus of policy and public discussion in which concern about resources has been countered by an accelerating search for organizational and managerial solutions. Major organizational changes were introduced in 1974 (DHSS 1972), 1982 (DHSS 1979) and, following the Griffiths Report (DHSS 1983), in 1984. It is this Report, introducing 'general management', that will be discussed in more detail in this Chapter. The post-Griffiths structure had barely settled down before the Conservative government published a new White Paper in March 1989 (Department of Health 1989) proposing yet more radical changes.

The first major reorganization in 1974 was introduced during a period of corporate rationalization which affected many other public services (Hunter 1988: 539). Three managerial tiers at regional, area and district level were established and local authority community health services were brought under NHS control. Management was provided by 'consensus' teams consisting of a medical representative, a nursing officer, an administrator and a treasurer. In 1978 a Royal Commission was established to look again at the organizational structure of the health service and this resulted in the 1982 reorganization, which abolished the area authorities, emphasized the role of districts and ad-vocated delegation as far as possible to hospital and community 'unit' level. Before this change had been fully implemented the government, responding to parliamentary concern about manpower levels in the NHS, asked Roy Griffiths, chief executive of the Sainsburys retail chain, to conduct a 'management enquiry' into the service and to make proposals for action.

The report was published in the Autumn of 1983 and quickly endorsed by the government. Its underlying theme was to bring in some of the principles and culture of good private-sector management into the health service. The report's recommendations included the setting up of a Supervisory and a Management Board at national level, the appointment of one accountable general manager 'regardless of discipline' at regional, district and unit level, an emphasis on delegation, the introduction of management budgeting, the involvement of clinicians (doctors) in management and finally, greater emphasis on consumer needs and satisfaction.

Would it be fair to say that the Griffiths Report on general management caught sociology on the hop? In carrying out an ethnographic study of the implemenation of general management in 1985–86 the author found little to be drawn on in the established traditions of medical or organizational sociology. In part, this reflected a relative neglect of the sociology of management in general and public-service management in particular.[1] There was a thriving neo-Marxist critical literature on the state and its problems at a macro-level but little research on what was happening within the organizational culture of the NHS.

The sociologists of medicine or health and illness seemed by and large to have accepted the argument that 'the NHS is different from business in management terms' (DHSS 1983: 10). Interest focused on aspects of health work that were unique, medical power, professional ideology, doctor-patient relationships.[2] While much of this literature was critical of medical domination and its effects, it tended to accept by implication the centrality of medical concerns and the medical model when looking at formal health-care organizational settings. Research on nursing, as an occupation and a practice, was minimal in comparison to the numerical importance of this group in the health service.[3] Health service administration was similarly left in the shadow of medicine and given little attention by sociologists apart from some interest in professional bureaucratic conflict or the lack of it (Green 1975).

For many sociologists, the most interesting thing about hospital and health service organization was its unique 'negotiated order', the lack of a traditional bureaucratic hierarchy and the interactions between various professional groups and administrators producing if not consensus, then a loosely structured order. Many of the classic works on health organizations were produced by interactionists, who found the paradigm examples of their visions of the social world in the intra-and inter-professional rivalries of hospital life.[4]

Even if Sir Roy Griffiths had taken the time to consult the strictly sociological literature on health service organization, it is unlikely that he would have been persuaded away from his simple recommendations. As one of Keynes' practical men he is firmly wedded to the classic principles of management where everyone in an organization needs one boss. The brief heyday of the sociologically informed Royal Commission was in the late 1960s and early 70s.[5] Sir Roy has (or had) the Prime Minister's confidence and a quick look and some decisive recommendations for action sufficed.

It may, however, be in the process of implementation that the sociologist is avenged. How has the complex social system of the health service responded to the new managerial styles, what are the unintended consequences of the new controls and have the doctors been really brought to heel? In a brief encouragement to medical sociologists to get involved in furthering an understanding of the management process, Hunter suggests the following:

> Out of ignorance, and a misguided faith in a conception of rationality that is at odds with practice, reformers have failed to recognise the NHS's power structure, the capacities of groups to bargain and influence, and the importance of historical legacy for the shape and character of organisational arrangements.
>
> (Hunter 1986: 9)

This Chapter looks at the recent history of administration in the health service, it then assesses the factors that have brought managerialism to the fore and reviews the social and political context of the Griffiths report. This is followed by an exploration of the impact of general management on relationships between staff groups and an assessment of the future prospects of managerialism in the health service. Has Griffiths imposed a new non-negotiable order on the health-care professionals or is the sociological scepticism suggested by Hunter justified?

The Chapter mainly draws on the growing 'post-Griffiths' literature, both academic and professional, but refers also to the author's own study of the implementation of Griffiths in one district health authority (Cox 1986). This is an ethnographic study based on observation and two rounds of semi-structured interviews with members of unit and district management teams and district officers during the critical period when the new structures and roles were being implemented from mid 1985 to mid 1986.

From administration to management

Klein (1983) emphasizes the administration vision, 'a radically managerial ideology' (ibid: 25) that contributed to the origins of the NHS. Important parts of the emerging consensus on the need for a national service were the 'rationalist paternalists, both medical and administrative . . . intolerant of muddle, inefficiency and incompetence' (ibid: 5). In the compromises between government and medicine, centralism and localism that characterized the NHS, the administrative disciplines in Whitehall and the authorities played a 'heroic' part in the 'sheer administrative slog' of establishing the Boards and the routines of the new systems. Even at ministry level there was a dual hierarchy of medical and lay officers and locally much distinction between lay, financial and medical administrators (ibid: 45).

A massive edifice of administrative lore became the underlying structure of the NHS organization but it was always built around the assumption of medical autonomy and expertise. The health service administrative tradition was established to enable a service to run rather than to run it. From the start the peculiar characteristics of the NHS institution created an environment and culture in which administration rather than management could thrive. As Klein states, the service was complex depending on the 'spontaneous interaction of a large variety of different groups with different skills, all dependent on each other'. And it was hetereogenous, delivering 'a wide range of service under one organisational umbrella' (ibid: 46). Administration provided, monitored and processed the complex web of guidelines, controls, financial and pay regulations, procedures and consultations that enabled this unique system to function.

At the time, the 1974 reorganization was seen as the high point of managerialism in the NHS. The mangerialist reforms of the public services at that time were about a systems approach, planning, economies of scale and a rationalized corporate structure, the 'New Rationalism' of Heclo and Wildavsky (1974). A measure of enquiry, research and consultancy was incorporated into process of change.[6] Critics like Draper and Smart (1974) felt that the new corporate management structure was inappropriate to a health service, which necessitated a more 'organic' form of organization. Similarly, Carpenter (1977) was critical of the Salmon structure for nurse management which, he held, was based on an inappropriate industrial model.

However, the 1974 restructuring, like the simplifications introduced in 1982, institutionalized further the unique tripartite 'consensus' organizational model. Indeed, writers like Jacques (1978) spent much time on 'social analysis' to demonstrate the characteristics of medical authority that rules out conventional line management. Around the power structure of the medical specialist consultants, with their firms and cogwheels, parallel administrative and nursing hierarchies and grading structures prospered. As Green (1975: 137) noted: 'If the administrators claim to be professionals where do you look for your professional bureaucratic conflicts?'

Within this well-established culture, the sociological literature continued to feature the unique and perhaps progressive nature of health service organization. Draper and Smart's enthusiasm for the 'organic' nature of health organization was picked up in a later study by Burns (1981) himself, in comments on the hospital's 'collaborative system', which might have served to discourage attempts to introduce commercial-style general management. This sociological viewpoint often seemed to reinforce the medical profession's desire for autonomy and special status and to defend a 'consensus' built around a medical dominance which was seen as preferable to managerial power.[7]

Thompson (1987) points to the neglect of intra-organizational conflict in comparison with this emphasis on the collaborative system. He develops a model which contrasts three coalitions – the political, the practitioner interest and the 'administrative ethic'. The latter coalition is seen as believing in 'patient need and social service' and as deriving its power from the information networks that it controls and its influence in the construction of agendas, recording of minutes and strategic roles in the planning and review processes. For Thompson, the key issue post-Griffiths is whether district general manager can build a new coalition 'to assert a dominance in order to create the conditions for profound transformation' (ibid: 148). If administrators have, or had, power, it is from the covert manipulative ability emphasized by Thompson (ibid: 149). Unlike managers, they are not expected to lead from the front nor give orders although many district and unit administrators under the 'consensus' system were informally using their position to manage rather than facilitate.

This covert administrative role was clearly too retiring for Griffiths. It is important for him and his version of managerial hierarchies that there is someone identifiable at each level who takes responsibility: 'By general management we mean the responsibility drawn together in one person, at different levels of the organization, for planning, implementation and control of performance' (DHSS 1983: 11) and: 'At no level is the general management role clearly being performed by an identifiable individual' (ibid: 12).

Griffiths creates a sharp focus for the managerial drive in the NHS because it can be identified with the courageous step of introducing the 'general management' role. Most public services have long survived with managerial roles, although as in local government and even the nationalized industries they may have been constrained by both political influence and professional power (see Hunter 1988: 543). The pressures to bring management to the top of the NHS agenda had been building up steadily throughout the 1970s. For administrators working at the large district general hospital in the author's case study, the industrial-relations crisis of the late 1970s had been where they had cut their managerial teeth. The local negotiations about emergency cover, the experience of militancy and picket lines had forced the unit management team to act cohesively, negotiate and make decisions. Similarly, crises in staffing wards and theatres, and the need to manage real budgetary cuts in order to move resources to the 'Cinderella services', had taken both administrators and some senior consultants far down the road towards general management ahead of Griffiths.

It was very evident that the difference between administration and management was a key issue amongst those implementing Griffiths. Management consultants ran seminars for senior staff on the theme 'From administration to management'. Whereas administration was seen as servicing the needs of the professionals (Harrison 1986), general management was a matter of taking overall responsibility for the delivery of a service.

For Griffiths, a managerial approach involved planning, setting targets, managing implementation and monitoring performance against pre-set criteria. The objective was a much more informed and determined approach to setting and keeping to budgets and in labour-intensive health care, this meant a stricter control over professional and manual labour costs, and performance (see Harrison 1986, 1988; Cousins 1987). The recurring themes of Griffiths' managerialism are action, effectiveness, thrust, urgency and vitality, management budgeting, sensitivity to consumer satisfaction and an approach to management of personnel which would reward good performance and ultimately sanction poor performance with dismissal. The appointment of general managers, coming soon after the enforcement of competitive tendering for ancillary services, was part of a new and more intensive form of managerial intervention. Whereas earlier reorganizations had brought some management techniques for planning into the NHS, the Con- servative government was now seeking to change managerial behaviour and introduce an approach to control and labour discipline derived from the competitive private sector.

The centrality of management

Why has the issue of management come to occupy a central place on the health-policy stage in recent years? With the NHS being one of the largest organizations in the world, it is perhaps surprising that its management has not always been a central issue. Issues of management – funding, resource allocation, planning, capital development, pay negotiation, industrial relations, etc. – have been on the agenda but perhaps in a subordinate and less focused way. Since the 1970s, organizational structure and managerialism have been seen as part of the solution to the problems of the NHS. What is new is the identification of a definite managerial role to take on the managerial tasks and the determination of a government to challenge existing ways of working.

The factors underlying this change are both structural and

ideological. Control of public expenditure has been a major concern of western governments since the oil crisis of the early 1970s. The 1974 structure may have been introduced to plan for growth (like so much of the restructuring of that period), but it arrived at a time of constraint. The present government's desire to contain public spending is a continuation of earlier retrenchment but motivated by monetarist convictions as much as external pressures. If public spending is to be pegged while costs increase because of new technology and an ageing population, then attention to the 'efficiency and effectiveness' of the public-health and caring services is a logical step (Harrison 1988). The fiscal crisis of the state is predicted as confidently by critical theorists of the left as it is by the monetarists of the right. The pressures on the public services created by the contemporary political economic scene are well summed up by Cousins (1987) and she shows that these are not unique to Britain or to the present government.

However, the enthusiasm for managerial solutions is driven by ideological factors as well as economic ones. Competitive tendering for ancillary services, the expenditure scrutinies of Lord Rayner (from Marks and Spencer plc), the invitations to join the NHS Management Board to businessmen like Roy Griffiths, Victor Paige and Len Peach, hints about new deals with the private health sector are part of an enthusiasm for 'business values' and 'the market'. They contain an explicit suspicion of the 'dependency culture' and restrictive practices of the traditional public sector.

Some of this policy drive from the Thatcher government may be seen as 'rational progressive managerialism' adopting techniques successful in private industry like performance monitoring, cost accounting and improvement schemes, management information systems, etc. Other aspects reflect a more ideological 'small-business' approach, with an emphasis on competition and contracts rather than a planned and rationalized corporate provision. The enforced contracting-out of cleaning is an example. This is insisted on from Whitehall when many managers feel that they would have more control over standards if they could employ their own staff.[8] The 1989 White Paper proposals continue this trend with the prospect of larger hospitals 'opting out' and becoming semi-independent contractors to health authorities and budget-holding general practitioners in an 'internal' competitive market in which private hospitals could also feature.

The implementation of Griffiths

If nothing else, the Griffiths Report (DHSS 1983) and its implementation has generated a lot of academic interest. There are several major studies of implementation, relationships, decision-making and management behaviour under the new regime. Most of these are still in progress or just about to be published, so definitive findings are still awaited. The main emphasis has been on comparative case studies across several districts and regions with some surveys, and much observation and structured interviewing.

As part of her critical study of the restructuring of the labour process in the public services, Cousins (1987) includes a chapter on Griffiths based in part on interviews in two DHAs. The 'Nursing Policy Studies Unit at Warwick have published two reports which concentrate particularly on the impact of general management on nursing and on the medical profession (Robinson and Strong 1987; Strong and Robinson 1988). This last report provides a wealth of ethnographic evidence on the process of introducing general management, mainly at regional and district level. Glennerster *et al.* (1988) have also looked at the impact of Griffiths on nursing in the North West Thames Region. Banyard (1988a and 1988b) provides some useful data from an interview and questionnaire study of how unit staff from two RHAs assess the impact of general management.

A major Economic and Social Research Council (ESRC) study is being carried out by Harrison *et al.* (1988). Harrison (1988) promises a systematic evaluation of the Roy Griffiths remedies taking his own 'diagnosis' as a base line. They are looking at the Supervisory Board's strategic role and the Management Board's success in protecting 'managers from the immediacies of politics'. They also want to know whether managers have been able to assert their authority over health professionals and how they relate to chairmen and authority members. They are collecting date on the impact of incentive payments and short-term contracts and asking whether the value of services has been systematically evaluated and whether it has become more responsive to consumers.

Meanwhile, the National Health Service Training Authority has sponsored two projects which are seen as feeding research directly into action and management development. Pettigrew *et al.* (1988) are engaged in action research on decision making the the implementation and management of change in twelve DHAs. They have focused on two major strategic service changes, the rationalization or development of acute services and priority group services. A team at Templeton College, Oxford, having been studying and helping DGMs find their feet (National Health Service Training Authority 1986), providing guidance on how major issues like quality are tackled.

The DGM or UGM who has not been included in some sociologist's or management specialist's sample must be feeling very left out! The high profile of health service matters in the press and Parliament has served to put both an academic and a public-interest spotlight on general management and general managers throughout their first short-term contracts.

An idea of the impact of Griffiths (DHSS 1983) on the relationships between managers, doctors, nurses and administrators can be obtained from the early publications of these projects.

The starting point for any assessment of the impact of general management on relationships within the NHS has to be the professional reactions to the original report and an assessment of the way the new key district and unit general-management posts were allocated. The Griffiths Report is very respectful of medical power and seeks to co-opt the doctors into management and budgetary responsibility. Professional medical reaction was 'reserved' and cautious but not entirely negative. The British Medical Association wanted some protection against managerial power – an appeal mechanism – and insisted on retaining regional contracts for consultants while the professional advisory machinery was to remain intact. The general-management jobs were to be open to clinicians with protection for salaries and conditions of service and the scope through part-time appointments to maintain clinical involvement. It would seem that the medical interest thought that Griffiths could be 'negotiated' and that doctors hoped to have the cake of clinical autonomy while still eating it if they chose to be managers.[9]

The reaction from the nursing profession and especially from nurse managers, who were largely ignored by Griffiths, was much more outspokenly critical. Implementation led to the dismantling nearly everywhere of post-Salmon functional management (Robinson *et al.* 1989). District officer posts disappeared or were marginalized in the new structures and few nurses obtained general management posts. A belated realization of this led to the famous Royal College of Nursing advertising campaign of early 1986 which sought public support for a nursing advisor, 'who understood nursing', at every level in districts (Clay 1987).

Petchey (1986) quotes data on regional, district and unit appointments to general-management posts and notes the ministerial level of interference which attempted to enforce an infusion of industrial and commercial managerial talent into the health service. Of regional and district general managers appointed by September 1985, around 60 per cent were ex-administrators, 9 per cent treasurers, 6 per cent medical officer, 2.3 per cent nursing officers and 1.4 per cent clinicians. The private sector contributed 10 per cent and the military nearly 6 per cent. By February 1986, a similar pattern emerged at unit level although with a slightly higher clinical involvement. Of unit general managers, 60 per cent were ex-NHS administrators, 19 per cent doctors, 10 per cent nurses, 2 per cent other NHS staff and 8 per cent non-NHS staff.

Similarly, Petchey (1986: 98–9) suggests that nurses, community physicians and consultants found their influence lessened on the formal management boards or teams of the post-Griffiths districts.

The next section will explore the impact of Griffiths on each of the key roles in district and unit organization, the general managers themselves, the administrators, the doctors and the nurse managers.

The general managers

Griffiths (DHSS 1983) argued that the health service needed a cultural change rather than a reorganization. In practice he produced a radical reorganization of the internal arrangements in most districts, not least because of the idea that districts could draw up a management structure to suit their own needs. The general-manager roles were specified but there was wide scope for restructuring units, redesignating 'support' and 'advisory' roles, designing management boards, etc. Whether real cultural change affecting behaviour and outcomes has been produced is perhaps debatable but there is little doubt that general management has become a new cultural force within the health service.

Strong and Robinson's (1988) research provides ample ethnographic evidence of how this early period of implementation affected attitudes and relationships at district and unit level. Above all, they capture, and are perhaps themselves captured by, the inspirational momentum that characterized the introduction of general management and the morale and self-esteem of the new generation of district general managers. The mixture of 60 per cent ex-administrators, with significant minorities from the private sector and from the clinical trades armed with the Griffiths message and supported by meetings and business consultants emphasizing leadership was an enthusiastic new cadre:

> The report capture the spirit of the age in a way managed by no other document.
> Many of those we observed, interviewed or heard lecture were deeply committed to the new way of doing things.
> In this heady atmosphere, a new organizational and moral vision was outlined. For this was both a new way of stucturing the health service and a moral crusade.
>
> (Strong and Robinson 1988: 54)

Griffiths (DHSS 1983) was launched at a time when British management generally was emerging with new self-confidence. The power of trade unions had been weakened by unemployment and legislation while management texts were becoming popular bookstall reading emphasizing culture, excellence, and leadership rather than the technical expertise of a management science (Peters and Waterman

1982; Peters and Austin 1984; Goldsmith and Clutterbuck 1984). Good NHS administrators came out of the closet and began to admit to managing and enjoying it. Clinicians and managers from the private sector felt obliged to prove themselves in the new roles. Furthermore, the problems of the health service – underfunding, pressure from government, new technologies, increased demand, closure of long-stay hospitals – all forced management to take action but gave little scope for avoiding unpopular decisions or for buying time or support.

Reading the extracts from Strong and Robinson's interviews with general managers and those close to them conveys a strong positive self-image of managers designing new organizational structures, making new appointments, taking decisions, obtaining and using information, facing up to problems, developing strategies and wishing to take responsibility for implementing them. As Strong and Robinson put it: 'For the moment and on present evidence Griffiths felt right; or at least more right than what had gone before' (Strong and Robinson 1988).

Now critics who can see little potential for any good management in public service may see much of this as self-serving hype and legitimation as Cousins says:

> To the extent that general managers can convince the public and employees, by their use of language, and by emphasising technical rationality, that their practices are in the public interest then their scope for further reductions in service and more coercive controls of the labour process are possible but, ... it is not clear that the managers have yet been successful in legitimating their practices.
>
> (Cousins 1987: 169)

It is interesting that both Strong and Robinson and Cousins pick up on the importance of what MacIntyre (1981) calls the 'histrionics' of modern management. It is not a science and is about commitment and persuasion, what Anthony sees as providing a narrative function for the organization or a governmental role (see Anthony 1986). Griffiths has created the cadre of general managers who can and indeed have to embody the new managerialism in a way that none of the roles or 'characters' produced by the 1974 or 1982 reorganization could do.

Strong and Robinson sum up Griffiths as follows:

> Griffiths, in fact, was based on a philosophy, a paradigm, a doctrine. It was not something that had been conclusively and scientifically demonstrated to be superior – nor, perhaps, could it ever be. For not only was management a practical discipline not a science, but it operated in that most complex of worlds, the social arena; the home of the soft, not the hard sciences. Thus the only way practical managers could proceed was by using a subtle brew

of hard evidence and gut feeling, of official statistics and qualitative data, of careful analysis and the charismatic enthusiasm of management gurus; variously stirred.

(Strong and Robinson 1988: 87)

Living up to the expectations of Griffiths in the unique political and professional environment of the health service and in face of government-funding policies and political interest was not an easy option, especially for those who came from outside the service. There was a shakeout of casualties claimed to be around 5 per cent (Alleway 1987), but including the Chief Executive, Victor Paige, and some highly publicized cases that hit national headlines. The replacement at District level came almost entirely from public service and mainly from the health service (Alleway 1987). It may be that Paige's resignation and the loss of ex-army or private-sector managers has served to reinforce the self-confidence of NHS general management – insiders know best and political interference at national and local level is seen as a shared and common problem and one of the major difficulties holding the Griffiths developments back.

Administration

'Mere administration was abolished. In its place came management' (Strong and Robinson 1988: 56). The Institute of Health Service Administrators grasped the message very quickly and opportunistically changed their name to the Institute of Health Service Management. Subsequently, the Institute has enthusiastically adopted a mangerialist stance in its training and publicity activities (IHSM 1985).

However, reviewing the general-management appointment process in 1986, the *Hospital and Health Services Review* editorial claimed that: 'On the whole administrators have had the roughest time, though they have received little sympathy in consequence' (1986: 4). Administrators were the most natural candidates for general-management posts and many succeeded but the 'discipline' lost its secure functional role and promotions ladder. Relatively little has been written about what has happened to administration since Griffiths, but some observations will be made from one district case study.

Successful unit and district administrators found themselves management posts, often moving rather than waiting on the outcome of interviews at their own authority. They knew that after Griffiths their influence and role would be curtailed if they remained. Older administrators unable or unwilling to make the transition to the new era would find themselves effectively demoted or taking early retirement. More problematic was the position of younger and more junior administrators who could see the career ladder withdrawn as they would have to compete with nurses, clinicians and outsiders for future management posts. Furthermore, the leaders of their 'profession' had taken up general-management posts and sometimes deliberately cut themselves off psychologically from the now-tainted image of administrator. Ideologically, administration had moved to management.

In practice, the administrators left behind divided into those locked into fairly routine but essential administrative work, servicing committees and running sites, and those whose talents and knowledge enabled them to find key roles in unit or district management, assisting UGMs and DGMs. These roles with management-development potential became at a premium for those interested in general management but without a clinical background. UGMs found that they needed the support of assistants who could prepare material for reviews, assist with planning, investigate problem areas or manage support services. Developing the next generation of general managers would have been very problematic without these posts unless there had been radical changes in the training and attitudes of nurses and doctors. The controversy about the 'fast-track' national general-management trainee scheme where trainees found on completion that suitable posts had not been identified for them to apply for is part of the same problem. Where there were posts, they were often too routine and did not offer much scope for the ideas, training and commitments generated by the course.[10]

Nursing

Nurses constitute half of the labour force of the NHS and provide the majority of patient contact and care. Since 1966 nursing had been managed on a functional basis with a hierarchy from ward sister/charge nurse through the Salmon gradings to a district nursing officer controlling a large budget and staff complement. The impact of Griffiths on this structure has been radical, at least above the unit level. Defensive lobbying by nursing pressure groups has aimed at preserving a route for nursing advice to both general managers and to district health authorities and at maintaining a line of professional accountability on matters of standards and ethics. At unit level, nursing interests have tried to maintain functional management and avoid the situation where non-nurse managers below UGM level are managing nurses. Meanwhile in some districts, at ward and sector level, more general-management responsibilities are being given to nurse managers as 'patient-service managers'.

This bald summary does not do justice to the traumatic effect of Griffiths (DHSS 1983) on the management of nurses and the roles of the most senior nurses. Griffiths hardly referred to nursing at all. His main aim was to exert some managerial power over doctors who were able to commit so much of the health service's resources. Chief nursing officers lost their empires and had to suffer the widespread, if muted, lack of sympathy from other disciplines and new managers who had often resented their power and expressed scepticism about the quality of nursing management. Those that stayed on rather than take early retirement found themselves in a variety of roles. In some cases, the role of chief nursing adviser was combined with a 'lead officer' hybrid role often for 'quality assurance' but sometimes for personnel. Elsewhere, the role of district nursing adviser was combined with line responsibility for nursing at unit level or with the role of director of nurse education. Strong and Robinson's (1988) evidence shows that amongst those who are left in district-level nursing posts, there are those who feel they were 'mugged' by Griffiths, while others have found new niches and valued roles within the new structures either through a 'staff' advisory function or as part of line management, and sometimes as both or more at once.

This exchange from Strong and Robinson indicates the problems that playing such hybrid roles might bring. The respondent is Chief Nursing Advisor, Unit General Manager and the District Director of Quality:

INT: So have you got at least two full-time jobs really?

CNA/UGM/DDQ: Absolutely. I'm between the devil and the deep blue sea. I'm being judged in many ways because of taking on the UGM post. All my nursing colleagues, if they ever thought me wrong before, now really think I'm letting the side down.'

(Strong and Robinson 1988: 112)

Banyard (1988c) recently summarized evidence given to the House of Commons Social Services Select Committee in 1987, which included views on the impact of Griffiths on nursing. The Royal College of Nursing said that 'many nurse managers were unhappy that lines of accountability within units now focussed on UGMs' (ibid: 883). They also comment on the diversity in senior nursing roles after the general-management structures were introduced. About a third of health authorities were reported to have retained a chief nursing post at district; another third had combined this with another function, while the remaining third had abolished the post (Baynard 1988c). Robinson *et al.* (1989) in a recent survey of 159 chief nursing advisers found 29 different job titles and no agreed core responsibilities and a lack of support staff and information.

Banyard (1988c: 883) reports that 'nurse managers at unit level had often found themselves with a wider range of responsibilities than before, because the district role had diminished'. Harrison (1988) also suggests that on balance, senior nurses have not fared as badly from

Griffiths as they may have anticipated. Their immediate loss of status has been compensated for to some extent by new career opportunities, particularly in areas like quality assurance, which have expanded as an outcome of Griffiths' emphasis on the impact of health care on the consumer. It is nurses at ward level who will be feeling the overall impact of increased managerial pressure on productivity and skill mix (Harrison 1988: 148–9).

Doctors

Many commentators see the desire to obtain some managerial control over doctors as being a principle objective of Griffiths and highlight the potential within general management for a challenge to medical hegemony (e.g. Harrison 1988; Scrivens 1988). Critiques of medical power have also been a central feature of sociological accounts of modern medicine and health services.[11] However, in the face of determined governmental efforts to contain health expenditure, medical independence becomes an important basis for defence and the new managers are widely suspected of being employed to carry out direct orders from Whitehall. To what extent has general management affected the role of consultants within the service?

Strong and Robinson (1988) claim that in the past, within the overall limits of the NHS, medical 'rule has been secure' and has weakened management and kept nurses 'ignorant' and in a subordinate role. The same thesis emerges from Harrison's (1986) work on the management culture of the NHS. General management offers a countervailing power for the first time which they see as a precondition of any fundamental change or reform including 'many forms of greater democratic control' (Strong and Robinson 1988: 6–7). Similarly, Petchey (1986) having indicated the ways in which the post-Griffiths management team and board structures had limited the involvement of the medical and nursing professions concludes: 'It is clear that the medical profession itself has to be controlled, and if Griffiths should achieve this, then strangely enough it may turn out that his impact will not be entirely regressive. (Petchey 1986: 101).

The challenge to medical hegemony is an important aim of general management. Thompson (1987) and Scrivens (1988) show how the development of information systems and clinical budgeting are part of an attempt to build up greater managerial control over how health service resources are deployed and committed. At present, the new general managers' powers over consultants are very limited. Nevertheless, challenging medical autonomy is an item on the general managers' agenda. Strong and Robinson's ethnography gives fascinating examples of the power games being played: 'Chief Nursing

Advisor describing a DGM known as "Big Bad Ian Hamilton": "What impressed me was the way that, from the beginning, he challenged the autonomy of medical staff" ' (1988: 135).

DGMs or their admirers tell of how they told the doctors straight what resources they had and what performance they wanted. Ex-military men went in and banged their paper down on the table and said: 'That's what we want,' even when in battle with the Royal Colleges. And it's not always quite such a macho confrontation. The new female managers can be assertive too: 'Jill (DGM) takes them on full frontal. There's a stunned silence at medical committees' (Strong and Robinson 1988: 76).

At present it is doubtful if these colourful scenarios in particular districts add up to any serious challenge to the substance of consultant power across the NHS. Banyard's survey suggests that the general managers have not yet effectively begun to control consultants and his respondents saw this as the principal constraint to general managers. There was little control over clinical targets and monitoring clinical activity was 'in practice . . . a somewhat spasmodic activity' (Banyard 1988b). Similarly, Pollitt *et al.* (1988) show how gingerly the general managers they interviewed are approaching the problem of involving consultants in management budgeting. The weakness of general management is not so much in its own arenas of district head quarters or even unit boards; here medical representation and the role of community physicians may have been marginalized (Strong and Robinson 1988). But in the world of the consultant with a regional contract and the mutual support of the medical advisory committees, things may not have changed very much. As one radiographer put it: 'consultants operate like a masonic lodge, and have considerable power to resist change' (Banyard 1988a: 825).

Harrison suggests that doctors have reacted critically to the formal challenge of general management but 'as yet there is no systematic evidence that such management initiatives are substantially affecting the behaviour of doctors' (Harrison 1988: 145). Scrivens (1988) documents the efforts by general managers to bring clinicians into management through involving them in policy and resource discussions. The appointment of clinical directors and heads of specialities accountable to the unit general manager have been popular. Developing a management budgeting system to encourage more financial accountability was seen by twenty-six of Scriven's DGM respondents as the key to clinician involvement in management (ibid: 31). It is a long way from this experimenting with budgets and the beginnings of dialogue to the full managerial control of medical employees.

The 1989 White Paper gives great emphasis to improved management accounting systems and proposes to extend management influence on clinicians in three ways. It recommends that district general managers become full members of the advisory appointments committees that appoint consultants. District general managers will agree detailed job descriptions for consultants each year. Managers will also be involved in the allocation of merit awards. Such payments should reflect commitment to the management and development of the service as well as clinical skills (Department of Health 1989). However, other aspects of the proposals such as the self-governing, revenue earning, hospital and the way clinical budgets and cost centres could be used in an internal market might lead to new forms of autonomy for consultants. Scrivens prophetically envisaged the possibility of 'a new type of health service, based, not upon the familiar notions of rational planning and equity in resource allocation, but based upon the entrepreneurship and the motivations of clinicians' (Scrivens 1988: 33).

Other health service staff and the issue of morale

Thus far, the overview has concentrated on the senior levels of the health districts where Griffiths (DHSS 1983) has had an immediate effect on individual roles, powers and relationships. Observing the long, complex and frustrating process of implementing Griffiths at district and unit level in 1985/6, it was always a surprise for the author to go onto wards or into the community services and find that the everyday process of operations, treatment, care and outpatient appointments was carrying on as usual. Most staff did not know the DGM's name and had only scant experience of a UGM, controversy about senior nursing roles, management boards and organizational structures only impacted on real life when wards were to be closed or changed, or a dispute flared up.

What little evidence we have from wider staff perspectives on the Griffiths changes are not encouraging. A range of organizations representing pharmacy, physiotherapy, dietetics and psychology submitted views to the House of Commons Select Committee on Social Services and bemoaned the loss of district-manager roles and a clear district-service perspective for their profession. Unitization often meant that these professions were not able to influence top-level management and opportunities for career development, rotation and an overall plan were lost (see summary in Anderson 1987: 635).

Banyard's survey suggests a downward gradient of enthusiasm about Griffiths and a loss of morale the further questions are asked away from the centres of managerial power. The Griffiths revolution had failed to improve confidence and direct-care staff did not feel that patients had benefited. To quote Banyard: 'General management has apparently failed to produce an improvement in the morale of unit staff – although clearly any blame for low morale cannot be placed exclusively at the door of general management' (Banyard 1988d: 916). Of his respondents, 68 per cent felt that general management had not improved morale and 57 per cent thought that it had not been beneficial for trade unionists. Cousin's interviews produced similar critical views:

> the undermining of the staff's moral commitment was evident in a number of ways: for some interviewees it was the loss of values of compassion and caring in the service, for others it was reduced public accountability . . . and for others it was the loss of trust and motivation of the lower-level members of the organisation.
>
> (Cousins 1987: 169)

General management, as introduced in the current political and economic context has been associated with wage restraint, competitive tendering, 'speed up' and an equivocal government policy towards the service and its future. For staff involved in care, service delivery and manual and non-manual support work, the imposition of a non-negotiable authority, and the exposure of protective functional interest groups in nursing but also in catering, works, transport, etc. is reinforcing the emergence of the industrial 'them and us' culture.

Harrison (1988) makes the point that while doctors and nurses opposed many of the formal challenges to professionalism of the new managerial approach, the substantive outcomes were not, yet, as radical as feared. However, 'for ancillary workers it is difficult to imagine anything more radical than the competitive tendering exercise' (ibid: 151). Whether contracts to go to internal or external contractors, the results have been job losses and reductions in earnings and hours, a narrow specification of duties and a weakening of trade-union influence.

This interview in the *Guardian* reinforces the picture painted by Cousins (1987), Banyard (1988c) and Harrison (1988):

> David Osborne, who works in the stores department at Guy's Hospital London and is branch secretary for the National Union of Public Employees, says morale among his members – nurses, clerical and ancillary workers – is at an all time low. Pay and conditions are the main grievances but the new managerial ethos niggles too.
> We have seen a dramatic increase in the number of managers walking around with clipboards and filofaxes, but they never seem to be doing any work. If you're a manager, you're OK. But if you're lower grade ancillary or clerical worker, it's sod you.
>
> (*Guardian* 12 October 1988)

Griffiths and decision making in the NHS

One aspect of general management was to be the devolution of decision making to the lowest possible level with managers being responsible for what they did and the centre maintaining control through accountability review and monitoring. For a systematic answer to how this has worked in practice, we will have to await results of the detailed studies promised by Harrison *et al.* (1988) and Pettigrew *et al.* (1988). Already, however, there has been a recurring theme in the literature about the ineffectiveness of the supervisory and management boards set up by Griffiths with the implication that governmental and civil service interference have constrained a managerial approach from the top. Similarly, the freedom of regional and district managers to made decisions and form policy had been limited by directives coming from the centre. At the unit level, there is some useful information on staff views in the Banyard (1988d) survey, which suggests some success in delegation to units and quicker decision making.

The controversies about the supervisory and management boards are reminiscent of Weberian concerns about the irrationality of the top of technically rational bureaucracies. Strong and Robinson (1988: 89) pick up the irritation of the DGMs and district chairmen at fudging and lack of consistency from Whitehall. Victor Paige's resignation was widely interpreted as a reaction against Norman Fowler and the political concerns that stopped action and delayed decisions (*Guardian* 6 June 1986).

Judge claimed recently that in contrast to the headway made by the Griffiths reforms at the local level, 'the changes at the centre have been less successful; in particular, the Management Board has not been allowed to function as originally envisaged and has been progressively neutered' (*Guardian* 12 October 1988). Similarly, the Institute of Health Service Management contrasted the benefits of general management at a local level with the confusion of responsibilities between health ministers, the NHS management board, the DHSS permanent secretary, and the supervisory board (Anderson 1987: 635).

Central intervention is criticized by the Institute of Health Service Management and by the National Association of Health Authorities. The latter's evidence suggests:

> There is a strong view from the authorities that the centre is still too involved in the day to day affairs of health authorities. There does not seem to have been any reduction in the number and frequency of central initiatives, both in the service objectives and management tasks, nor in the detailed information required for central monitoring and control.
>
> (Anderson 1987: 635).

In the contrast to the problems of the interface between the government and the health service, there is some evidence of progress towards Griffiths objectives of speedier, delegated and accountable decision making at least down as far as the unit. Banyard's respondents thought that there had been delegation to units and that decision making was quicker and clearer. Managers were more involved in setting and controlling budgets and there was a greater awareness of costs. However, the Royal College of Nursing has not been won over to general management and claimed that the quality of decision making had been reduced because of inadequate consultation and participation of professionals (Banyard 1988c). Until more detailed case studies are published, it will be difficult to test assertions about whether better decisions are being made by general management. If the government press ahead with their current programme of changes, managers will be making decisions within a very new arena, which will make any comparative assessment very difficult.

The outlook for the managerial approach in the health service

There is little certainty within the health service at the moment with arguments raging about the government's 'Working for Patients' White Paper (DH 1989) and continued worries about an underlying determination to contain costs and force through a more pluralistic pattern of health care and health finance. However, it is inconceivable that the general management genie having been finally let out of the bottle and given considerable momentum and encouragement could ever be squeezed back in. It was clear at the 1987 election that the Labour opposition would have retained general management had they won, while perhaps setting different targets. There will be continued struggles between the management viewpoint and that of the clinicians, together with exasperation at the frustrations of trying to exercise industrial-style authority in health care, but general management is here to stay. Furthermore, economic and social pressures on the health service and the development of more powerful information and accounting systems will all serve to increase the managerial influence.

The extent of the managerial revolution in health care is summed up by the outspoken DGM for Gloucester Health Authority, Ken Jarrold: 'If someone five years ago had said all senior NHS managers would be on short-term contracts with performance-related pay and individual performance review, I would have thought they were wierd. But here we are,' (quoted in *Guardian* 12 October 1988). There has not been much evidence yet on the consequences of these radical conditions of service on managerial behaviour but the changes are indicative of the way in which a cultural and organizational revolution has been engineered.

Those of us who wish to preserve and enhance the range of public services needed to enhance social citizenship cannot seriously entertain services entirely run along lines dictated by the needs of the dominant professions and especially not the medical profession. Public services need good management and Griffiths (DHSS 1983) has begun to enhance standards of managerial effort and skill in the health service. The political interest that has forced the changes through has not always had the strength of its convictions about managerial independence, nor the good sense to provide a secure direction and funding base for the service. Managers have not been left to manage, the service has been starved of funds at a time when the exchequer was full. Ideological objections to a 'socialist' service have led to an insistence on competitive tendering and other forms of privatization which have harmed the income and morale of lower-paid staff and prevented general managers from developing the 'culture of excellence' that their management training may have taught them to pursue.

One of the most interesting perspectives on Griffiths and general management in the health service is derived from comparisons with social services. Here, morale is reportedly low with nearly a quarter of directors of social services 'losing their jobs' this year (*Guardian* 19 October 1988). Problems seem to relate to low public esteem following repeated scandals and the lack of managerial autonomy because of political not professional interference. *Social Services Insight* (1987: 2) considers that in there is 'a beefed-up (remoralized?) health service management' and points to the LGTB/DHSS survey of forty-seven local authorities which sees 'the biggest blockage to management development perceived by managers themselves at all levels was the lack of an appropriate culture or vision within which they could work' (Ibid). The evidence thus far from Strong and Robinson and from Banyard is that the post-Griffiths general managers are loyal to the health service and have some confidence that they can contribute to its future and success. The limitations they face are the reluctance of the government and Whitehall to trust management and provide a consistent policy and funding framework, the resistance of the powerful medical lobby and the lack of positive action to improve the morale and prospects of many non-managerial staff.

Conclusion

Since 1983 the management and organization of the British health service has seldom been off the front pages of national and local newspapers. Managerial initiatives have been seen by the government as a way forward when caught between the continued popularity of the National Health Service and a determination to contain public expenditure in the face of increasing costs. In the Griffiths Report (DHSS 1983), the approach was to move towards a conventional corporate line-mangement structure, more recently the 1989 White Paper advocates a more open and diverse internal market and greater autonomy for local managements. In both scenarios, general managers and financial accountants might be expected to be playing an increasingly significant role in the production and control of health care.

It was suggested in the introduction to this Chapter that the organization and management of health care had been hitherto relatively neglected in the sociological literature. The response to the Griffiths initiative has indicated a growing sociological research interest in health service management and demonstrates the range and scope of a sociological contribution to current debates. Inevitably, most of the research and writing being done is interdisciplinary and sociological perspectives are informing work which draws also on social policy, public administration, policy analysis, organization theory and management science. The importance of a sociological approach can be summarized in three areas.

The pace and diversity or organizational change in the health service means that there is considerable value in surveys, descriptions and more sophisticated ethnographic accounts of the process of policy implementation. This can vary from basic surveys like Banyard (1988a) to the more detailed and ethnographic accounts like that of Strong and Robinson (1988). The latter study, in particular, brings out the changes occuring in senior roles and professional cultures and shows the realities of organizational diversity and confusion. There is great potential for medical and organizational sociologists using this perspective to explore the impact of reorganization and change on health service personnel at all levels. Ethnographies which threw light on clinical budgeting, new ward-management arrangements, clinical director roles, the impact of competitive tendering, etc. would greatly enhance our understanding of a changing health service and link up with much established work in medical sociology.

There is a strong tradition of sociologically informed 'administrative science' which researchers like Hunter (1986, 1988) and Pettigrew *et al.* (1988) have developed in a health service context. The research base is a detailed analysis of the way organizations and decision-making work and a strong critical awareness of the limitations of 'one best way' solutions to managerial structures and tasks. The distinctive context of health care organization, its division of labour and culture are shown to limit the simplistic importation of inappropriate industrial models (Hunter 1988: 544–5). Hunter (1988: 548–9) indicates some frustration that such policy-relevant work is not having much influence on national policy makers. However, he also shows that at a local managerial level, sociologically informed and realistic analysis of organizational problems and opportunities may be seen as more valuable and indeed incorporated into training and staff-development activities.

Cousins' (1987) work is distinctive in opening out a much broader critical framework within which to assess developments in the management of health care. By linking her empirical work to the labour-process tradition in industrial sociology, Cousins shows up the important parallels in the intensification of labour and the increased pressure on low-paid and predominantly women workers. There is clearly much more research to be done which looks at the impact of the restructuring of the health service and the new managerial approach on health service staff at all levels.

The current ideological debates about health care between the political right and the left, and the respective roles of markets and private capital and of state intervention and organization are in part premised on assumptions about the effects on staff and on consumers of different patterns of health-care organization. The outcome of the 1989 White Paper may well generate a diverse range of organizational options' which should be the subject of critical research and evaluation.

Acknowledgements

I am particularly grateful for the comments provided on an earlier draft of this paper by David Hunter who was the discussant at the BSA Seminar and by the editors, Jonathan Gabe, Michael Calnan and Michael Bury.

Notes

1. Storey (1983) and Cousins (1987) are attempts to remedy this deficiency in general and public-sector management, respectively.
2. Hart (1985) provides a useful overview.
3. See Davies (1977); Dingwall and McIntosh (eds) (1978).
4. As in the popular reprinted extract by Strauss *et al.* (1973).
5. See Bulmer (1982), but Royal Commissions of any kind have become a rarity under the present Conservative government.
6. See Jacques (ed.) (1978); Rowbottom (1973).
7. For example, Cousins (1987); Carrier and Kendall (1986); Widgery (1988).
8. See Cousins (1987: 174).
9. See Ross (1984); *British Medical Journal* 10 December 1983.
10. See Millar (1988); Edmonstone (1988).
11. See Turner (1987).

David Cox

References

Alleway, L. (1987) 'Back on the outside looking in', *Health Service Journal* 16 July: 818.

Anderson, F. (1987) 'Griffiths – set to survive 11 June', *Health Service Journal* 4 June: 635.

Anthony, P.D. (1986) *The Foundation Management*, London: Tavistock.

Banyard, R. (1988a) 'How do UGMs perform ?' *Health Service Journal* 21 July: 824–5.

——(1988b) 'Management mirrored', *Health Service Journal* 28 July: 858–9.

——(1988c) 'More power to the units', *Health Service Journal* 4 August: 882–3.

——(1988d) 'Watching the revolution', *Health Service Journal* 11 August: 916–17.

British Medical Journal (1983) 'Lukewarm reception for Griffiths Report', *British Medical Journal* 10 December; 1811-12.

Bulmer, M. (1982) *The Uses of Social Research: Social Investigation in Public Policy Making*, London: Allen & Unwin.

Burns, T. (1981) 'A comparative study of administrative structure and organizational processes in selected areas of the NHS' SSRC Research Report.

Carpenter, M. (1977) 'The new managerialism and professionalism in nursing', in M. Stacey and M. Reid (eds) *Health and the Division of Labour*, London: Croom Helm.

Carrier, J. and Kendall, I. (1986) 'NHS management and the Griffiths Report', in *Year Book of Social Policy in Britain 1985/6*, London: Routledge.

Clay, T. (1987) *Nurses: Power and Politics*, London: Heinemann.

Cousins, C. (1987) *Controlling Social Welfare, A Sociology of State Welfare Work and Organisations*, Brighton: Wheatsheaf.

Cox, D. (1986) 'Implementing Griffiths at district level', paper presented to the British Sociological Association Medical Sociology Group conference, York, September.

Davies, C. (1977) 'Continuities in the development of hospital nursing in Britain' *Journal of Advanced Nursing* 2: 479–93.

DH (Department of Health) (1989) *Working for Patients*, London: HMSO, Cmnd 555.

DHSS (Department of Health and Social Security) (1972) *Management Arrangements for the Reorganised National Health Service*, London: HMSO.

——(1979) *Patients First*, London: HMSO.

——(1983) *NHS Management Enquiry (Griffiths Report)*, London: HMSO.

Dingwall, R. and McIntosh, J. (eds) (1978) *Readings in the Sociology of Nursing*, London: Churchill Livingstone.

Draper, P. and Smart, A. (1974) 'Social service and health policy in the United Kingdom: some contributions of the social sciences to the bureaucratisation of the National Health Service', *International Journal of Health Services* 4: 433–70.

Edmonstone, J. (1988) 'Trained in the fast lane, *Health Service Journal* September: 997–9.

Glennerster, H., Owens, P. and Kimberley, A. (1988) 'The nursing management function after Griffiths in the North West Thames Region' Second Interim Report, London: London School of Economics.

Goldsmith, W. and Clutterbuck, D. (1984) *The Winning Streak*, Harmondsworth, Penguin.

Green, S. (1975) 'Professional/bureaucratic conflict: the case of the medical profession', *Sociological Review* 23 (1): 121–41.

Harrison, S. (1986) 'Management culture and management budgets', *Hospital and Health Service Review* pp. 6–9, January.

——(1988) 'The workforce and the new managerialism', in R. Maxwell (ed.) *Reshaping the NHS;* London: Policy Journals.

Harrison, S., Hunter, D., Marnoch, G. and Pollitt, C. (1988) 'Check out on Griffiths: general management in the NHS', *ESRC Newsletter* 62 27–8, June.

Hart, N. (1985) *The Sociology of of Health and Medicine,* Ormskirk: Causeway.

Heclo, H. and Wildavsky, A. (1974) *The Private Government of Public Money,* London: Macmillan.

Hospital and Health Service Review (1986) 'The general managers', *Hospital and Health Service Review* January: 4–5.

Hunter, D. (1986) *Managing the National Health Service in Scotland: Review and Assessment of Research Needs,* Scottish Health Service Studies No. 45 Edinburgh: Scottish Home and Health Department.

——(1988) 'The impact of research on restructuring the British National Health Service', *The Journal of Health Administration Education* 6 (3) 537–53, Summer.

Institute of Health Service Management (1985) 'NHS general management implementation: issues on authority and unit general management'.

Jacques, E. (ed.) (1978) *Health Services: Their Nature and Organisation and the Role of Patients, Doctors and the Health Profession,* London: Heinemann.

Klein, R. (1983) *The Politics of the National Health Service,* London: Longman.

McIntyre, A. (1981) *After Virtue: A Study in Moral Theory,* London: Duckworth.

Millar, B. (1988) 'GMTS I: an elite or a waste of resources?' *Health Service Journal* 1 September: 990–1.

National Health Service Training Authority (1986) 'Tracer study of district general managers', research and discussion papers, Oxford: Templeton College.

Petchey, R. (1986) 'The Griffiths reorganisation of the National Health Service: Fowlerism by stealth?, *Critical Social Policy* 17 87–101, Autumn.

Peters, T.H. and Waterman, R.H. (1982) *In Search of Excellence,* New York: Harper & Row.

Peters, T.H. and Austin, N. (1984) *Passion for Excellence,* London: Collins.

Pettigrew, A.M., McKee, L. and Ferlie, E. (1988) 'Understanding change in the NHS', *Public Administration* 66: 297–317; Autumn.

Pollitt, C.J., Harrison, S., Hunter D and Marnoch, G. (1988) 'The reluctant managers: clinicians and budgets in the NHS' *Financial Accountability and Management* 4 (3): 213–33.

Robinson J. and Strong, P. (1987) *Professional Nursing Advice After Griffiths: An Interim Report*, Warwick: Nursing Policy Studies Centre.

Robinson, J., Strong, P. and Elkan, R. (1989) *Griffiths and the Nurses: A National Survey of CNAS*, Warwick: Nursing Policy Studies Centre.

Ross, P. (1984) 'How to doctor the Griffiths Report', *Health and Social Service Journal* 26 July: 880.

Rowbottom, R. (1973) *Hospital Organisation*, London: Heinemann.

Scrivens, E. (1988) 'The management of clinicians in the National Health Service' *Social Policy and Administration* 22 (1): 22–34.

Social Services Insight (1987) 'A cultural revolution for social services?', *Social Services Insight* 25 September: 2

Storey, J. (1983) *Managerial Prerogative and the Question of Control*, London: Routledge.

Strauss, A., Schatzman, L., Ehrlich, P., Bucher, R. and Sabshin, M. (1973) 'The hospital and its negotiated order', in G. Salaman and K. Thompson (eds) *People and Organisations*, London: Longman.

Strong, P. and Robinson, J. (1988) *New Model Management: Griffiths and the NHS*, Warwick: Nursing Policy Studies Centre.

Thompson, D. (1987) 'Coalitions and conflict in the National Health Service: some implications for general management', *Sociology of Health and Illness* 9 (2): 127–53.

Turner, B.S. (1987) *Medical Power and Social Knowledge*, London: Sage.

Widgery, D. (1988) *The National Health: A Radical Perspective*, London: The Hogarth Press.

Chapter five

Evaluating the outcomes of health care

Angela Coulter

'The problem of evaluation is the first priority of the NHS.'
(Cochrane 1972: 25)

Introduction

Evaluation is an essential component of the rational approach to decision making. Health-care evaluation involves defining the objectives of care, monitoring health-care inputs, measuring the extent to which the expected outcomes have been achieved and assessing the extent of any unintended or harmful consequences of the intervention. As Klein has pointed out, evaluation can be seen as a technical process, where performance is measured against an agreed set of fixed goals, for example, the extent to which professionally defined 'needs' are being met, or as an interactive process where the goals are shifting and defined by the economic and political market place and where the emphasis may be on the extent to which consumer-defined 'demands' are satisfied (Klein 1982). The history of evaluation in the NHS has been characterized by tension between these two approaches. The consequent failure to resolve the problem of objectives has contributed to the difficulties inherent in measuring outcomes.

Policy within the NHS has been shaped by a number of powerful political forces, but of the various factions involved, including politicians, administrators and health-care professionals, the doctors have usually had the upper hand. Although the assumptions behind the creation of the NHS were those of paternalistic rationalism (Klein 1983), policy can be said to have developed through a process of disjointed incrementalism, or 'muddling through' (Lindblom 1982).

In the NHS the incrementalist approach to policy development through consensus management could not effectively challenge the autonomy of the professional groups and demands for greater professional accountability made little headway. In recent years, however, there have been attempts to shift the balance of power away from the health-care providers towards corporate control by managers. Following the Griffiths (1983) recommendations, the new generation of health service managers has been charged with two major, and possibly conflicting, responsibilities: to control expenditure and to improve quality. The assessment of performance is seen as central to both these tasks.

This chapter looks at some of the factors underlying this concern with quality in the health service and the means available for evaluating specific medical interventions. As an illustration of the complexities involved in evaluating the outcomes of health care, the chapter focuses on one common surgical procedure which has been the subject of a number of evaluative studies. This is followed by a discussion of strategies for the incorporation of outcomes data into the policy-making process.

The case for evaluation

There are at least four levels of evaluation which need consideration in the health service context:

1. evaluation of specific treatments, e.g. drug therapies or surgical procedures;
2. evaluation of patterns of care for particular patient groups, e.g. the organization of antenatal care, or the care of patients with chronic conditions such as diabetes;
3. evaluation of organizations, e.g. a hospital or a day centre;
4. evaluation of health systems, e.g. the effects of different methods of payment for health care.

Each level raises considerable design and analytical problems. Sociologists have engaged in evaluative studies at each level: see, for example, Fitzpatrick and colleagues' study of the medical management of headaches: level 1 (Fitzpatrick *et al.* 1983); Hall, Macintyre and Porter's study of an innovative system of antenatal care: level 2 (Hall *et al.* 1985); Smith and Cantley's evaluation of a psychogeriatric day hospital: level 3 (Smith and Cantley 1985); and the Health Insurance Study conducted by the Rand Corporation in the USA: level 4 (Ware *et al.* 1986). Most of the examples in this chapter are taken from level 1 studies of specific treatments and it should be remembered that different strategies may be appropriate at different levels of evaluation.

In his now classic Rock Carling Monograph, Cochrane drew attention to the lack of evidence of effectiveness for many common treatments (Cochrane 1972). He outlined three criteria or components of quality by which medical therapies should be judged: effectiveness – does the treatment alter the natural history of the disease for the better? efficiency – does the input justify the output, in other words, is the treatment or service cost-effective? and equality – is there equal access to the treatment or service on the part of the population served? The further additional criterion of social acceptability was later proposed by Doll (1974).

There have been subsequent refinements and redefinitions of these criteria. For example, economists use the term 'cost-effectiveness' to mean one specific methodological approach to the relation of inputs to outputs, others being cost-benefit analysis, cost minimization analysis, and cost-utility analysis (Drummond *et al.* 1987). In this chapter I have used the term in its all-embracing sense. Similarly, the term 'effectiveness' as used by Cochrane, meant the measurement of outcomes in experimental research (efficacy), but here the term has been used in its more general sense of the effects or outcomes of treatment as practised in the real world of the NHS.

Since the inception of the NHS, it has become increasingly apparent that the supply of health service resources would be unable to satisfy the demand for health care. Despite the increases in public expenditure which occurred throughout the 1960s, unmet needs appeared to increase rather than diminish. As attention focused on lengthening waiting times and cancelled operations, there was doubt about the ability of the service to cope with increasing demands. The imposition of cash limits following the economic recession of the mid-1970s exacerbated many of these problems and political pressure built up for a radical reassessment of the method of delivery of health care, in particular the extent to which the service was efficient and cost-effective.

The implementation of general management following Sir Roy Griffiths' recommendations introduced a new managerial culture into the NHS. Managers were encouraged to set performance objectives and to monitor progress towards them. To assist them in this task, they were to have a set of performance indicators (PIs) designed to point up areas of inefficiency. Although statistics on hospital activity had been collected since the early days of the NHS, it is only very recently that developments in computer technology have made easy manipulation of the data possible. The performance indicators were included in user-friendly computer-software packages containing information about a large number of measures of hospital performance, including admission rates, lengths of stay, waiting times, etc. The packages were designed in such a way that individual districts or units could see how their performance compared, by means of ranking, with those in others parts of the country.

The problem with the performance indicators, as many commentators have acknowledged (Goldacre and Griffin 1983), was that they focused on the process of care rather than on health outcome. They were based on the premise that there were inefficiencies in the health service which could be identified and ironed out by monitoring and comparing the performance of different sectors and dealing with anomalies. The assumption was that performance which lay within the normal range was unproblematic, but the problem lay with the outliers, i.e. those hospitals which had longer lengths of stay, performed fewer procedures as day cases or had higher unit costs of care. The goal set by the government was the achievement of faster throughput in order to reduce waiting lists and hold down costs. If managers could identify the problem areas, it was assumed inefficiencies could be eradicated. What the performance indicators could not do, and indeed were not designed to do, was to question the effectiveness of the treatments and processes of care within the health service.

That there was a need to question the effectiveness of medical interventions was demonstrated by the growing evidence of large, unexplained geographical variations in the rates at which many common procedures were carried out. Health services researchers in a number of countries had documented startling international variations in hospital utilization rates which could not be explained by morbidity differences and there was increasing evidence of wide variations within countries as well (Bunker 1970; Vayda 1973; Wennberg and Gittelsohn 1980; McPherson *et al.* 1981; Sanders *et al.* 1989).

A number of recent studies have demonstrated variations between geographical areas in Britain. For example, twofold variations in tonsillectomy rates were observed between adjacent small areas in Scotland (Bloor *et al.* 1978); a child in Oxford, Wessex or South West Thames Region was found to be twice as likely to have surgery for glue ear as a child in Trent or South Western Region (Black 1985); hysterectomy rates were found to vary threefold between eighteen general practices in one English district (Coulter *et al.* 1988) and there were large differences between towns in south-east England in admission rates for the most common operations (Jessop 1988). Hospital admission rates for appendicitis varied threefold between Welsh districts (West and Carey 1978); regional treatment rates for end-stage renal failure varied by twofold (Dowie 1984) and a smaller rate of variation was observed within North West Thames Region (Dalziel and Garrett 1987). There were fivefold differences between English regions in cardiac surgery rates (English *et al.* 1984), and large differences were observed between regions in rates of cataract extraction (Sanderson 1980), in caesarean sections (Macfarlane and Mugford 1986), in lengths of stay (Heasman and Carstairs 1971) and in out-patient attendances (Fowkes and McPake 1986). General practitioners' referral rates to out-patients clinics (Wilkin and Smith 1987) and use of diagnostic tests (Epstein *et al.* 1984) are also known to vary very widely.

Many investigators have tried to identify underlying patterns in the variations, or associations with other variables such as morbidity rates, resource or demographic factors, in an attempt to explain them. Most observers discount the possibility that underlying differences in morbidity rates could explain such wide differences in admission rates. While differences in the supply of beds, staffing and other resources explain some of the variation, they cannot account for it all (McPherson *et al.* 1981). It is worth noting that much of the evidence on regional variations in hospital admission rates within Britain has emerged since the implementation of the Resource Allocation Working Party (RAWP) recommendations, which were designed to distribute resources more equitably than previously. Unexplained variations have been found between regions receiving similar levels of funding (Haynes 1984; Holland 1986). Differences in patients' expectations may be an important factor (Coulter and McPherson 1986), but when, as in many of the aforementioned studies, the differences arise between adjacent small areas serving similar populations, the most plausible explanation is that the common underlying factor is the absence of a professional consensus about the effectiveness of these treatments (Wennberg 1984; McPherson 1989).

There are of course major cost implications here: if all procedures were carried out at the highest rate, costs could double or triple in some cases. On the other hand, if these interventions were performed uniformly across the country at the lowest rate, considerable savings could be made. There has been a tendency to assume that high rates are evidence of unnecessary intervention and low rates suggest deprivation, but in reality, of course, the problem is not that simple. In the absence of evidence of the impact of these procedures or admissions policies on the health status of the population served, it is not possible to draw sensible conclusions. This was the problem facing the Social Services Select Committee of the House of Commons in its deliberations on future directions for the NHS:

> The last major weakness of the National Health Service is that it is not possible to tell whether or not it works. There are no outcome measures to speak of other than that of crude numbers of patients treated. There is little monitoring on behalf of the public. As a result, the correct level of funding for the NHS cannot be determined and the public and politicians cannot decide whether or not they are getting value for the resources pumped into the National Health Service.
>
> (Social Services Committee 1988: xi)

The apparent unanimity of the multi-party Select Committee on this issue was interesting, because it appeared to represent a convergence of concerns from different ends of the ideological spectrum about the need to evaluate the effectiveness of medical interventions. On the one hand, the libertarian left had long been concerned to establish greater professional accountability in order to challenge medical dominance. The critical assessment of medical treatments and redefinition of health needs was seen as an essential part of the process of democratization of health care (Doyal 1979). On the other hand, right-wing moves to promote competition and market forces as a means of controlling costs also represented an attempt to transfer power from the providers to the consumers of health care. Information about effectiveness was seen as an essential prerequisite for informed choice in a market system where consumers are expected to select the most appropriate form of care.

This, then, is the context in which the concern about the evaluation of the outcomes of health care has developed. But was the Select Committee correct to conclude that there are no means of measuring effectiveness in the NHS? I shall argue that although outcome indicators have not, as yet, been included among the information tools available to health service managers, the barriers against doing so are as much structural and political as technical. There are outcome measures which could be used, but what has been lacking up until now has been the organizational structure and managerial power to use them to implement change. First of all though, it would be helpful to consider a model for evaluating health services proposed by Donabedian.

Quality assessment and medical audit

In a series of influential volumes on the subject of quality assessment, Donabedian proposed three aspects of health care which are amenable to evaluation: structure, process and outcome, where structure is the resources, facilities and organizational settings; process is the set of activities that go on between practitioners and patients; and outcome is the change in a patient's current and future health status which can be attributed to the health care they have received (Donabedian 1980).

Of the three, Donabedian saw outcomes as 'the ultimate validators of the effectiveness and quality of medical care' (Donabedian 1966: 169). Exclusive emphasis on process, he argued, can simply encourage the perpetuation of unscientific and unnecessary interventions. The natural optimism of physicians about the effectiveness of the therapies they have been trained to provide and of patients wanting to place their faith in these therapies, can promote a bias in favour of intervention. Furthermore, unnecessary intervention can involve risks which might otherwise have been avoided (Bunker 1985). On the other hand, the awareness of the scarcity of resources for treatment may also affect the clinical judgement of physicians, possibly causing them to refuse or delay treatment which might have been beneficial (Schwartz and Aaron

1988). The benefits and risks can only be assessed by comparing the outcomes of medical interventions against non-intervention.

However, process is clearly important, too, since within process is included the interpersonal aspects of care which are of considerable concern to patients. Furthermore, the process of care is very likely to affect the outcome. Many examples of beneficial effects of placebos and of patients' level of satisfaction with the treatment they have received provide evidence that this can be the case (Fitzpatrick *et al.* 1983). In addition, an understanding of the process of care is essential if the objectives of the various actors are to be understood and the relationship between structure and outcomes explained (Smith and Cantley 1985). So in some ways the separation of process and outcome is an artificial one; the two are obviously interlinked, and no evaluation should ignore one or the other.

Many of Donabedian's ideas have been incorporated into the health-care quality assurance movement, which is now fashionable in health service circles. Imported from the United States and promoted by the Regional Office for Europe of the World Health Organization and such bodies as the Nuffield Provincial Hospitals Trust and the King's Fund, quality assurance has been defined as: 'The measurement of the actual level of the quality of services rendered plus the efforts to modify when necessary the provision of these services in the light of the results of the measurement' (Vuori 1982). Although the terminology is slightly different, the measures of quality which have been proposed are essentially the same as those outlined at the beginning of this chapter: effectiveness, efficiency, equality and social acceptability.

A related term which is increasingly being used is medical audit. This is usually taken to mean self-review or peer review by clinicians themselves, usually involving an examination of medical records and a discussion of individual cases (Shaw 1980). In the United States, concern about the increasing costs of health care and the suspicion that there was a high level of unnecessary intervention, resulted in the imposition of a formal, external system of audit, supervised by the Peer Review Organizations and the funding agencies. Until the publication of the 1988 White Paper on the NHS (Secretaries of State 1989), audit was a purely voluntary activity in Britain, although influential voices within the medical profession had argued that audit should be an essential part of continuing medical education and there had been several professional initiatives in this regard (Hoffenberg 1987; Ham and Hunter 1988). The White Paper required all doctors to participate in regular systematic medical audit. This was to be based on a peer review system, although managers were to have the right to initiate external review if necessary.

121

Measuring outcomes

How does the reality of quality assurance match up to the rhetoric? In 1988 an exercise in quality assurance in the NHS was conducted by the *Sunday Times*, in conjuction with the NHS Management Board, in the form of a competition for health authorities designed to identify examples of good practice. Entrants were asked to describe the processes of care and the outputs, including the efficient delivery of services, quality, the position of the consumer, cost-effectiveness, community-care policies and health promotion. The final report containing the entries from the 'five best-run health authorities' (Deer 1988) provided an impressive demonstration of new managerial thinking within the health service, but was revealing for what it did not contain. Although there were plenty of examples of a new consumer awareness, and there was predictable emphasis on cost-efficiency, usually seen as synonymous with faster throughput and lower unit costs, there were few examples of attempts to identify whether or not the services on offer were effective. In other words, the emphasis was mainly on structure and process, with little or no evidence that issues of outcome, or effectiveness, had been addressed.

If this nettle is to be grasped in order to improve standards of quality in the NHS, what methods could be used to measure the outcomes of care? In discussing the measurement of the outcomes of care, Cochrane drew attention to the problem of establishing a causal linkage between the process of care and its outcome (Cochrane 1972). For Cochrane, the answer was to subject medical treatments or systems of care to scientific assessment by means of randomized controlled trials (RCTs). This technique, developed in agricultural science and first applied to the study of medical care in the 1950s, involves comparing the experience of a group of patients randomly allocated to a treatment with a similarly randomized group receiving another treatment or a placebo. The assessment of outcome is preferably made 'blind', i.e. by someone who does not know which patients have received the treatment under study. RCTs are commonly used to evaluate new drugs, and sometimes used in the evaluation of new health-care technology, but much less commonly used in health services research to evaluate established modes of treatment or patterns of care.

Conventionally, RCTs have been designed to measure outcomes on only a limited number of dimensions: death, or recurrence of disease, or clinical side effects being the most obvious ones. Sociologists have tended to reject the experimental approach to evaluation, arguing that goals and outcomes are often hard to define and measure and that the approach assumes a greater degree of control over extraneous variables than is usually possible or desirable in social research (Smith and

Cantley 1985). However, others have argued the importance of establishing efficacy under controlled conditions in order to avoid the over-hasty adoption of procedures and practices of doubtful effectiveness (Hall *et al.* 1985). The ethical problems associated with RCTs are often overstated, whereas the dubious ethics of promoting interventions which have not been rigorously evaluated are sometimes ignored (Rachlis and Kushner 1989). There seems to be no a priori reason why RCTs could not be used to examine a wider range of outcomes including psychosocial variables and patient satisfaction.

However, RCTs are often costly to set up and raise particular practical problems. Ideally, an RCT might be the end point in a programme of evaluation, but in practice it is unlikely that such trials will be established to evaluate every medical intervention in which there is some doubt about effectiveness. Most health-care evaluation therefore relies on observational studies. These obviously have major drawbacks, since it is often impossible to directly attribute the observed outcomes to the process of care. There are, of course, many social influences which can affect the course of illness, and isolating those aspects in which medical intervention can be expected to have an impact is by no means unproblematic.

A further problem is the timing of outcome measurement. It is often the case that immediate or short-term outcomes are measured, but longer-term ones are not, for example, studies of surgical procedures which fail to consider readmissions for complications or related conditions. Chronic conditions pose particular problems in this regard. At what point should you measure the effectiveness of care for arthritis sufferers, where there is unlikely to be an easily definable end point, or for children suffering from otitis media, where the condition is likely to be self-limiting? A long interval before measuring outcome may result in an over optimistic view of the value of treatment in a self-limiting condition, and an interval that is too short may miss important long-term effects.

It may be unrealistic to try to evaluate all possible outcomes of care. To what extent should an evaluation attempt to be comprehensive, and to what extent selective? If selectivity is the aim, how should one decide which of the outcomes are most important? The objectives of medical interventions are often inexplicit, both at the individual level of clinical decision making and at the population level of health authority planning. Some are designed to save lives, others to cure disease, many are designed to control or alleviate symptons in chronic conditions, yet others are intended to be prophylactic or preventive. All can have potentially harmful as well as beneficial consequences. To what extent is it possible or desirable to adopt a common approach to measuring the effects of such a diverse range of activities? If the outcomes of care are to be evaluated in relation to the objectives, whose definition of objectives is the most relevant? Patients and doctors may differ in the objectives they consider to be important. Clinicians may place more stress on physical outcomes, whereas for patients, the social impact of treatment may be more relevant. The effect of treatment or patterns of care may also have a considerable impact on carers and close relatives, so it may be important to include their perspective in the evaluation. If the selection of outcomes is confined to one or two easily measurable clinical outcomes, the results may be more clear cut but the evaluation will be partial. If a variety of outcomes are selected, the chance of an unequivocal result which will provide a clear guide to decision making is greatly reduced.

Patrick has argued that 'the linkage of theories and concepts from medicine with those from the social sciences and the humanities is nowhere more important than in conceptualizing the outcomes of disease and treatment' (Patrick 1986: 224). He proposed six categories of disease and treatment outcomes: death, disease, physical wellbeing, psychological wellbeing, social wellbeing (under which heading he included social integration, social contact and intimacy) and quality of life (including health perceptions, satisfaction and relative disadvantage). This multidimensional model of health outcomes may seem utopian. To what extent has evaluative research attempted to address all these dimensions of health care?

The hysterectomy example

There is a vast literature on the measurement of health outcomes and it would be impossible to review it all here. Instead, I shall concentrate on some studies which have looked at the outcomes of one common surgical procedure in order to illustrate the range of approaches adopted in health services research.

Hysterectomy is one of the most commonly performed surgical operations; in 1985 more than 66,000 women had this operation in NHS hospitals in England and Wales: a rate of 28 per 10,000 women per annum (DHSS/OPCS 1987). The costs to the health service are considerable (we estimated that the hysterectomies performed in 1983 would have cost the NHS around £50 million (Coulter and McPherson 1986)), but more importantly, the individual woman undergoing hysterectomy faces costs, risks and benefits which are less easy to quantify. Hysterectomy rates have been rising since the inception of the NHS and the recent increase in the number of people holding private health insurance may have fuelled the demand for this operation. About 20 per cent of hysterectomies in Britain are now performed in the private sector.

On current rates, at least one-fifth of women living in England and Wales will have a hysterectomy before the age of 65. Most hysterectomies are carried out to relieve menstrual disorders: menorrhagia ('excessive' menstrual bleeeding) is the main presenting symptom in about 60 per cent of cases. Only about 10 per cent of hysterectomies are performed in response to a diagnosis of cancer. This operation is carried out in most cases, therefore, to improve the quality of a woman's life rather than to save her life.

There has been considerable debate about the use of hysterectomy for non-life-threatening conditions. About a third of all uteri removed at hysterectomy are pathologically normal and some have argued that these hysterectomies are performed unnecessarily, on the grounds that this operation can only be justified if there is evidence of organic dysfunction. However, this may not be the most valid criterion on which to judge whether the operation is necessary or not and anyway it appears that large numbers of women proceed to surgery in the absence of such evidence (Coulter *et al.* 1988). Menstrual blood loss is rarely measured in clinical practice, so for the most part the decision to operate is taken on the basis of the patient's subjective account of the severity of her symptoms.

There is debate about the extent to which the decision to operate ought to be based on diagnostic criteria (the 'needs' criterion) and the extent to which it should be decided on functional grounds (i.e. making an assessment of the effect of the symptoms on a woman's daily life and taking into account the extent of her desire for the operation – the 'demand' criterion), but little is known about the relative weights given to such factors in practice. What we do know is that hysterectomy rates vary considerably between small areas and internationally, suggesting a lack of professional consensus about when this operation is indicated. These variations can only partly be accounted for by variations in available resources and it seems unlikely that morbidity rates vary to such an extent (McPherson 1988). Hysterectomy presents, therefore, a suitable case for evaluation.

A woman recommended for hysterectomy, at the average age (in Britain) of 40–45, to relieve symptoms of heavy menstrual bleeding, faces a number of important consequences. On the benefit side, the operation will result in the cessation of menstrual bleeding, thus removing the problem for which she sought help; she will no longer have to worry about contraception; she will no longer run a risk of uterine cancer; and there may be other social and psychological advantages to her. One the cost side, she will have to undergo a major operation with associated risks of mortality, morbidity and complications; she will be unable to carry out her normal activities for a period of time; she will no longer be able to bear children; if her ovaries are removed at the same time, as is sometimes the case, she will undergo an immediate artificial menopause, and she will probably have to undergo a course of hormone replacement therapy with a further set of associated risks; and she may risk other social and psychological complications. Weighing up the risks and benefits of this procedure is, therefore, no easy task, either at the individual level, or at the population level when determining health policy.

There have been a number of studies of the outcomes of hysterectomy, the majority emanating from North America and Canada where there has long been concern that many of the hysterectomies performed are unnecessary. For the most part each study has looked at only one or two aspects of the spectrum of outcome categories: death, disease, physical wellbeing, psychological wellbeing, social wellbeing and quality of life.

To start with death: as we have noted, hysterectomy is only rarely carried out as a life-saving procedure and it carries a low risk of operative mortality. However, there are certain prophylactic effects of hysterectomy: for example, the risk of uterine cancer is obviously removed if the entire uterus is removed at surgery. On the other hand, there may be a slightly increased risk of myocardial infarction (Rosenberg *et al.* 1981). A number of studies have used decision-analysis techniques to assess the net effect on life expectancy. These studies rely on the calculation of risk probabilities derived from existing data on mortality and survival rates. They are always open to the charge that the risk estimates on which they were based were incorrect, and these risk estimates will obviously change over time as new techniques and new data become available. Using these techniques and basing their analysis on estimates derived from American data, Bunker and colleagues estimated that a healthy woman aged 40–50 stood to gain 4½ days additional life expectancy, if she had a hysterectomy without an associated oophorectomy. An older woman with a higher operative risk could be expected to have a slightly reduced life expectancy as a result of the operation (Bunker *et al.* 1977). Another American study found a somewhat more optimistic gain of 73 days life expectancy for a healthy woman aged 35 (Cole and Berlin 1977). A more sophisticated US study, which included quality-of-life estimates and a cost-effectiveness analysis, concluded that a 40-year-old woman could expect to gain 104 additional days of quality-adjusted life expectancy (Sandberg *et al.* 1985). The authors of the first two papers concluded that hysterectomy could not be justified on prophylactic grounds, while the authors of the third paper felt it could.

There are a number of problems with these studies. In the first place, they are based on an implicit assumption that increased life expectancy is the important factor in the decision making. In practice, some patients may prefer to accept the risk of reduced life expectancy in return for elimination of the symptoms for which they are seeking treatment, even if the risk of treatment is greater than the risk of non-intervention. Second, they are based on partial data. The first two studies contained no estimates of the quality-of-life outcomes of the operation, although the authors drew attention to the need for such data. The authors of the third study based their quality-of-life calculations on estimates of gains or losses of quality of life resulting from physical disability, pain and discomfort, emotional problems, social dysfunction and threat of unarrested cancer, derived 'from the medical literature and judgements of clinicians', but not, apparently, from patients. And in the third place, they illustrate the different and inconclusive results obtained from different estimates of the life-enhancing or life-threatening effects of the procedure.

A number of studies have looked at the short-term clinical outcomes, or complications of hysterectomy. One such study reviewed the hospital records of a sample of over 12,000 patients undergoing hysterectomy in 1,300 hospitals in the United States and compared them with patients undergoing appendectomy and cholecystectomy (Ledger and Child 1973). While patients undergoing hysterectomy had less than half the mortality rate of patients having an appendectomy and less than one-eighth that of cholecystectomy patients, post-operative complications were highest in the hysterectomy group, of whom 48 per cent had to be given antibiotics for post-operative fever and 16 per cent had to have blood transfusions. The complication rate was much higher for non-white patients in these hospitals and the authors speculated that this might be a reflection of 'unequal responses to surgical stress from different socio-economic groups' (ibid).

A Canadian study used a large administrative data set to investigate the health service contacts of women undergoing hysterectomy, as compared with a group of women undergoing cholecystectomy and an age- and sex-matched population sample (Roos 1984). The time period examined was two years before and two years after surgery. Four per cent of the 2,300 women undergoing hysterectomy required re-hospitalization for complications in the two years following the operation. In addition, the women who had undergone hysterectomy visited their physicians more frequently after the operation than they had before for such problems as neurosis, nervous debility, headaches, urinary-tract infections and menopausal symptoms. They were more likely to make such visits than were women in the age-matched population. This study provides a neat demonstration of the way in which a routinely-collected linked data set can be used to study the outcomes of medical and surgical treatments. However, such studies are limited in the data at their disposal since administrative data sets do not usually contain any information about the social wellbeing or quality of life of the people undergoing treatment. Once again, only a partial analysis is possible.

A number of studies have been undertaken to investigate the social and psychological outcomes of hysterectomy. There has long been concern that hysterectomy carries with it the risk of significant psychological disorder and this concern has generated a considerable body of research. Many of the early studies used a retrospective design and non-standardized measures of outcome. A more recent study, which did not exhibit these deficiencies, was conducted by Gath and colleagues in Oxford (Gath *et al.* 1982). The prospective design of this study involved interviews with a consecutive series of patients undergoing hysterectomy for menorrhagia of benign origin. The interviews, which were conducted four weeks before hysterectomy, and at six and eighteen months afterwards, covered demographic and social factors, gynaecological history, understanding and expectations of the operation, psychosexual functioning, physical and psychiatric health, family health, marriage and social adjustment and three standardized instruments: the Present State Examination, the Eysenck Personality Inventory and the Profile of Mood States. This is a much broader range of variables than were included in the studies just described but perhaps not surprisingly, since the study was carried out in a university department of psychiatry, the major emphasis was on the psychiatric outcomes of hysterectomy, using clinical definitions of psychiatric disorder as the main outcome measures. The results demonstrated lower levels of psychiatric morbidity in the group as a whole after the operation than before, but overall levels of psychiatric morbidity were much higher, even after the operation, than had been observed in general-population studies. This finding raises the question of whether some women may be receiving gynaecological treatment when some form of psychiatric therapy or counselling might be more appropriate. None of the studies of the psychological consequences of hysterectomy can address this problem because they have not included comparison groups of women receiving alternative forms of treatment for gynaecological disorders.

Another prospective study of the outcomes of hysterectomy used a nursing perspective to undertake what the authors claimed was 'a wider, more humanistic evaluation of outcome than that which has previously been employed' (Gould and Wilson-Barnett 1985). In this study, 85 women undergoing hysterectomy in one district general hospital were interviewed a few days post-operatively, and at four and eleven months after surgery. As has been reported in other studies, patients expressed high levels of satisfaction with the operation, and there was no evidence of an adverse effect on sexual functioning, but half had experienced serious physical symptoms in the eleven months following the operation. The investigators also attempted to evaluate the impact of the operation on physical and social functioning, but reported some difficulties with the measures they had adopted. Once again, the absence of a control group makes these findings somewhat difficult to interpret.

In summary, then, we can see that the studies of hysterectomy outcomes that have been conducted so far have between them attempted to address most of the categories outlined earlier (i.e. death, disease, physical wellbeing, psychological wellbeing, social wellbeing and quality of life), albeit with varying degrees of success. However, for the most part, the analyses were limited to only a few of the possible outcomes. The objectives of treatment were implicit in the outcome measures chosen, but limited by the empirical data to hand, rather than explicitly selected from a range of alternatives. Most of the studies focused on potential ill-effects of the treatment, and most ended by recommending further research to answer problems they were unable to address. All the studies were bound by one particular perspective. In summary, they present a fragmented and inconclusive picture.

An evaluation strategy

How far could such disparate approaches to evaluation be used to inform a rationally based policy? Wennberg and colleagues have proposed a strategy for the evaluation of established procedures or patterns of care which might produce the required synthesis (Wennberg *et al.* 1988). They are currently adopting this strategy to evaluate the outcomes of prostatectomy by means of international collaborative studies in a number of countries including Britain. The strategy has four stages:

The identification of uncertainty

The starting point for their programme of evaluation, which assumes the active involvement of clinicians, is the identification of professional uncertainty. Examination of utilization rates and the identification of geographical variations helps to highlight the particular treatments which lack a professional consensus about when and on whom they should be performed. The first stage of the strategy involves the evaluation of published evidence and current clinical opinion, in order to identify the hypotheses underlying current practice and to understand the major controversies. In order to highlight the extent of uncertainty, the literature review is supplemented by surveys of clinicians. The 'vignette' or case-study approach, where doctors are asked to say how they would deal with a range of hypothetical cases, has proved illuminating on occasions (Rutkow 1982).

Clinical outcomes

The second stage involves the use of large, linked data bases to obtain estimates of the probabilities for survival and complications. Large linked data bases do exist in England (the Oxford Record Linkage Study) and in Scotland (the Scottish Hospital Inpatient System) and they could be used for such a purpose. Their advantage is that they enable the analysis of person-based, as opposed to only episode-based, records of hospital admissions and can therefore be used to follow up patients' subsequent hospital admissions to study the outcomes of care (Goldacre et al. 1988). In theory, such data bases should be available at district level following the full implementation of the Korner proposals and could provide information about readmissions to hospital and, possibly, mortality, for use as outcome indicators (Goldacre 1985). In addition, the rapid development of computerized records in general practice may eventually extend the horizons of such research considerably (Coulter et al. 1989).

The first two stages in this strategy, therefore, raise technical problems of measurement and analysis, but the data are now, or will shortly become, available within the NHS for evaluating the impact of procedures in terms of mortality and subsequent hospital admissions or GP consultations. Although subsequent health service contacts clearly have limitations as outcome indicators, they could be an improvement on the current absence of routinely collected measures and it is not beyond the bounds of possibility that clinical indicators such as these could be incorporated into performance indicators. Quality-of-life and health-status indicators present many more problems in this regard.

Health status and quality of life

The third stage in the strategy is to conduct prospective interview studies with patients to assess the nature of their symptoms and their feelings about them, and their functional status and quality of life. Although these concepts are not easy to define and quantify (Fowlie and Berkeley 1987), great strides have been made in recent years by social scientists working on the development of subjective and objective measures of quality of life, including disability scales, health profiles and health indices (Hollandsworth 1988). In a useful review, Teeling Smith has described a number of such measures which have been developed for use in Britain (Teeling Smith 1985). One such instrument, the Nottingham Health Profile, has been used in a number of studies designed to measure the outcomes of treatment (Hunt et al. 1986), although it has been the subject of some criticism (Kind and Carr-Hill 1987). This measure recognizes the multidimensional nature of health and avoids the simplicities of counting years of life or numbers of symptoms, but it appears to lack discriminatory power when used as a tool for measuring the health status of basically healthy populations and this may limit its usefulness.

The development of standardized health-status and quality-of-life measures has become a major industry in North America. The Dictionary of Behavioral Assessment Techniques lists 286 different measures which are intended for use by clinicians or researchers to measure a wide range of psychosocial variables using a variety of methods, including behavioural observations, self-reports, judges' ratings, semi-structured interviews, etc. (Hersen and Bellack 1988). In the introduction to another review of standardized instruments, the authors recount their experience as research consultants where the greatest problem was to persuade researchers not to invent their own unique measurement scales until they had carefully reviewed the methods that are already available (McDowell and Newell 1987).

However, in spite of all this activity, there is not yet a great deal of evidence that these instruments are being widely adopted for use in clinical trials. Clinicians remain resistant to what are seen as 'soft' measures and it will require a major effort of education to persuade them of the relevance of subjective experiences of medical interventions (Read 1987). In addition, there is still a need to continue to refine the measures. If they are ever to be used to evaluate care on a routine basis, they will have to be simple and easy to administer. These are complex issues, not easily refined down to a few dimensions, and it seems likely that their use and development will be confined to specific research studies rather than routine data collection for some time to come.

Decision analysis

Clearly, stages one to three of this strategy will produce a mass of data measuring a large number of health-care outcomes. The most difficult task is the final stage of synthesis of all the aforementioned information in a decision-analysis model. This is the ultimate goal of most economic analyses of health care and it for this purpose that QALYs (Quality-adjusted Life Years) were devised. Based originally on research into how people value varying levels of disability and distress, QALYs attempt to measure judgements about various states of health (utilities) in order to calculate the benefits and risks of medical treatments in terms of quality-adjusted life years (Williams 1983).

QALYs have been enthusiastically received by some, because they appear to offer a solution to the apparently intractable problem of combining patients' perspectives on the effects of treatment with an economic analysis of cost-effectiveness. However, even the most enthusiastic advocates of QALYs acknowledge that they are currently based on extremely limited data about the actual impact of medical therapies on quality of life (Williams 1987). They have also been criticized on methodological and ethical grounds (Avorn 1984; Harris 1987; Mulkay *et al.* 1987; Smith 1987). The effects of using QALYs to prioritize resource allocation, say the critics, will be to discriminate against elderly people and against those with expensive diseases, on the grounds that greater utility can be obtained by treating younger people or those whose care is relatively cheap. The use of QALYs to direct resource allocation could result in some highly unpalatable decisions not to treat certain groups of patients. The utilitarian principle on which QALYs are based, negates individual autonomy and precludes a needs-based principle of allocation of resources. Many of the objections to QALYs are reflected in the philosophical debate about utilitarianism (Gillon 1985). The most acceptable and useful role for QALYs may be the comparison of alternative therapies for specific groups of patients. It seems both unlikely and undesirable that they should be used to inform the allocation of resources on a grander scale.

Nevertheless the debate about QALYs has served to underline the need for more research into the quality-of-life outcomes of medical treatments, and the need to work on better ways to synthesize this information with data on clinical outcomes. Clearly, a massive inter-disciplinary research effort is required. Who will do such work and how will it be used to change priorities within the health service?

Evaluation and the policy process

Health services research has traditionally been a low-status activity in Britain, lacking the glamour and funding power of, say, molecular biology or cancer epidemiology. For the most part it has been small scale and lacking in impact. There are at least four reasons why health service evaluation has remained underdeveloped as a research activity.

Methodological problems

As I have tried to indicate in the previous section, evaluative research is not easy and many methodological problems remain unresolved. The problems of goal definition, measuring inputs, identifying extraneous variables and selecting and measuring outcomes are particularly acute in the real world of health services. The experimental model of scientific research in controlled conditions is hard to apply in this context. The pluralistic alternative recommended by Smith and Cantley (1985) attempts to accommodate the real world of incremental change, but by giving equal legitimacy to a wide range of objectives and success criteria, it leaves unresolved the problem of providing directions for change. As such, it is arguably conservative in effect.

The multidisciplinary nature of evaluation

The hysterectomy example has served to illustrate the extent to which evaluation should be a multidisciplinary effort, involving the co-operation of clinicians, epidemiologists, social scientists and users of health services. Unfortunately, effective collaborations between multi-disciplinary teams are relatively rare in Britain, due in part to mutual suspicion of each other among practitioners of the different disciplines and in part to organizational fragmentation and funding difficulties.

The need for a long-term view

Traditionally, applied research has been funded by government departments or local health authorities, leaving the research councils and the charities to fund basic medical research. When decisions about research funding are in the hands of national or local government, there is a tendency to favour projects which will address short-term political priorities rather than those which require a long turn-around time between problem identification and the implementation of change.

The challenge to vested interests

Evaluative research is essentially a subversive activity. Attempts by out-siders to evaluate the outcomes of medical interventions often provoke intense professional resistance. Arguments about the sanctity of clinical freedom and the inability of non-specialists to understand clinical issues are invoked in order to discredit such research. Thus, it is not surprising that process research has been emphasized at the expense of outcomes studies. The former is less threatening since it rarely offers a challenge to professional decision making. In addition, the lack of effective sanctions or incentives seriously inhibits the extent to which externally imposed evaluative research can be used to change clinical behaviour (Strong and Robinson 1988).

If evaluative research is to make an impact on what goes on in the NHS, it will probably have to involve clinicians from the outset. On the face of it the apparently widespread acceptance of the government's plans to encourage medical audit are encouraging. However there were signs in the British Medical Association's response to the 1989 White Paper that clinicians would be happy with such a system only as long as it remained within professional control: 'It is inappropriate for the operation of medical audit to become a management function' (British Medical Association 1989: 13).

Neither should it be assumed that the adoption of medical audit represents a major step in the direction of accountability to the users of the health service. In his analysis of the American health care system, Alford argued that in the conflict between the professional monopolizers on the one hand and the corporate rationalizers on the other, neither side has an incentive to release information which would allow users to assess the quality of health services (Alford 1980). Thus, we see the incorporation of patient satisfaction surveys into quality-assurance programmes on the market-research model, but resistance to the release of information on outcomes on the grounds that lay people are unqualified to judge professional decisions. The health care market has no incentive to expose its shortcomings.

Conclusions

The question of how the results of outcomes research should be used to inform policy remains an important area for debate. A possible solution which could incorporate the demand for user participation in decision making, would be to make the results available to patients so that they can make their own judgements and choices. This has been advocated by many of those who have evaluated the use of hysterectomy in the United States. However, a policy of extending patient choice may be incompatible with a system designed to achieve equitable distribution. The alternative strategy of using the information for making more informed decisions on behalf of users falls more easily within the paternalistic tradition of the NHS, but would appear to run counter to the new demands for a participatory style of decision making.

The reliance on market solutions to achieve cost control appears to underestimate the amount of information required to make a health-care market function effectively (Quam 1989). It seems unlikely that the necessary expansion of investment in information technology and research will occur in the current political climate. So far the thrust of the managers' efforts has centred on the measurement of efficiency and patient satisfaction, but attempts to measure cost-effectiveness make no sense unless careful analysis of effectiveness precedes the analysis of costs.

It is clear that more data on health-care outcomes and better techniques of decision analysis are no panacea. Decision making can never be a purely technical exercise and there are many barriers which must be overcome before policy decisions are taken on the basis of evaluative research.

Acknowledgement

I am very grateful to Ray Fitzpatrick for his comments on an earlier draft of this chapter.

References

Alford R.R. (1980) 'The political economy of health care', in D. Mechanic (ed.) *Readings in Medical Sociology*, New York: Free Press.

Avorn, J. (1984) 'Benefit and cost analysis in geriatric care', *New England Journal of Medicine* 310: 1294–301).

Black, N. (1985) 'Geographical variations in the use of surgery for glue ear', *Journal of the Royal Society of Medicine* 78: 641–48.

Bloor, M.J., Venters, G.A. and Samphier, M.L. (1978) 'Geographical variation in the incidence of operations on the tonsils and adenoids', *Journal of Laryngology and Otology* 92: 791–801.

British Medical Association (1989) *Special report on the Government's White Paper Working for Patients*, London: British Medical Association.

Bunker, J.P. (1970) 'Surgical manpower: a comparison of operations and surgeons in the United States and England and Wales, *New England Journal of Medicine* 282: 135–44.

—— (1985) 'When doctors disagree', *The New York Review* 25 April.

Bunker, J.P., McPherson, K. and Henneman, P.L. (1977) 'Elective hysterectomy', in J.P. Bunker, B.A. Barnes, and F. Mosteller (eds) *Costs, Risks and Benefits of Surgery*, New York: Oxford University Press.

Cochrane, A.L. (1972) *Effectiveness and Efficiency*, London: Nuffield Provincial Hospitals Trust.

Cole, P. and Berlin, J. (1977) 'Elective hysterectomy', *American Journal of Obstetrics and Gynecology* 129: 117–23.

Coulter, A. and McPherson, K. (1986) 'The hysterectomy debate', *Quarterly Journal of Social Affairs* 2: 379–96.

Coulter, A. McPherson, K. and Vessey, M. (1988) 'Do British women undergo too many or too few hysterectomies?' *Social Science and Medicine* 27: 987–94.

Coulter, A., Brown, S. and Daniels, A. (1989) 'Computer-held chronic disease registers in general practice: a validation study', *Journal of Epidemiology and Community Health* 43: 25–8.

Dalziel, M. and Garrett, C. (1987) 'Intraregional variations in treatment of end stage renal failure', *British Medical Journal* 294: 1382–3.

Deer, B. (ed.) (1988) *The Best of Health*, London: *Sunday Times* and PA Consulting Group.

DHSS/OPCS (Department of Health and Social Security/Office of Population Census and Surveys) (1987) *Hospital In-patient Enquiry*, London: HMSO.

Doll, R. (1974) 'Surveillance and monitoring', *International Journal of Epidemiology* 3: 305–14.

Donabedian, A. (1966) 'Evaluating the quality of medical care', *Millbank Memorial Fund Quarterly* 44: 166–206.

—— (1980) *Explorations and Quality Assessment and Monitoring, Vol. 1: The Definition of Quality and Approaches to its Assessment*, Ann Arbor, Michigan: Health Administration Press.

Dowie, R. (1984) 'Deployment of resources in treatment of end stage renal failure in England and Wales', *British Medical Journal* 288: 988–91.

Doyal, L. (1979) *The Political Economy of Health*, London: Pluto Press.

Drummond, D.F., Stoddart, G.L. and Torrance, G.W. (1987) *Methods for the Economic Evaluation of Health Care Programmes*, Oxford: Oxford University Press.

English, T.A.H., Bailey, A.R., Dark, J.F. and Williams, W.G. (1984) 'The UK cardiac surgical register, 1977–82, *British Medical Journal* 289: 1205–8.

Epstein, A.M., Hartley, R.M., Charlton, J.R., Harris, C.M., Jarman, B. and McNeil, B.J. (1984) 'A comparison of ambulatory test ordering for hypertensive patients in the United States and England, *Journal of the American Medical Association* 252: 1723–6.

Fitzpatrick, R.M., Hopkins, A.P. and Harvard-Watts, O. (1983) 'Social dimensions of healing: a longitudinal study of outcomes of medical management of headaches', *Social Science and Medicine* 17: 501–10.

Fowkes, F.G.R., McPake, B.I. (1986) 'Regional variations in outpatient activity in England and Wales', *Community Medicine* 8: 286–91.

Fowlie, M. and Berkeley, J. (1987) 'Quality of life – a review of the literature', *Family Practice* 4: 226–34.

Gath, D., Cooper, P. and Day, A. (1982) 'Hysterectomy and psychiatric disorder: 1. Levels of psychiatric morbidity before and after hysterectomy', *International Journal of Psychiatry* 140: 335–50.

Gillon, R. (1985) 'Utilitarianism', *British Medical Journal* 290: 1333–413.

Goldacre, M.J. (1985) 'Development of outcome measures: what are the deficiencies in existing data?', paper given at DHSS seminar *Outcome indicators – their application in the NHS*, Guy's Hospital, 12 June.

Goldacre, M. and Griffin, K. (1983) *Performance Indicators: A Commentary on the Literature*, University of Oxford: Unit of Clinical Epidemiology.

Goldacre, M.J., Simmons, H., Henderson, J. and Gill, L.E. (1988) 'Trends in episode-based and person-based rates of admission of hospital in the Oxford Record Linkage Study area', *British Medical Journal* 296: 583–4.

Gould, D. and Wilson-Barnett, J. (1985) 'A comparison of recovery following hysterectomy and major cardiac surgery', *Journal of Advanced Nursing* 10: 315–23.

Griffiths, R. (1983) *NHS Management Inquiry DA (83) 38*, London: Department of Health and Social Security.

Hall, M., Macintyre, S. and Porter, M. (1985) *Antenatal Care Assessed*, Aberdeen: Aberdeen University Press.

Ham, C. and Hunter, D.J. (1988) *Managing Clinical Activity in the NHS*, London: King's Fund Institute.

Harris, J. (1987) 'QALYfying the value of life', *Journal of Medical Ethics* 13: 117–23.

Haynes, R. (1984) 'Regional anomalies in hospital bed use in England and Wales', *Regional Studies* 19 (1): 19–27.

Heasman, M.A. and Carstairs, V. (1971) 'Inpatient management: variations in
some aspects of practice in Scotland', *British Medical Journal* 1: 495–8.
Hersen, M. and Bellack, A.S. (1988) *Dictionary of Behavioral Assessment
Techniques*, New York: Pergamon Press.
Hoffenberg, R. (1987) *Clinical Freedom*, London: Nuffield Provincial
Hospitals Trust.
Holland, W.W. (1986) 'The RAWP review: pious hopes', *Lancet* ii: 1087–90.
Hollandsworth, J.J (1988) 'Evaluating the impact of medical treatment on
the quality of life: a 5-year update', *Social Science and Medicine* 26:
425–34.
Hunt, S.M., McEwan, J. and Mckenna, S.P. (1986) *Measuring Health Status*,
London: Croom Helm.
Jessop, E.G. (1988) 'Equity of access? Small area variations in surgery',
Community Medicine 10: 1–7.
Kind, P. and Carr-Hill, R. (1987) 'The Nottingham Health Profile: a useful
tool for epidemiologists?' *Social Science and Medicine* 25: 905–10.
Klein, R. (1982) 'Performance, evaluation and the NHS: a case study in
conceptual perplexity and organisational complexity' *Public
Administration* 60: 385–407.
——(1983) *The Politics of the National Health Service*, Harlow: Longman.
Ledger, W.J. and Child, M.A. (1973) 'The hospital care of patients
undergoing hysterectomy: an analysis of 12,026 patients from the
Professional Activity Study', *American Journal of Obstetrics and
Gynecology* 117: 423–33.
Lindblom, C.E. (1982) 'Still muddling, not yet through', in G. McGrew and
M.J. Wilson (eds) *Decision Making: Approaches and Analysis*,
Manchester: Manchester University Press.
McDowell, I. and Newell, C.C. (1987) *Measuring Health: a guide to Rating
Scales and Questionnaires*, New York: Oxford University Press.
Macfarlane, A. and Mugford, M. (1986) 'An epidemic of caesareans?'
Journal of Maternal and Child Health 11: 38–42.
McPherson, K. (1988) 'Variations in hospitalisation rates: why and how to
study them', in C. Ham (ed.) *Health Care Variations: Assessing the
Evidence*, London: King's Fund Institute.
——(1989) *International Differences in Medical Care Practice*, Paris: OECD.
McPherson, K., Strong, P.M., Epstein, A. and Jones, L. (1981) 'Regional
variations in the use of common surgical procedures: within and between
England and Wales, Canada and the United States of America' *Social
Science and Medicine* 15A: 273–88.
Mulkay, M., Ashmore, M. and Pinch, T. (1987) 'Measuring the quality of life:
a sociological invention concerning the application of economics to health
care' *Sociology* 21: 541–64.
Patrick, D.L. (1986) 'Measurement of health and quality of life', in D.L.
Patrick and G. Scambler (eds) *Sociology as Applied to Medicine*,
Eastbourne: Bailliere Tindall.
Quam, L. (1989) 'Post-war American health care: the many costs of market
failure', *Oxford Review of Economic Policy* 5: 113–23.
Rachlis, M. and Kushner, C. (1989) *Second Opinion*, Toronto: Collins.

Read, J.L. (1987) 'The new era of quality of life assessment', in S. R. Walker and R.M. Rosser (eds) *Quality of Life: Assessment and Application*, Lancaster: MTP Press.

Roos, N.P. (1984) 'Hysterectomies in one Canadian Province: a new look at risks and benefits', *American Journal of Public Health* 74: 39–46.

Rosenberg, L., Hennekens, C.H., Rosner, B., Belanger, C., Rothman, K.J. and Speizer, F. E. (1981) 'Early menopause and the risk of myocardial infarction', *American Journal of Obstetrics and Gynecology* 139: 47–51.

Rutkow, I.M. (1982) 'The reliability and reproducibility of the surgical decision-making process' *Surgical Clinics of North America* 62: 721–35.

Sandberg, S.I., Barnes, B.A., Weinstein, M.C. and Braun, P. (1985) 'Elective hysterectomy: benefits, risks and costs', *Medical Care* 23: 1067–85.

Sanders, D., Coulter, A. and McPherson, K. (1986) *Variations in Hospital Admission Rates: a review of the Literature*, London: King's Fund.

Sanderson, H.F. (1980) 'Regional variation in cataract extraction rates and their relationship with resource supply and need', *Journal of the Royal Society of Medicine* 73: 492–6.

Schwartz, W. B. and Aaron, H.J. (1988) 'Rationing hospital care: lessons from Britain', in J. Dowie and A. Elstein (eds) *Professional Judgement: a Reader in Clinical Decision Making*, Cambridge: Cambridge University Press.

Shaw, C.D. (1980) 'Aspects of audit 1: the background', *British Medical Journal* 281: 1256–8.

Smith, A. (1987) 'Qualms about QALYs', *Lancet* i: 1134–6.

Smith, G. and Cantley, C. (1985) *Assessing Health Care: a Study in Organizational Evaluation*, Milton Keynes: Open University Press.

Social Services Committee (1988) *The Future of the National Health Service*, Fifth Report, London: HMSO.

Strong, P. and Robinson, J. (1988) *New Model Management: Griffiths and the NHS*, University of Warwick: Nursing Policy Studies Centre.

Teeling Smith, G. (1985) *Measurement of Health*, London: Office of Health Economics.

Vayda, E. (1973) 'A comparison of surgical rates in Canada and England and Wales', *New England Journal of Medicine* 289: 1224–9.

Vuori, H.V. (1982) *Quality assurance in health services: Concepts and Methodology*, Copenhagen: Regional Office for Europe, WHO.

Ware, J.E., Brook, R.H., Rogers, W.H., Keeler, E.B., David, A.R., Sherborne C.D., Goldberg, G.A., Camp, P. and Newhouse, J.P. (1986) 'Comparison of health outcomes at a Health Maintenance Organisation with those for fee-for-service care', *Lancet* i: 1017–22.

Wennberg, J. (1984) 'Dealing with medical practice variations: a proposal for action', *Health Affairs* 3: 6–32.

Wennberg, J. and Gittelsohn, A. (1980) 'Small area variations in health care delivery', in D. Mechanic (ed.) *Reading in Medical Sociology*, New York: Free Press.

Wennberg, J. E., Mulley, A.G., Hanley, D., Timothy, R.P., Fowler, F.J., Roos, N. P., Barry, M.J., McPherson, K., Greenberg, E. R., Soule, D., Bubolz, T., Fisher, E., and Malenka, D. (1988) 'An assessment of prostatectomy for benign urinary tract obstruction: geographic variations and the evaluation of medical care outcomes', *Journal of the American Medical Association* 259: 3027–30.

West, R.R. and Carey, M.J (1978) 'Variations in rates of hospital admission for appendicitis in Wales' *British Medical Journal* 1: 1662–4.

Wilkin, D. and Smith, A.G. (1987) 'Variation in general practitioners' referral rates to consultants', *Journal of the Royal College of General Practitioners* 37: 350–3.

Williams, A. (1983) 'The economic role of "health indicators" ', in G. Teeling Smith (ed.) *Measuring the Social Benefits of Medicine*, London: Office of Health Economics.

——(1987) 'Measuring quality of life', in G. Teeling Smith (ed.) *Health Economics: Prospects for the Future*, Beckenham: Croom Helm.

Chapter six

Recent developments in general practice: a sociological analysis

Michael Calnan and Jonathan Gabe

General practice has a key position in the provision of health care under the British National Health Service. On the one hand, it provides free of charge primary care to the vast majority of the population. On the other hand, the general practitioner (GP) acts as a gatekeeper and controller of access to a range of expensive hospital specialist services. The aim of this chapter is to examine changes that have taken place in general practice over the last twenty years and to identify the major influences on this development. More specifically, the intention is to attempt to develop a sociological account of the development of general practice, drawing on the literature about medicine as a profession. Work in this area has traditionally conceptualized medicine as an occupation which has obtained and maintains professional status. However, it has tended to focus mainly on hospital specialist medicine and has neglected other branches like general practice, which have developed less quickly. In this chapter, we want to rectify this situation and consider the extent to which these sociological perspectives adequately explain development in general practice over the last twenty years.

Professionalism: theoretical approaches

Since the demise of the taxonomic approach to the professions in the late 1960s, two theoretical frameworks have dominated this field of study in Britain and North American – the neoWeberian and Marxist approaches (Saks 1983). As one might expect, both approaches contain within them differences of emphasis and these will be noted in the following account of their distinguishing features.

Taking Weber's concern with the market as a starting point, those adopting a neoWeberian perspective have focused on the way in which professions have sought to regulate market conditions in their favour by limiting and controlling the supply of entrants. According to Parkin (1979), this represents an exclusionary form of social closure, based on credentialism. In the health field, it is Parry and Parry (1976) who most clearly illustrate this approach. Their historical analysis of the emergence of the British medical profession showed how the Medical Registration Act of 1858 provided a basis for occupational closure by creating a statutorily mandated framework for the self-control of medical education, training and qualifications. According to the Parrys, it also provided the basis for the formal amalgamation of the low-status apothecaries and surgeons with the physicians, thereby providing the opportunity for the former groups to become upwardly mobile and achieve higher status.

As Saks (1983) has pointed out, other sociologists employing a neoWeberian framework in the 1970s were not always so firmly wedded to the mainstream of Weberian thought. Freidson (1970), for instance, focused on the US medical profession's control over work rather than the market place, although a concern with the market and social closure were implicit in his analysis. For him, the profession's ability to control its own work and at times that of other health-care occupations was its distinguishing feature. He argued that a profession could be differentiated from other occupations in that it had been given the right to control its own work by a dominant elite or by the state. Having established itself and its monopoly over medical work, the medical profession was able to control the growth of a division of labour around it as a result of its expertise and its ability to monopolize such knowledge, supported by legal and formal state regulations.

Johnson (1972), writing about the professions in Britain, took a different position. For him the provider–consumer relationship represented the key to understanding professional control and autonomy. He argued that the type of occupational control found in the provider–consumer relationship depended on the social and economic resources available to the two parties and, more crucially, on the distance created by the difference in specialized knowledge and skills between the producer and consumer. The greater the distance between the producer and consumer, the greater the level of uncertainty in the relationship, and thus the greater the dominance of the provider and the dependence of the consumer. Johnson felt that medicine represented a form of collegiate control because of this ability to impose on consumers its own definition of need and the way in which such need should be catered for. This social distance in the doctor–patient relationship evolved when medicine tied itself to science for its cognitive base (Larson 1978). According to Saks (1983) this emphasis on control over consumers, rather than the market, is related to the concept of closure and thus lies within the general spirit of the neoWeberian approach.

A further approach which fits broadly within the neoWeberian framework has been articulated by Haug (Haug 1975; Haug and Lavin 1983). Writing about more recent developments in the US health-care system and the consequences for doctoring, she has argued that the relationship between doctors and patients has changed, leading to the deprofessionalization of medicine. This conclusion is premised on the argument that the 'knowledge gap' between the medical profession and the consumer has diminished, reducing the consumer's unquestioning trust. Moreover, consumers, armed with this increased knowledge, are said to have become more willing to shop around for medical services, as they do for other commodities in the market place. From this stand-point consumers, not physicians, will dominate health care in future, and medicine will become just another health occupation like all the others which have arisen around different specialist bodies of knowledge and skills. Such an approach, then, relates to several of the concerns of earlier neo-Weberians in so far as the focus is on the degree of control over consumers and the market for medical specialists. However, the conclusions drawn are somewhat different and reflect perceived changes in the distribution of knowledge about health and health care.

In contrast to these writers, others concerned with professional development have adopted a Marxist framework centred on the relations of production. Such an approach is illustrated by Johnson who, in his more recent writing (1977), has argued that medicine has fulfilled the global functions of capital in the phase of monopoly capitalism, by appropriating official definitions of illness and health and legitimizing the withdrawal of labour through certification. In this sense the medical profession is centrally involved in the surveillance and reproduction of labour power.

Navarro (1978) has also emphasized the medical profession's social control function and has suggested that this function provides it with its source of power. As far as he is concerned, the profession acts as an agent of social control by translating the collective and political problem of health and illness into an individual one. Medicine, according to Navarro, 'ameliorates or makes palatable those diswelfares generated by the economic system' and legitimates them in the eyes of the general population. Applying his analysis to Britain, he argues that the medical profession contributes to capital accumulation by its actions and that its interests are similar to those of the ruling class.

More recently, the class position attributed to the medical profession has been challenged by others within the Marxist tradition. For instance, McKinlay and Stoeckle (1988), writing about the difference in the USA between self-employed physicians of the 1900s and salaried physicians working in bureaucratic institutions in the late 1980s, have argued that the latter have experienced a process of proletarianization. This they define as 'the process by which an occupational category is divested of control over certain prerogatives relating to the location, content and essentiality of its task activities, thereby subordinating it to the broader requirements of production under advanced capitalism'. Although this process is difficult to recognize, they argue that evidence for its development includes an increased emphasis on managerial imperatives (productivity, cost efficiency) and greater specialization/deskilling with other health workers taking over some of the medical profession's functions.

This proletarianization thesis, along with the deprofessionalization approach, have recently been criticized from within the neoWeberian tradition by Freidson (1984, 1985, 1986). He argues that those advocating these approaches have failed to take seriously that the profession is a corporate organization rather than simply an aggregate of individuals doing their daily work with others. For Freidson, this has consequences for both theses in that 'it is the organised character of the profession and the connection of its organisation to state policy making and institutional chartering that pose a major barrier' to them. Thus, like McKinlay and Stoeckle (1988), Freidson does see that professional dominance could be diminishing, although only at the level of everyday work. This work is being carried out by a large rank and file of doctors who are increasingly becoming divorced from elite groups who are responsible for knowledge, training, discipline and administration within the profession. It is at this elite level that the corporate body of medicine is well able to retain its position of dominance. In contrast, the Marxist approach implies an equivalence between the macro- and microlevels.

As we noted earlier, both the neoWeberian and Marxist perspectives have been developed in an attempt to understand the professional development of hospital medicine. How relevant, then, are they to general practice in Britain and, in particular, what light can they shed on recent developments in this field? For instance, can the professional dominance of GPs be so easily undermined by consumerism or the requirements of capital accumulation?

We intend to explore these issues by focusing on developments in general practice since the publication of the GP charter of 1965, an event which had significant consequences for the organization and professional status of general practice. Three main themes will be explored: general practitioners' relationship with hospital doctors and other health-related occupations, their relationship with the state and their relationship with their patients. Separating out these issues in this way is admittedly somewhat artificial and has been done mainly for heuristic reasons. However, one or more of them have been identified in the accounts of professionalism just described as being crucial to the understanding of occupational development.

The relationship between GPs, hospital doctors and related occupations

Here, we focus on the extent to which the professional dominance model is suggested by recent developments in the relationship between GPs and other health-related professions. In order to understand this relationship, we need briefly to situate it historically. If this is done we find that the professional development of general practice has been shaped to a large extent by the development of hospital medicine. The control that hospital doctors gained over the medical market place in the nineteenth and early twentieth century set the agenda for future debates about the role of general practitioners and the identification of the most effective strategy for enhancing professional development. Should general practitioners follow the path of hospital specialists or should they try to create a distinct speciality of their own? In recent years, as we shall see, general practice in many respects appears to have opted for the second course of action.

This decision was informed by a recognition that specialized hospital doctors had made further progress in their professional development in the decade following the introduction of the NHS in 1948. At the same time, general practitioners had become an isolated and defensive group who had lost interest in challenging the dominance of hospital specialists. Their professional development was at a standstill and in many respects their poor conditions of work, low income and long hours of work were the price they were paying for owning their own practice and being independent. Their position can be likened to the small shop-keeper and this approach has left its legacy in more recent proposals (Maynard 1984; Enthoven 1985) where the general practitioner has been prescribed the role of the small-scale entrepreneur. In the decades after the creation of the NHS, however, the professional fortune of the generalists slowly began to change.

These changes began in some respects with the GP charter of 1965 which recommended that the methods of remuneration and terms of service of GPs be changed. The charter stemmed from a build-up of pressure for improved conditions of service from the profession, although one of the most obvious catalysts was the setting up of the College of General Practitioners in 1952. Certainly, the charter did result in a change in GPs' working conditions and there was a decline in the proportion of doctors in single-handed practice, a decrease in the amount of home visiting and a more extensive use of appointment systems and deputizing services (Cartwright and Anderson 1981). Similarly, Wilkin and colleagues report significant changes in the organization of general practice in the years immediately after the charter's introduction:

Between 1968 and 1975, 553 new health centres were opened in
the UK and over 1,400 loans to convert and construct new premises
were taken up. The trend towards larger practices continued, so
that the proportion of doctors in practices with three or more
partners increased from 42% in 1964 to 60% in 1973. In the five
years from 1968 to 1973 the number of wholetime equivalent
clerical staff went up by 10% each year and the number of
employed nurses by 26% overall. . . . A new concept of the primary
health care team began to emerge.

(Wilkin *et al.* 1987: 4)

Thus, in the mid-1970s, twenty-five years after the introduction of
the National Health Service, general practitioners had gained control
over their working conditions and created a distinct environment in
which a profession could flourish. Not only that, but general
practitioners had started to become employers and could assert their
dominance over the primary health-care team.

These changes, while improving the working conditions of the
doctor, appear to have increased the social distance between doctor and
patient by creating barriers between the two. This may account for the
finding from Cartwright and Anderson's (1981) study examining
changes in patient views about primary care between 1964 and 1977,
which showed that despite marked changes in the organization of
general practice during this period, there was no indication of any
greater understanding between doctors and patients. Indeed, from the
patient's point of view, the quality of care they received had actually
diminished in some respects.

While these organizational changes may have created further barriers
between GP and patient, the new specialist body of knowledge which
the official representatives of GPs were trying to develop appeared to be
aiming to bring the doctor and patient closer together. If further
professional development was to be achieved, general practice appeared
to require a distinct specialist body of knowledge, at least distinct from
their rivals in the hospital. Up until this time GPs' professional
aspirations were still modelled closely on hospital medical practice,
reflecting the continuing dominance of the content and ideology of
hospital medicine. For example, Armstrong (1979) has shown how
problems or crises in general practice were defined through the
perspective of the hospital paradigm, however inappropriate it may have
been for a community-based service response to the demands of the
public. The recurrent concern about trivial demands, the desire for
hospital work, and the emphasis on academically acceptable
foundations are all examples of the continuing influence exerted by the
consultants over their generalist colleagues during this period.

About the same time, however, a different solution to the more traditional 'medical' approach was emerging from discussions initiated by the Royal College. This solution has been described by Armstrong (1979) as the biographic approach to medicine as it places emphasis on the need to consider the patient as a whole and to concentrate on the signs and symptoms in the context of the patient's own biography and environment. This holistic approach is represented in the work of Balint and colleagues (Balint and Norell 1975) and appears to have been largely accepted by the profession's leaders, if the official pronouncements of the RCGP are anything to go by.

The extent to which this model has been adopted in the surgery at the expense of the traditional hospital-dominated model is, however, difficult to assess. Results from a recent study (Calnan 1988a) suggest that the GP population as a whole is split down the middle in that a large proportion support the clinical model and another large section support the holistic model. One way that this evidence might be interpreted is that a clear difference is emerging between the world of the official representatives of GPs and the world of everyday general practice. In some respects the elitist and radical approach of the RCGP is becoming increasingly distant from the view of the majority of general practitioners. Yet, as Freidson has pointed out (1985), professional status does not hinge on the activities of an aggregate of individual general practitioners but on the activities of the profession's representatives. Hence, the holistic model may perform the function of providing the profession with a distinct ideology which can be used at the official level even though it is not accepted by a large segment of working GPs. In some respects, it merely acts as political rhetoric.

Over the last decade or so some of the developments which have affected hospital medicine have worked in favour of the development of general practice. There is evidence of the growing popularity of general practice as a career choice for medical students, in spite of the low esteem in which specialist teachers hold general practice. Between 1979 and 1984 GPs contracted for general medical services increased by 11 per cent from 26,000 to 29,000. This increase in popularity is probably due in part to the improved financial prospects of GPs and in part to relative freedom to practice medicine without the constraints of cash limits. Indeed, it is perhaps only in the last ten years that the independent contractor status of GPs has come to work in their favour when compared to the position of specialists. In addition, general practice may become a more popular career option, not so much because of its new holistic model propagated by the RCGP but because of the failure of hospital specialists medicine to make progress. Certainly, over the past couple of decades, specialist medicine has seen relatively few major advances which have affected large numbers of people. The hospital-based specialists have made relatively little progress in dealing with the major chronic and life-threatening illnesses and this may have had the effect of raising the status of general practice compared with specialist medicine. In this respect, the cultural critique of scientific medicine has shaped doctors' perceptions as well as the public as a whole.

In some respects, then, this period saw an increase in the professional status of general practitioners which was further illustrated by the emergence of the debate about the content and quality of general-practitioner care. The debate about the content of general practice focused on which areas GPs should expand into. It was shown previously that general practitioners as a whole were divided into those with a clinical approach and those with a more social orientation. The difference is reflected in the two distinctly different schools of thought which have emerged in the debate (Calnan 1988b) about the broad areas of service in which general practitioners could be involved.

The first school argues for a deepening involvement with clinical care, extending the general practitioners' range of activities into areas such as minor surgery. One advocate of this position is the General Medical Services Committee of the British Medical Association (1983) which argues that 'too many medical skills and aptitudes are laid to rest when doctors enter general practice. If general practitioners were given the opportunities and resources to use their wasted skills, it would result in a redistribution of work in the NHS'. Clearly, then, the concern is not with just creating a sounder base for the professional discipline but also with resource allocation and the money apparently saved if GPs rather than hospitals carry out certain medical treatments. This shows how broader developments in the health-care system have implications for the professional development of GPs.

The other school of thought, rather than looking for a deepening involvement in clinical care, advocates shifting the focus and extending the GP's role into the area of health promotion and disease prevention. Much of the impetus for this change appears to have come from within general practice itself, although it clearly resonates with cultural and political discourses about healthy living and self-help (Crawford 1984).

One such advocate of change is Tudor Hart (1984) whose proposal for a community general practitioner involves the doctor combining clinical skills with those of population medicine. Central to this approach is the idea of anticipatory care where a team of health workers would actively seek out people's needs by, for example, identifying high-risk groups within the practice population.

Other suggestions for developing preventive care in general practice have also been put forward. For example, the RCGP has published a series of reports on prevention which would seem to reflect at least two other approaches. First, there is the traditional approach of opportunistic health education or screening of the patient who consults. Second, the general practitioner could become more involved with the local community and develop initiatives in collaboration with other professionals working within the community.

Criticism of the initiative from the RCGP has been made on a number of levels. Some have interpreted it as another example of the creeping medicalization which is inherent in western industrial society (Davies 1984). It is argued that the medical profession – or one section of it – is furthering its empire by attempting to claim jurisdiction over people's life styles, or over aspects of life style which are claimed to influence disease. Others have suggested more plausibly that the RCGP's crusade in the area of prevention is a further attempt to maintain or enhance general practice's professional identity independent of hospital medicine. For example, Honigsbaum states:

> They (the RCGP) fear most any move that will carry general practitioners closer to hospital medicine, so much so that it might be fair to describe their proposals as the 'keep general practitioners busy in the community' school. For them, almost any activity will do as long as it leaves general practitioners free from entanglement with consultants.
>
> (Honigsbaum 1985: 826)

Thus, for some commentators, even recent attempts to define the role or content of general practice are largely coloured by the profession's concern about the higher status and greater power of their hospital colleagues.

The profession's increasing confidence was also reflected in its concern with and willingness to openly discuss the quality of care in general practice. In 1985, a consultation document (Royal College of General Practitioners 1985) was published entitled 'Towards the quality of general practice'. The document identified five areas in which the attainment of consistently high standards would have beneficial consequences for the care that patients received: the professional development of the doctor, practice management and teamwork, the regular review of the quality of clinical care, contracts and incentives and the availability of resources.

Apart from, or in addition to, the development of primary care in this country being shaped by intraprofessional rivalry, its development has to some extent also been influenced by interprofessional rivalries. There is still some debate (Armstrong 1976) about whether the professional development of certain paramedical groups such as social workers, health visitors, nurses, pharmacists and physiotherapists has led to a decline in medical authority. Larkin (1983), for example, suggests that

148

while paramedical workers may have wrested some control from doctors in the division of labour, they have not been able to challenge their dominance.

Certainly, in general practice there has been a shift towards larger partnerships with primary-care teams which has meant the involvement of health visitors, nurses and social workers amongst others. How far such developments have threatened the authority and power of general practitioners is difficult to gauge. Stacey presents evidence to show that this development may pose a threat. She quotes from the General Medical Council as stating:

> Doctors must be educated in the implications of their clinical decisions for members of the other professions, and the doctor must exercise his/her overall responsibility for the patient as a leader of the team and not as an autocrat. Nevertheless . . . the leader of the health team in general practice must continue to rest with the doctor in charge of the patient and not with other professions or administrators.
>
> (Stacey 1988: 186)

Some empirical studies (e.g. Jefferys and Sachs 1983) have shown little evidence of rivalries and tensions between general practitioners and other occupational groups. However, in certain areas of work there is evidence, at least at the political level, of a struggle between general practitioners and the allied occupations over authority, responsibility and jurisdiction. One such area where tensions over the division of labour are marked is in child health surveillance. The territorial disputes over this area have involved both intraprofessional rivalries (between GPs, hospital paediatricians and community health doctors) and interprofessional struggles particularly between general practitioners and health visitors (Butler 1989). For example, in 1983 the RCGP published a report which, while acknowledging the role of the health visitor, suggested that the key agent in child health surveillance was the general practitioner. The Health Visitors' Association viewed this development with unease and responded swiftly by producing a policy document a year later which gave a prominent role to health visitors and limited the role of GPs to dealing with 'cases' selected by thorough screening.

Overall, then, it would seem that as general practitioners as a profession have grown in confidence, they have increasingly attempted to establish the kind of dominance traditionally exercised, according to Freidson (1970), by their hospital colleagues. They have established control over their working conditions, attempted to develop a specialized body of knowledge and striven to maintain a superordinate position in relation to allied occupational groups.

Involvement with the state

In this section, we explore the state's role as a mediator between GPs and patients and whether this has changed over time. In particular, has the state moved from confering legitimacy on the medical profession and general practice's status within it to actively seeking to regulate and control general practice? Historically, the state's role with regard to general practice has been facilitative. For example, through the National Insurance Act of 1911, it gave GPs some economic security, releasing them from the controls of private and contract patients. Similarly, when the 1946 Act came into force in 1948, they retained their independence, contracting their services to the NHS through the newly created executive councils and they received slightly better incomes and gained more job security. At the same time, however, the Act gave greater support to the hospital doctors who were given a guaranteed salary and financial incentives and the freedom to engage in private practice. Thus, the 1946 Act perpetuated the division between the GP and the hospital doctor and also made the hospital doctor less financially dependent on the general practitioner's referral of private patients. The Act represented a further stage in the development of the hospital doctors' professional autonomy, for they could now formally be accessed only through the general practitioners. This is important because the control of patients' access is (and probably always will be) one of the problems that the general practitioner faces in a setting in which the work is client- rather than colleague-dependent (Calnan 1982). They are on the receiving end of decisions made by the public rather than by professionals. However, as will be seen, GPs did attempt to develop strategies for controlling patient access and for distancing patients, which appears to help them in their pursuit of a professional identity.

One advantage for general practice supposedly stemming from this legislation is that it retained its independence. However, it is unclear whether this benefit was gained against the wishes of the state or whether it was a benefit to which the state was indifferent. It is quite clear that Bevan (the minister responsible for the Act) and his colleagues were concerned with trying to placate the powerful hospital lobby (Webster 1988) and thus may have been happy to leave the less-powerful general practitioners to carry on as they wished. Anyway, the idea of being an 'independent' contractor tends to be misleading. If a general practitioner wished to opt out of the newly formed NHS, he or she had only a very limited range of choices for alternative careers in medicine because of the monopoly of one employer. Also, as Johnson (1977) has argued, it was in the interests of the state and the economy that doctors were available to treat the health problems of the mass of the population to ensure that a functionally able labour force was always available.

It appears, then, that up until 1950 the state had done more to enhance the professional dominance of the hospital doctors than their colleagues in general practice. During the 1950s, as we have seen, general practitioners managed to negotiate better terms of employment, but it is only recently, since the mid-1980s, that the state has become more interested in general practice, frequently intervening between the producers and consumers of medical care to regulate and control aspects of general practice and consumer satisfaction. This is partly because it is seen as the key for controlling expenditure on health care. General practitioners are seen as important as they control access to the expensive hospital technologies and they could also provide a prevention service which is believed to be less expensive than curative care.

The state's increased interest in general practice is reflected in their involvement in vocational training which is now mandatory and the introduction of the limited list for prescribed medicines. While making vocational training mandatory enhanced the professional status of general practitioners, there was vociferous opposition to the limited list both from the medical profession, including GPs, and the pharmaceutical industry. It is difficult to assess how far this has affected GPs' professional independence. Recent research on the effects of the limited list in general practice indicates that GPs generally have had relatively little difficulty finding suitable alternatives to black-listed drugs – the main problems being with cough medicines and multivitamins (*Drug and Therapeutics Bulletin* 1987). On balance, the limited list has probably had more severe constraints on hospital specialists' clinical freedom than on GPs, both in terms of restrictions on the patients they can treat and in terms of controls on prescribing, through policies such as generic substitution and the use of antibiotics.

The recent Green and White papers on primary care are also illustrative of the state's more active stance with regard to primary care. The White Paper which confirmed many of the proposals outlined in the Green Paper, had the following aims:

1. to make services more responsive to the consumer;
2. to raise standards of care;
3. to promote health and prevent illness;
4. to give patients the widest range of choice in obtaining high quality primary care services;
5. to give better value for money;
6. to enable clear priorities to be set for the family-practitioner service in relation to the rest of the health service.

(DHSS 1987)

Raising standards of care and increasing involvement in health promotion were to be achieved by changing the means of remuneration;

151

other policy recommendations included making 70 the compulsory retirement age, increasing financial support to improve practice premises, extending the role of nurses as prescribers, developing ways of giving consumers better information and a wide choice of providing financial incentives for vocational training.

Why has the state published these documents? As with the limited list, one reason is economic – the perceived need to get 'value for money' and to control the use of resources by linking it to performance. Care provided by general practitioners is also believed to be a less expensive option than the ever increasing costs of hospital based, high-technological medicine. Hence, the recent focus on the problem of the 'referral' behaviour of general practitioners and the attempt to shift the care of certain types of patient from the hospital to the community.

There are also political factors to be taken into account. Evaluating the performance of GPs is in line with the state's policy of attempting to limit the autonomy of certain professional groups. The White Paper makes it clear that if GPs do not monitor the quality of their performance, then they are at risk that the state will do it for them. Such a proposal, of course, appears to threaten professional autonomy and may be one of the reasons why the Royal College developed its 'Quality of care initiative' in 1985. Alternatively, the emphasis on evaluation may be seen as another device for enhancing professional status through the use of scientific methods.

In addition, the plan to give nurses more responsibility for prescribing certain drugs is also in line with the state's attempt to restrict professional autonomy. In this case the strategy adopted challenges the profession's monopoly of certain skills on the grounds that the state is best equipped to decide how patients' needs should be met.

Third, and finally, there are important ideological forces at work. For instance, the White Paper's discussion of prevention would seem to reflect the state's current predilection for encouraging individual responsibility and self-care. Likewise, the recommendations for action on quality control and the need to increase patient choice are related to the state's attempts to promote consumer sovereignty in the market economy. It should be noted, however, that this market approach is not the only one found in these documents. As Day and Klein (1986) have noted in their comment on the Green Paper a 'paternalistic' model (provider-defined need) of health care can also be found in the proposals for strengthening the role of FPCs.

The contract which emerged out of negotiations about the implementation of the 1987 White Paper has produced vociferous opposition from general practitioners, as have the recommendations in the most recent White Paper on the NHS (Department of Health 1989). The essence of these proposals is similar to that which has affected their hospital colleagues in the past, i.e. an attempt to cash limit general practitioners.

The proposals suggest that general practitioners in some larger practices have the option of controlling their own budgets for a range of treatments and hospital services. With their own practice budgets they are expected to contract with hospitals for certain services and to provide a full range of primary care services for their patients. The aim is to create a competitive health care system in which GPs in medical groups are to be at financial risk for their practice decisions. These GPs would be given the option of being more economically independent with less of their salary being derived from allowances and more being directed from capitation (increased from 45 per cent to 60 per cent) and payments for services provided. Such a proposal in turn means that funding would become increasingly like that found for health maintenance organizations in the United States (Petchey 1989).

These government proposals have also led to general practice being affected by the same managerialism which has been imposed on their hospital colleagues (DHSS 1983). General practitioners are now under contract to Family Practitioner Committees (FPCs), which will have the task of monitoring their performance against the indicative prescribing budgets set by the FPCs and taking appropriate action to maintain expenditure within these budgets. In this sense, then, they will be managed by the FPC.

What are the implications for professional sovereignty? Certainly, as with the previous White Paper, the government is intervening in the professional lives of general practitioners. Also, these initiatives come from the government and not from the profession as the quality of care, initiative did. However, the proposals about practice budgets do give more economic independence to the GPs even if they create the possibility of greater economic dependence on the patient through capitation fees. At the same time, general practitioners will have more economic control over their rivals – the hospital specialists. In essence, it is a return to the pre-NHS days where GPs were economically dependent on patients and hospital doctors were more economically dependent on GPs. In this sense, then, the professional sovereignty of GPs is being both enhanced and circumscribed by the White Paper.

In addition, these proposals, and those from the previous White Paper (Department of Health and Social Security 1987), open up the possibility for deprofessionalization and proletarianization. If patients come to appreciate the extent to which GPs are economically dependent on them, they may use this to exert power over their doctors. Also, the increased scope given to nurses as prescribers suggests that GPs may be facing the beginning of a process of specialization and hence deskilling.

Michael Calnan and Jonathan Gabe

Moreover, this process may be enhanced by the new managerialism which larger practices are being encouraged to embrace.

General practioners and patients

In this section we consider the extent to which professional dominance has been challenged by the collective and individual acts of patients. Or, to put it another way, is there evidence of deprofessionalization?

The influence that patients have on general practice can be analysed at the political and cultural levels. Taking the *political* level first, this can be conceptualized in both collective and individual terms. *Collectively*, the patient may have an influence through formal institutions such as community health councils (CHCs) and patient groups. Doubts have been expressed about the extent to which such bodies are influential. For example, Watkins describes the influence of CHCs as follows:

> Many CHCs, however, have been able to bring new ideas to light and to be a potent force for change in the NHS, although it must be recognized that many have had only a limited impact. The personality and politics of the CHC secretary seem to have been more important than those of the members in determining the behaviour of the CHCs, so that what started out as an attempt to graft democracy on to a technocratic structure has evolved into a system of licensed health campaigners employed by the NHS.
>
> (Watkins 1987: 154)

Patient groups tend to be found only in the more enlightened practices (Shaw 1978). Some experimental schemes have been set up such as patient committees to advise their general practitioners about the way in which services should develop (Watkins 1987). According to Hall (1980), the setting up of these committees is best understood as a voluntary relinquishment of status and power by the GP, aimed at lessening the power imbalance while at the same time increasing the patients' obligations to a system in which they are more involved. The initial response to these groups by the BMA, through its ethical committee, was critical; it was argued that the doctors who set them up were effectively advertising, since the groups would publicize the practices. That criticism has been quietly dropped (Watkins 1987) and the movement has continued to grow, albeit at a modest pace. This suggests that the medical profession no longer sees such groups as a major threat to their authority.

Other collective forces for change include the women's movement which has campaigned on issues such as the power exerted over female patients by male doctors, for services to be provided to meet the specific needs of women (such as well-woman clinics and antenatal clinics), and the demedicalization of childbirth where the preference is for maintaining a balance between hospital and home care. It is difficult to identify the influence of these different groups but, at least amongst some practices, services for women have become more widely available.

At the *individual* level, how far can patients challenge GPs over the type of service and care that they receive? There is a formal complaints procedure which, according to some commentators, has many defects (Watkins 1987). Less formally, patients may be able to voice their opinions through direct contact with their general practitioners and other staff. How often patients do voice their opinions directly and how sensitive practices actually are to patients' views is also difficult to estimate. Survey evidence (Jefferys and Sachs 1983) appears to suggest a relatively high level of satisfaction with primary care. However, evidence from Blaxter and Paterson's ethnographic study (1982) showed a greater level of criticism amongst the younger generation of women compared with the older generation. This may reflect the effect of ageing in that older age groups are more dependent on the doctor and thus less critical, or that the younger generation brought up under the NHS have higher expectations about health care. Also, evidence from Cartwright and Anderson's (1981) study examining changes in patients' views about primary care between 1964 and 1977 showed that despite marked changes in the organization of general practice during this period, there was no indication of any greater understanding between doctors and patients. Indeed, from the patients' point of view, the quality of the care they received had actually diminished in some respects. This evidence appears to suggest that there had been little change in the structure of the doctor-patient relationship during this period or in the communication styles of general practitioners. More up-to-date evidence is needed to see if there have been recent changes in patients' views.

Recent government proposals have placed a major emphasis on increasing consumerism in general practice (DHSS 1987; DH 1989). This is illustrated by the proposal to get GPs to provide patients with more information about the services they offer in order to facilitate patient choice, and the suggestion that patients should be able to change their GP without first approaching their existing doctor and the FPC. The idea of consumerism inherent in this proposal does not imply increased public participation in decision making but is aimed at increasing 'individual' choice, as it is derived from a model of health care which suggests that its provision should be determined by a market economy. Medical care should be treated like any other commodity and be subject to market forces. Whether such a system will increase patient

155

choice is difficult to say. However, there is evidence to show that professional control and influence over provision and resource use is also prevalent in the market-economy model, primarily because health care has special qualities that differentiate it from other consumer products. In a market economy, there is a greater risk of overprovision for those who can pay and lack of access for those who cannot.

Turning to the *cultural* level, there appears to be an increasing scepticism, at least among some social groups, about the value and benefits of modern medical care. General practice has not escaped this scrutiny. Moreover, this scepticism has been encouraged and/or amplified by the mass media. For example, there is evidence that patients' perceptions of the dangers of tranquilliser dependence have been heightened considerably by recent media coverage (Gabe and Bury 1988). It may be that it is at the cultural level that general practitioners have been influenced most. To continue with the example of tranquilliser use, there is recent evidence of a marked decline in tranquilliser prescriptions which could be explained in part by the adverse media coverage.

Evidence at the cultural level provides at least some grounds for the view that professional dominance is being challenged. At the political level, however, the weight of evidence is against such a view. There is little to suggest that patients have in general become less satisfied with the care and service of their GP in recent years nor do they seem to have become more willing to take individual or collective action if they are dissatisfied. Furthermore, there seems to have been little change in the structure of the doctor-patient relationship or in GP communication styles. The deprofessionalization of GPs therefore seems to have made little headway in Britain, although the 1989 White Paper may encourage this process in future.

Conclusions

A number of questions emerged out of this analysis of developments in the field of general practice. First, at the substantive level, it was shown that the explanation for the present professional position of general practitioners had its roots as far back as the nineteenth century, when GPs' low status in relation to hospital doctors and their isolation and economic dependence on patients at that time encouraged them to become the independent small business men and women that they are today. However, while their independence from the state and their social distance from the hospitals hindered their professional development, it has in many ways cushioned them from the managerial controls over resources and clinical freedom that the hospital sector was experiencing. Coupled with that, the doubts about the effectiveness and efficiency of high-technology medicine have meant that general practice has become a more attractive option. In some ways the past successes of hospital specialist medicine hindered the professional development of general practice, while the recent failures of hospital specialist medicine have enhanced its development. However, in the last few years, concerns with the quality and efficiency of care have focused on general practice. Indeed, it increasingly looks as if general practitioners are going to be facing the same managerial controls and cash limiting that their hospital colleagues had to face some time ago. In addition, they are being asked to be more accountable to the patient.

Second, our analysis has theoretical implications for the professional dominance thesis. To start with, it has provided empirical support for two of the forms of occupational control identified by Johnson (1972) – namely collegiate control and mediation. Collegiate control has been illustrated by the activities of the RCGP, while mediation has been highlighted by the state intervening in the relationship between GPs (producers) and patients (consumers). Indeed, mediation has increasingly become the form of occupational control in the late 1980s as the state has taken on the role of redefining the ways in which patients' needs are to be met. One explanation for such a development would seem to be the present government's desire to restrict public spending (e.g. on NHS prescriptions) so that taxation can be reduced and the opportunities for capital accumulation increased. Another is ideological, the desire to make individual consumer choice the dominant value in welfare policy. And a third is the political calculation that the power of the oldest professions, such as medicine, should be curtailed.

At the same time, we have shown that the state is not the only mediator. The medical profession and general practitioners in particular have also been forced into this role in recent years: mediating the demand of the state to control resources and the demands of the patient to provide good quality care. Moreover, this role is likely to become more important in the 1990s if the recent White Paper is implemented in full. In such an event GPs will be expected to have regard to financial considerations in their prescribing and referral activities while ignoring those considerations when it comes to the selection of patients (Petchey 1989). If this interpretation is accepted, the idea of professional autonomy conferred by the state, as put forward by Freidson (1970), needs to be modified to take into account the changing demands of the state and also the patient population.

In addition, our account of the recent history of general practice has provided little support for either deprofessionalization or proletarianization. There appears at present to be relatively little evidence of patients being dissatisfied with their GP, challenging their authority and shopping around for an alternative opinion. Nor is there much evidence of GPs succumbing to the new managerialism or being deskilled. This suggests that McKinlay and Stoeckle (1988) are incorrect to argue that the professional dominance thesis may have explained the position of doctors in the 1960s but does not do so now. On the contrary, we have shown that it is still of value, if suitably modified to take account of the GPs' new role as mediator and the state's attempt to define the ways in which patients' needs should be met.

Professional dominance's prospects as an explanatory force within the British context is, however, less certain and depends in large part on the outcome of the current political negotiations around the 1989 White Paper. Certainly the process of corporatization and hence proletarianization is being encouraged by the recent White Paper in that large practices are being invited to opt out and make greater use of private health care. Furthermore, proposals to extend the role of the nurse as prescriber in the Health and Medicines Act may also enhance this process. Likewise, deprofessionalization may be encouraged by the rhetoric of consumerism and the current White Paper's proposals to increase information about GP services to aid patient choice, and to enable patients to change GP without approaching their existing one or the FPC first. In the longer term, however, the scope for proletarianization and deprofessionalization are likely to depend on whether the NHS is replaced by a privately funded system, as the United States' experience suggests that such a system provides a major impetus for such developments.

Third, a range of more specific questions emerge from the analysis. One of these revolves around the issue of consumer sovereignty and the extent to which this current emphasis in policy will actually influence the position of the patient. Maybe a look at other countries such as the United States, where the market economy of health care and the ideology of consumer sovereignty has been in existence for a longer period might provide some evidence to answer this question. There has been considerable sociological research in the area of illness and help-seeking behaviour although the picture about how, when and why patients use general practice still remains blurred. More specifically, little is known about the level of 'shopping around' (Salisbury 1989), whether patients actually like this idea and whether recent government policy will actually lead to such behaviour becoming more prevalent.

There is also a related question as to whether recent policy proposals will lead to general practitioners having a greater involvement in providing private health care. Evidence from a national survey (Calnan and Butler 1988) showed that the average number of hours that general practitioners in the sample spent per week on private practice was 0.4 hours out of an average time spent each week on activities within their practices of 39.2 hours. Evidence from this national survey (Calnan

1988a) also suggests that there may be a large amount of resistance among GPs as a whole to becoming more involved in private practice because a large proportion still tend to have a social and altruistic approach to general practice rather than an 'entrepreneurial' approach. This and other evidence (Horder *et al.* 1986) also raises doubts about 'the effectiveness of proposals' (Maynard 1984) which advocate the benefits of financial incentives for changing or modifying general practitioners' behaviour.

Other major policy questions concern the quality of care in general practice and how far will the increasing state involvement lead to improved care. Certainly, there are still considerable gaps in our understanding of what are the most significant factors that influence the pattern of care provided in general practice. Examination of the influence of structural factors such as partnership size or list size suggest that they have a negligible impact and maybe a more fruitful line of investigation would be to look at the beliefs of the general practitioners as well as their social characteristics. For example, there is evidence to suggest that female general practitioners have longer consultations than male general practitioners. There are a number of possible explanations, including gender differences in these practitioners' beliefs. It also raises the question about whether the increasing involvement of women in general practice will lead to an improvement in some aspects of quality of care, particularly in the relationship between doctor and patient.

Acknowledgements

We should like to thank our discussant, Patricia Day, and also David Armstrong and David Wilkin, for their comments on an earlier draft of this paper.

References

Armstrong, D. (1976) 'The decline of medical hegemony', *Social Science and Medicine* 10: 157–63.
——(1979) 'The emancipation of biographical medicine', *Social Science and Medicine* 13A: 1–8.
Balint, E. and Norell, J.S. (1973) *Six Minutes for The Patient: Interactions in General Consultation,* London: Tavistock.
Blaxter, M. and Paterson, E. (1982) *Mothers and Daughters,* London: Heinemann.
Butler, J. (1989) *Review of Child Health Surveillance,* London: HMSO.
Calnan, M. (1982) 'The hospital accident and emergency department: what is its role?', *Journal of Social Policy* 11: 483–502.
——(1988a) 'Images of general practice; the perceptions of the doctor', *Social Science and Medicine* 27: 579–86.

Michael Calnan and Jonathan Gabe

Calnan, M. (1988b) 'Variations in the range of services provided by GPs',
Family Practice 5(2): 94–104.
Calnan, M. and Butler, J.R. (1988) 'The economy of time in general practice:
an estimate of the influence of list size', *Social Science and Medicine*
26(4): 435–551.
Cartwright, A. and Anderson, R. (1981) *General Practice Revisited*, London:
Tavistock.
Crawford, R. (1984) 'A cultural account of "health": control, release and the
social body, in J. McKinlay (ed.) *Issues in The Political Economy of
Health Care*, London: Tavistock.
Davies, C. (1984) 'General practitioners and the pull of prevention',
Sociology of Health and Illness 6: 267–89.
Day, P. and Klein, R. (1986) 'Weighing up opposing models of health care',
Health Service Journal 1: 618–19.
DH (Department of Health) (1989) *Working for Patients*, HMSO: London.
DHSS (Department of Health and Social Security) (1983) *NHS Management
Enquiry (Griffiths Report)*, London: HMSO.
—— (1987) *Promoting Better Health*, London: HMSO.
Drug and Therapeutics Bulletin (1987) 'The Limited List: effects in general
practice' *Drug and Therapeutics Bulletin* 25(6): 21–4.
Enthoven, A.C. (1985) *Reflections on The Management of The National
Health Service*, London: Nuffield Provincial Hospitals Trust.
Freidson, E. (1970) *The Profession of Medicine*, New York: Dodd Mead &
Co.
—— (1984) 'The changing nature of professional control', *Annual Review of
Sociology* 10: 101–20.
—— (1985) 'The reorganization of the medical profession', *Medical Care
Review* 42(11): 11–35.
—— (1986) 'The medical profession in transition', in L. Aiken and D.
Mechanic (eds) *Applications of Social Science to Clinical Medicine and
Health Policy*, New Jersey: Rutgers University Press, pp. 63–79.
Gabe, J. and Bury, M. (1988) 'Tranquillisers as a social problem', *The
Sociological Review* 36(2): 320–52.
General Medical Services Committee (1983) *General Practice: A British
Success*, London: BMA.
Hall, D. (1980) 'Prescribing as social exchange', in R. Mapes (ed.)
Prescribing Practice and Drug Usage, London: Croom Helm.
Haug, M. (1975) 'The deprofessionalisation of everyone', *Sociological Focus*
8(3): 197–213.
Haug, M. and Lavin, B. (1983) *Consumerism in Medical Care – Challenging
Physician's Authority*, Beverley Hills: Sage Publications.
Honigsbaum, F. (1985) 'Reconstruction of general practice: failure of reform'
British Medical Journal 290: 823–6.
Horder, J., Bosanquet, N. and Stocking, B. (1986) 'Ways of influencing the
behaviour of general practitioners', *Journal of the Royal College of
General Practitioners* 36: 516–21.
Jefferys M. and Sachs, H. (1983) *Rethinking General Practice*, London:
Tavistock.

Johnson, T. (1972) *Professions and Power*, London: Macmillan.
—— (1977) 'The professions in the class structure', in R. Scase (ed.) *Industrial Society: Class, Cleavage and Control*, London, Allen & Unwin.
Larkin, G. (1983) *Occupational Monopoly and Modern Medicine*, London: Tavistock.
Larson, M. (1978) *The Rise of Professionalism: A Sociological Analysis*, California: California University Press.
McKinlay, J. and Stoekle, J.D. (1988) 'Corporatization and the social transformation of doctoring', *International Journal of Health Services* 18: 191–201.
Maynard, A. (1984) 'Reassessing NHS evaluation could prove a "blooming" success', *Health and Social Services Journal*, 13 December, p. 1467.
Navarro, V. (1978) *Class Struggle, the State and Medicine*, London: Martin Robertson.
Parkin, F. (1979) *Marxism and Class Theory: A Bourgeois Critique*, London: Tavistock.
Parry, N. and Parry, J. (1976) *The Rise of the Medical Profession*, London: Croom Helm.
Petchey, R. (1989) 'The politics of destabilisation' *Critical Social Policy* 9(1): 82–97.
Royal College of General Practitioners (1985) Towards Quality in General Practice, London: Royal College of General Practitioners.
Saks, M. (1983) 'Removing the blinkers? A critique of recent contributions to the sociology of professions', *Sociological Review* 31(1) 1–21.
Salisbury, C.J. (1989) 'How do people choose their doctor? *British Medical Journal* 299: 608–10.
Shaw, I. (1978) *Patient Participation in General Practice*, Cardiff: Welsh Consumer Council.
Stacey, M. (1988) *The Sociology of Health and Healing*, London: Unwin Hyman.
Tudor Hart, J. (1984) 'Community general practitioners', *British Medical Journal* 288: 1670–3.
Watkins, S. (1987) *Medicine and Labour: The Politics of a Profession*, London: Lawrence & Wishart.
Webster, C. (1988) *The Health Services Since the War*, London: HMSO.
Wilkin, D., Hallam, L., Leavey, R. and Metcalfe, D. (1987) *Anatomy of Urban General Practice*, London: Tavistock.

Chapter seven

Knowledge and control in health promotion: a test case for social policy and social theory
Alan Beattie

Introduction

One of the principal features of health promotion as a field of practice and enquiry is that is very difficult to pin down for descriptive purposes. 'What health promotion is' the subject of fierce and incessant disputes among professional practitioners and policy makers, and it must be said that the battles are waged for the most part on decidely ill-formed theoretical grounds. It has long seemed to me in itself highly significant, and in itself a matter deserving social enquiry, that the large and growing enterprise of health promotion in Britian is so centrally torn apart by disagreements about its basic purposes and methods, and yet that these disagreements have received so little systematic clarification or fundamental review in the light of social theory. A major aim of this chapter, therefore, is to offer a conceptual framework for deliberation on different forms of contemporary health promotion, and to use this framework:

1. to illustrate the tensions and conflicts that mark the development of policy and practice in this field;
2. to highlight some of the points at which debates around health-promotion policy and practice may benefit from re-thinking within the wider terms of reference of social theory;
3. to indicate some directions in which future social enquiry in health promotion could usefully proceed.

This chapter is written from the standpoint of someone extensively involved in the practice of health promotion as well as in its academic scrutiny. What follows should be seen as an example of a practitioner attempting to think through the social issues encountered in this field of work, excited by the possibilities opened by harnessing the sociological imagination, but at every point concerned to see whether (or not) socio-logical insights can help to transform contemporary practice.

The different forms of health promotion: problems of definition and classification

Before the 1980s, the term in general use in this field in Britain was 'health education', and practice was located almost exclusively within public health and preventive medicine. Sociology and psychology were drawn upon in a strictly limited way to provide tools to broaden the scope of epidemiology, for example, to support the use of social epidemiology and behavioural epidemiology to pinpoint suitable targets for intervention, and to improve the success of health education programmes in bringing about behaviour change in target populations. But already in the 1970s, debate on the definitions, purposes and methods of health education had become widespread, prompted in particular by two challenges to the prevailing orthodoxy.

The first challenge was from those who identified within mainstream health education (as an arm of preventive medicine) what they labelled a 'medical model', which they contrasted with a so-called 'educational model' (Engel 1978). This critique in part reflected the views of those health education practitioners who worked in the school system, or who had come into NHS health education units from that occupational background. But there was support from social scientists in contesting the assumption (embodied in the 'medical model') that the principal aim of health education should be to bring about attitude change and behaviour change in 'at-risk' populations (Van Parijs 1980). The alternative (often called the 'educational model') typically took as its focus the giving of information about health risks to permit individual choice of behaviour (Department of Education and Science 1977, HMI 1978). By 1977 there were already several publications which set out this approach as a basis for work in schoools (Dallas 1972, McPhail 1977; Schools Council/Health Education Council 1977)

The second challenge was from those who drew attention to the almost exclusive ambition of recent health education (and preventive medicine generally) to bring about individual change. These critics characterized this as an example of 'blaming-the-victim' philosophies (Crawford 1977); and advocated a move 'up-stream' towards social change models for health education (Freudenberg 1989). Whereas the first challenge reflected (in large measure) a critique of preventive medicine from professional groups outside it (teachers, behavioural scientists, etc.), the second challenge emerged more from a distinctive political grouping (broad left), in which a wide varity of professionals found themselves in alliance (with medical workers often prominent among them.)

There was a rapid proliferation of attempts from the late 1970s onwards to classify the emerging repertoire of different approaches within contemporary health education. None of them is founded on any reasoned basis of broader sociological theory; they offer descriptive typologies that give little or no purchase for wider analysis. But they are all of interest, and they all served a useful purpose in taking forward debate on the changing boundaries of health education.

Tuckett (1979) identified three distinct rationales for health education: (1) to produce changes in belief and behaviour in order to reduce mortality and morbidity; (2) to influence norms and values governing the use of health services; (3) to produce a general understanding of certain more diffuse health issues in order to obtain a population which has a general understanding of health issues and to avoid certain forms of 'undesirable' or not directly definable unhealthy behaviour. In what was one of the earliest attempts to pin down the varieties of health education, Tuckett also hinted at a broader sociological analysis of these various forms:

> Views concerning health and illness in society are always related to the distribution of power and authority within it . . . Health Education is and must be a political and ethical activity. The choice of a health education strategy will both reflect and influence social and political organisations.
>
> (Tuckett 1979)

These remarks were tantalizingly brief, however, appearing only at the end of his paper. His subsequent work reflected his own choice: he went on to develop in a partisan way the particular health education strategy which he favoured (Tuckett *et al.* 1985).

Draper has suggested two different classification schemes. The first in 1980, closely resembled Tuckett's, suggesting that there are three types of health education: (1) education about the body and how to look after it; (2) education about health services and the 'sensible' use of health care resources; (3) education about the wider environment within which health choices are made (Draper *et al.* 1980). The article argued that 'Type 3', described as 'part of the moribund public health tradition', was neglected and deserved more attention. In a later paper Draper extended this scheme to five types as follows: (1) education about the body (including the mind) and how to look after it; (2) education about health services; (3) education about the context, the human habitat, the environment, and how the environment affects health; (4) education about the politics of health, about power and accountability, about impotence or disadvantage; (5) education about health education itself, about its effectiveness and its ethics (Draper 1983). These two schemes go beyond the orthodox 'medical model' in a useful way. But they are essentially lists of content of information of *what* a health educator might seek to transmit to the public. They do not attend to the disputes widespread among professional practitioners at the time he wrote and still common now, about methods, and about *how* health education may be conducted.

Tones, in a series of publications, has developed an increasingly complex typology of health education. A key paper (Tones 1981a) identified 'four different philosophical approaches to the practice of health education'. These were: (1) 'the educational approach', based on the 'principle of informed choice'; (2) 'the preventive approach', to 'modify the behaviours which are responsible for disease'; (3) 'the radical approach', which seeks the roots of health problems and finds them in social, economic and political factors' (4) 'the self-empowerment approach', with the aim of encouraging personal growth – by enhancing self-esteem and self-assertiveness; he notes that this is a way of facilitating the 'informed choice' of approach no. 1, which might otherwise be 'an illusory goal'.

This scheme makes an important advance in attending to process as much as to content; but it has two obvious internal shortcomings. First, the distinction between approaches 1 and 4 seems logically arbitrary – it is as if no. 1 is an end, and no. 4 is the complementary means. Second, the terminology is awkward and confusing 'radical' evokes political reputation, 'preventive' refers to social purposes and 'educational' draws attention to a particular occupational location. Again, the lack of a broader conceptual framework of analysis is apparent. By the early 1980s, commentators on this field in Britain were beginning to link health education with 'health promotion'. This term came into use on the international scene from the late 1970s onwards, principally through the WHO (World Health Organisation 1978), the Canadian National Health and Welfare Office (Canadian Public Health Association 1974) and the US Department of Education, Health and Welfare (1978). The US DEHW definition in 1979 was as follows: 'Health Promotion begins with people who are basically healthy and seeks the development of community and individual measures which and help them to develop lifestyles that can maintain and enhance their state of well-being'.

A subsequent publication from the same source (US Department of Health and Human Services 1982) sees health promotion and health education as inseparably linked within the work of health maintenance organizations 'a combination of motivational, organizational and environmental supports for behaviour conducive to the health of members'.

The WHO European Region Programme on 'Health Education and Lifestyles' (World Health Organization 1981) makes the following remarks on health promotion '[it is] . . . opposed to disease prevention and secondary and tertiary care systems . . . a state of positive well-being. Whereas a health prescription approach could well be dealt with in one system, in the medical care system, a health promotion approach depends on the coordinated efforts of all units of society'.

In Britain, Draper and colleagues published a paper in 1982 which seeks to make a sharp distinction between health promotion and health education:

> The terms Health Promotion and Health Education are not interchangeable. Health promotion covers all aspects of those activities that seek to improve the health status of individuals and communities. It therefore includes both health education and all attempts to produce environmental and legislative change conducive to good public health. Put another way, health promotion is concerned with making healthier choices easier choices.
>
> (Dennis *et al.* 1982)

Tones observes that health promotion is taken by some to describe a distinctive approach to 'marketing' health, that is those more powerful initiatives, within (what he calls) the preventive model, which uses mass-media persuasion tactics borrowed from the worlds of commercial sales and advertising. He sees this as another facet of the 'social engineering' approach – alongside legal, fiscal and other environmental devices; and suggests that such health promotion strategies raise ethical problems, especially that of 'coercion' versus 'voluntarism'. He argues that such social engineering measures need to be accompanied by Health education programmes, to 'operate synergistically' with one another (Tones 1984).

Several other schemes and typologies have subsequently been published that attempt to enumerate the different forms of health education and health promotion (Burkitt 1983; Ewies and Simnett 1984; French and Adams 1986). They are all, with minor variations, similar to those I have already cited, and none of them reaches out to any wider theoretical perspectives to achieve a more systematic and coherent analysis. Likewise, a few studies have been carried out which examine the concepts of health and health education held by different professional groups, approaching the question in a strictly inductive fashion (Collins 1984, Nutbeam 1984). And one recent study has surveyed the views which health education officers (employed in the NHS) take of the most commonly cited models of health education; this study sets out to relate the views held by HEOs to a social-psychological theory of 'work values and action programmes' within occupational groups (Rawson 1985). But again, none of these empirical studies seeks to make connections with a broader analysis of social theory and social organizations. I shall not attempt here to summarize any of this other typological or empirical work. Instead, I shall now move on to present an analytical scheme of my own which does offer possibilities for explicit reference to wider social enquiry.

The repertoire of health promotion: a structural map

My own scheme adopts the device of cross-classification, recommended by C. Wright Mills (1959) to enumerate some of the logical possibilities within the field that is under scrutiny. It sets out the different strategies that are available in contemporary health promotion in terms of two bipolar dimensions namely 'mode of intervention' and 'focus of intervention', as shown in Figure 7.1 (see Beattie 1982).

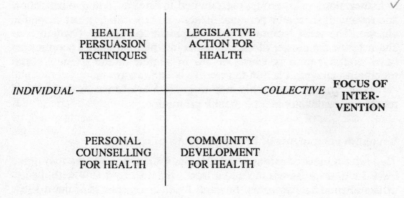

Figure 7.1 Strategies of health promotion
Source: Beattie 1982.

The dimensions of cross-classification used in this map (Fig.7.1) are not taken directly from any single source, and later in this chapter I will comment on some of the wider theoretical frameworks with which the map can usefully be aligned. In this initial formulation, the map deliberately invokes two familiar and long-standing dichotomies in the analysis of social policy. The authoritative/negotiated dimension can serve to draw a parallel with debates about paternalist, prescriptive or top-down forms of social intervention versus participative or 'bottom-up' forms (Hardy 1981; Room 1979). The individual/collective dimension stands in its own right as one of the most stable and enduring axes of conflict in social theory and social policy (Taylor-Goodby and Dale 1981).

I offer the map at this stage in order to summarize and draw attention of some of the key features of the alternative strategies around which debate rages in contemporary health promotion. In this light 'health persuasion techniques' is the term I will use to characterize the cluster of interventions which employ the authority of public-health expertise to re-direct the behaviour of individuals in top-down prescriptive ways. The term 'legislative action for health' I will use to characterize the cluster of interventions which employ the authority of public health expertise to change civic policies so as to improve health – e.g. through environmental controls, taxation, etc. – again in top-down prescriptive ways. The term 'personal counselling for health' I will use to characterize the cluster of interventions in which individual clients (whether alone or in groups) are invited to engage in active reflection and review of their own personal lifestyle and their individual scope for change. The term 'community development for health' I will use to characterize the cluster of interventions in which groups of people who have similar health concerns or are in similar circumstances, come together to take joint action to improve health prospects.

I now propose to use this map to guide a brief historical sketch of recent policy development in health promotion.

Recent developments of health promotion: a sketch

This brief review of recent developments will proceed along two lines. First, I will try to assess the major trends that can be traced within each of the alternative strategies. Second, I will try to pinpoint the overall shape of health-promotion policies within different sectors and at different levels – how the alternative strategies have been mixed and combined, which health-promotion strategies are favoured, and why.

The persistence of health persuasion tactics

This strategy has long historical roots, including temperance campaigns in the nineteenth century, anti-VD propaganda at the time of the 1914–18 war and better-eating campaigns on the 'home front' during the 1939–45 war. The establishment of the Health Education Council (HEC) in 1968 was itself a response to the Cohen Report of 1963 which specifically demanded that much more effort should be put into applying the mass media techniques of commercial advertising for the purposes of 'health persuasion' (Cohen Committee 1964). Many of the campaigns which the HEC itself ran on road safety, on alcohol abuse, on the hazards of smoking, etc. became familiar features of the cultural landscape – on hoardings, in newspapers, in public service announcements on TV or in cinemas, etc. So also did similar campaigns which the HEC in turn subcontracted to the Family Planning Association, on contraceptive choices, on VD risks, etc.

Such tactics have, on the surface, some obvious attractions for policy-makers. They are visible and apparently straightforward as a means of social intervention, and they possess the virtue of being simple to plan: merely requiring selection of relevant messages from current medical knowledge about the risks associated with a particular behaviour and presentation of these messages to appropriate audiences through convenient media (Cust 1979).

Reviews of research on the effectiveness of this strategy, however, have repeatedly shown that it is for the most part strikingly unsuccessful, on its own, in bringing about changes in lifestyles (Gatherer *et al.* 1979). Ever more elaborate socio-psychological theories have been brought to bear on the design of health promotion campaigns, discarding the simplistic 'knowledge–attitude–behaviour model' in favour of the 'health beliefs model' based on Lewin's 'field theory' of motivation (Becker 1985); or in favour of the 'health action model' based on Fishbein's 'value expectancy theory' of personal choice (Fishbein 1976). But even with these impressive and sophisticated tools for 'persuasive communications', the results of such mass-media campaigns have continued to be disappointing (Tones 1981b).

What is most intriguing however about this is the extreme reluctance of the major state agencies of health promotion to accept this solidly founded conclusion. A Health Education Council consultation exercise in 1979 (Beattie 1979a) (in form of a three-day retreat for HEC Officers and Council Members), explored the policy implications of this conclusion but the report was never given the full circulation that had been agreed. An extended piece of action research on the HEC's publications policies which I directed between 1981 and 1985, carried out by Wendy Farrant and Jill Russel, likewise showed that a majority of senior officers of the HEC were not unaware of the scientific evidence on the shortcomings of top-down, one-way campaign strategies focused on individual behaviour change (Farrant and Russel 1985). The reports from this research also proved to be unwelcome to the HEC, and attempts were made to suppress their publication. Ironically, our work during the latter project brought to light a substantial and scholarly research report – for its time definitive – written by senior staff within the HEC some ten years previously (Jones and Grahame 1973). This had come to exactly the same familiar conclusions about the lack of scientific justification for health persuasion campaigns, but this report, also, had been effectively suppressed.

The fallacy of persuasion lingers, since the HEC was dismantled and replaced by the HEA (Health Education Authority) in April 1987, major mass-media campaigns have again been initiated on heroin use and on HIV/AIDS. Both were widely criticized by independent health education experts at the time, to no avail, and both have been found to be of very doubtful worth (DHSS/Welsh Office 1987). The question that emerges quite unmistakably, therefore, is why this strategy has continued to be supported and defended by the major state agencies for health promotion.

Two vivid insider accounts point the finger firmly at government departments as the source of directives to persist with campaign tactics. A brief account of one particular episode by a former research officer at the HEC (St George 1981) suggests that the HEC was manipulated in a puppet-like manner by the DHSS, to serve its own expedient interests. A more extended account by the first Director of Education and Training at the HEC (Sutherland 1987) paints a vivid and colourful picture of the pressures and machinations that consistently led to an over-emphasis on mass campaigns, and to a deliberate avoidance of confrontations with vested interests inimical to more wide-ranging health-promotion initiatives. Our own Health Education Publications study, with privileged access to archival information and informal insider testimonies (Farrant and Russel 1985) showed that the medical establishment were one axis of power that was consistently appeased in the construction of health messages (to the detriment of the agendas of interests on the part of intended clients that were revealed in the develop- mental testing of publications); but that their professional authority was in turn overridden when other powerful lobbies (e.g. in food manufacture and agriculture) seemed likely to be threatened (Farrant and Russel 1986).

The dubious and discredited strategy of health persuasion regularly finds enthusiastic champions in Parliament. Numerous politicians, in both Houses, have made it their personal mission to resurrect the most blatant tactics of medico-moral persuasion around such issues as food and health, and sexuality and health. And indeed, there has emerged a new-right theorist of health promotion, the Director of the Conservative Party-supported Unit for Social Affairs, Digby Anderson. He has made repeated attacks on the 'unprofessional attitudes, inefficient methods, and hopeless dreams' of health educators; and has directly argued the case for behaviour manipulation for example: 'Health Education is about changing people. Those who find this distasteful and would rather "facilitate environments wherein people can make their own health decisions" could realise that their techniques do not become any more practical by being nicer' (Anderson 1980; 1982).

Renewed calls for legislative action for public health

This strategy also has long historical roots. The reinterpretation by McKeown (1976) and Powles (1973) of the relationship between the rise of modern medicine and the transformation of mortality figures in the late-nineteeth and early twentieth centuries has become familiar. Their analysis points of course to environmental interventions – clean water, sanitation, improved diet, better housing and hygienic school buildings – as the major factors that had brought about the dramatic decrease in infant and child mortality before the invention of specific remedies for the cure of bacterial infections in the 1930s and the 1940s.

Other studies have identified more recent instances where legislative measures introduced on a large scale have produced striking benefits for public health. Winter (1985) has shown how the emergency rationing imposed on the home population in Britain during the 1939–45 war led to marked improvements in physical stature and reductions in mortality. Scarrow (1972) has documented the spectacular impact of the 1956 air pollution legislation in reducing mortality and morbidity from respiratory diseases. And Leathard has recounted the effects on the incidence of unwanted pregnancies, of legislation and resource provision related to family planning and abortion clinic services (Leathard 1980). This is to name but a few of the citations that can be invoked in identifying the scientific credentials of this strategy in health promotion. Similar claims are made (with as yet less clear-cut evidence of the social arithmetic of success) for food policies as a factor in coronary mortality; work hazards as a factor in industrial accidents and occupational cancers (etc); fluoridation of public water supplies as a factor in dental health; traffic controls as a factor in road safety statistics; fiscal policies regarding cigarettes and alcoholic drinks as factors in ill-health associated with these products; benefit levels for old-age pensioners as factors in avoidable morbidity in elderly; and so on.

The case for intervention to improve health by legislative and environmental measures has been argued with increasing force and vigour throughout the 1980s (Draper *et al.* 1977; Kennedy 1983; Politics of Health Group 1974; Doyal 1981). A decisive thread of evidence supporting this case in general has been inexorably spun by a series of reports documenting the growing social and regional inequalities in health and disease in Britain (Black *et al.* 1980; Whitehead 1987; King's Fund 1988). And each of these major reports in turn has made systematic recommendations for fiscal, economic, environmental and legislative action to diminish the widening divide between the health experience of different social classes. The WHO initiatives and guidelines on 'Health for All by the Year 2000' specify 'addressing inequalities' as a major aim (World Health Organization 1985); and they endorse a range of environmental measures in support of this.

My overall impression (although I know of no research that documents it), is that awareness of the logic and merits of this strategy is now more prominent among health promotion professionals than it has ever been. The 'ecological' model of health, which supports and informs legislative action for public health has become more familiar during the 1980s (Baric 1982) – which may perhaps have some links with the wider growth in environmental awareness and in the green movement. The wider ecological parameters that need to be encompassed for successful coronary prevention initiatives – related to the food industry, agricultural policies, legal and fiscal controls over cigarette smoking, etc. – are being acknowledged (HEC/CPG/DHSS 1984). More concerted policy directives concerning the 'health environment' are becoming widespread, for example, food and health policies right across district health authorities (Eskin 1983), anti-smoking policies agreed at the level of a school, a hospital, an office, or even across a health district, ASH (Action on Smoking and Health), CPG (the Coronary Prevention Group) and LFC (London Food Commission) have been prominent in providing 'action-guides' for agencies and authorities willing to move towards such policies for a healthy environment (Olsen *et al.* 1981, London Food Commission 1986).

It should not escape attention though, that this upsurge of awareness and activity has mostly been within well-defined limits. The environment that has come under the scrutiny of the new health legislators so far has been the local environment, the immediate environment – the environment in which the larger vested interests of commerce and industry have least stake; the environment which probably has the least salience in the determination of larger social inequalities in health. This is not to say that these renewed activities at the legislative level have not been worthwhile – and perhaps a valuable political education also for those engaged in such activities; it is merely to recognize the limits of action so far.

More far-reaching in their ambition are the recent activities of the 'Healthy cities' project in Britain, which is part of a European programme initiated by the WHO in 1985 (Ashton *et al.* 1986). This is based on a recognition by WHO that an important implication of an ecological and social view of health is that human habitats – the settlement, the city – can provide a specific focus for bringing together good practice in health promotion. By 1988, twenty-four European cities were designated as part of the programme, including four in Britain: Camden/Bloomsbury in London, and Liverpool, Glasgow and Belfast (Ashton and Seymour 1988).

Against these signs of revival of the 'moribund public health tradition' (Dennis *et al.* 1982) needs to be set the most striking feature of the recent vicissitudes of the ecological/legislative strategy for health promotion. This is – I suggest – the consistent rejections that the major reports have met with at the hands of government ministers. Both the Black Report in 1980, which had been commissioned by the DHSS; and the Whitehead Report in 1986, which updated the Black Report, and which had been commissioned by the HEC (Black *et al.* 1980) were not merely 'rubbished' by government representatives; they were both in effect suppressed – plans to publish them were abandoned. In the case of 'The Health Divide' the publicity it was nevertheless given by HEC Officers coincided closely in time with the dismantling of the HEC (as a Quango) and its replacement by the HEA. The episode appeared to lend credence to the idea that the government was seeking to tighten its grip on the health promotion experts, to forestall and eliminate unwelcome public attention to health inequalities.

Concern at the government's suppression of health statistics and of health promotion policy recommendations which it finds uncongenial, should not blind us though to other questions that need to be asked about attempts to revive the grand tradition of legislative action for health promotion. Sooner or later, some serious debate would be in order, to examine the dangers as well as the benefits of renewed intervention along those lines. A recent paper by Pat Garside (from within the new public health movement) has suggested that 'we need to be aware of the cultural, moral, and ethical dimensions' of the key instances of successful reform on the part of the 'old' public health movement (Garside 1987). She argues that earlier reformers (Chadwick, Booth) were 'not so democratically sound that their precedents can be followed with any political confidence, rather there were (and are) dangers of 'collectivist authoritarianism' in social reform focused too exclusively on health itself (as against 'the problems of the community at large').

The spread of personal counselling for health

The adoption of counselling and group-work techniques and personal-development programmes for the purpose of health promotion has been rapid and far-reaching in many different settings within the last 10 years or so. The cluster of theories and methods associated with this line of work have their origins in psychodynamic and post-Freudian 'humanistic' psychology and social psychology: and they have recognizably emerged within the context of the 'mental health movement'. The most obvious strands – frequently intertwined in complex ways – have been in 'biographical medicine' within psychiatry, general practice, psychiatric nursing, etc. (Armstrong 1979), in progressive or 'pupil-centred' education, initially in primary schools, subsequently in personal tutoring and personal – social education in secondary schools and further education colleges (Walkerdine 1984); and in individual casework among social workers, probation officers, marriage-guidance counsellors, hospital chaplains and several other kinds of therapists and professional and lay helpers (Campbell 1984). As with individual persuasion techniques, an elaborate range of detailed psychological models – what Ingleby calls the 'Psy-complex' (Ingleby n.d.) – has been brought to bear on the personal counselling process, but there are significant common features in the style of intervention that they underpin. They focus on 'life-review', on eliciting the personal story or narrative of the client, and prompting identification and (in a variety of different ways) clarification and interpretation of the social situations or subjective impulses that trouble the client; leading to systematic reflection on the scope for personal choice and change, then moving on to rehearsal of the processes that will be entailed in accomplishing the changes that are desired – e.g. confidence building, self-assertion, decision making, action planning, contract making, etc. (Kanfer and Goldstein 1975).

Such help may be provided by an individual counsellor on a 1:1 basis; and/or through the processes within a group of peers (with a group leader); but increasingly these forms of face-to-face help may be supplemented or even replaced by printed health promotion/health education resources, in the form of self-study materials. These texts offer the process 'in print' – triggering life-review by questions, by case histories or incidents that resonate with the circumstances of the reader, etc.; then structuring the full sequence of self-empowerment through to personal action plans and even to negotiation and bargaining (over a life change) with a partner: lover, spouse, work-mate, boss . . . (Open University 1982).

A number of studies are available which report marked benefits for the clients of personal counselling for health (PCH). One set of examples concerns the success of 'anticipatory guidance' programmes in diminishing severe depression and other psychiatric disturbance in people who have suffered a bereavement (Murray-Parkes 1979). Another self of examples refers to the impact of programmes of training in 'generic' social skills (so-called 'life skills') on young people (adolescents), who turn out to be better able to resist unwanted social pressures (e.g., as regards smoking, drinking, sexual relationships), and to be better able to persevere with 'healthier lifestyles' on a wide front (Botvin 1984). What is striking in such programmes is that they do not need even to mention specific risks to health (smoking, drugs, etc.), and that 'selling' a particular line in a one-sided way appears to be counterproductive. The major precept in such PCH work is therefore frequently summed up as 'self-empowerment', and the non-directive and client-orientation of the helping process is highly prized by many of its proponents (Rogers 1969).

The increasingly widespread resort to the PCH strategy on the part of clients perhaps reflects their enthusiasm in turn for the personal autonomy and self-determination that it promises (Blackham 1978). But there has been criticism, inevitably, from those who favour other standpoints in health promotion. One set of commentators point to the dangers of covert invasion of the private domain – of policing of values, of infringement of personal rights and of surveillance of intimate biography – that irresponsible or professionally inexpert use of such techniques may encounter (Halmos 1965).

Another critique is that in its emphasis on self-conscious verbalization and self-disclosure, and on future-oriented life planning, the PCH strategy puts a premium on middle-class values and attributes, which may perpetuate problems of poor accessibility for working-class clients (Bernstein and Henderson 1974) – which may raise hopes and expectations within a privileged 'pastoral' space, which are rapidly confounded in all other departments of a client's life (Radical Therapy Collective 1974).

Finally, while the PCH strategy may be more disposed than are persuasion methods to grant the client an active role, its emphasis is clearly and almost exclusively on helping individuals to learn to cope (rather than to change their circumstances), and it therefore does not escape the charge of 'victim blaming', even if it is a more benign version (Pattison 1988; Pearson 1973).

Many of the major health-promotion agencies, in the statutory and in the voluntary sector, have been prominent throughout the 1980s in supporting and developing PCH as a major element within their overall programmes, – including the HEC/HEA, the Family Planning Association, MIND, National Marriage Guidance Council (Relate), and training in the associated techniques has become widely available in the general professional preparation and continuing education of doctors, nurses, schoolteachers, chaplains, social workers and youth workers (Priestley and McGuire 1983).

The rise of community development for health

This is perhaps the most recent addition to the repertoire of health-promotion strategies in Britain. Its relative newness, as well as some of its unfamiliar features, perhaps explains why community development for health (CDH) does not even appear on the map for most commentators on the changing forms of health promotion and health education. Like PCH (as seen in the previous section), CDH appears in many different guises and under different labels (sometimes misleadingly): e.g., self-help health; community-oriented health education; health outreach; community health action, etc. (Watts 1985). And also like PCH, it has emerged in several different contexts with a set of ideas and working methods that are broadly similar across those diverse contexts. The pedigree includes community-oriented social work, adult and community education and direct voluntary action by embattled groups; women's groups (Smith 1981), black and minority ethnic groups (McNaught 1988; Anionwu 1988), local residents' groups (Rosenthal 1981), etc.

The very form of the action that the strategy of CDH favours is one that emphasizes self-organization and mutual assistance within groups of like-minded people; so, as a consequence, 'expertise' or theory that is external or extraneous to the group is a less urgent requirement and a less prominent feature within CDH initiatives (Beattie 1986). Certain precepts, however, are commonly emphasized in the working processes and styles of CDH projects. A group or groups of like-minded people, who recognize themselves as having common experiences in health matters, come together to discuss and review their concerns, to take stock of their situations, to identify mutual problems and to share in the process of clarifying options, working out appropriate joint action and setting about the process of trying to change their circumstances. As in PCH, the agenda of action would be expected to reflect the concerns of the 'client', but in the case of CDH the client is the group – the collectivity whose common interests and joint action plans are canvassed through the style of work characteristic of this strategy. As many proponents of CDH have observed, it is a way of helping groups of people who are otherwise alienated or depowered in matters of health – the most deprived or oppressed groups – to 'find a voice' for themselves (Rosenthal 1980).

The role of the health promotion worker in CDH initiatives is also one of the features that is relatively novel and unfamiliar, frequently misunderstood and often difficult to sustain (Henderson and Thomas 1980). It may include helping to identify potential groups, by community surveys and consultative exercises, and to bring them together. It may include acting as a facilitator to a group, as an 'animateur' who ensures that the process of sharing and joint deliberation and action proceeds – by managing the necessary debate, by mobilizing resources to support the work of the group, by securing access to significant power-holders in local health and welfare services, etc. The CDH worker may also act as an advocate for such a group in wider circles and within official channels, and may 'network' by bringing together groups and other people who can act as resources on a larger scale – from immediate neighbourhood to region, etc. (Chaplin and Adams 1986).

One of the sources of puzzlement and confusion around CDH as a strategic option, is that it is frequently perceived in ways that reflect the preoccupations of the other health-promotion strategies, and which merely assimilate CDH to those other priorities (Beattie 1986). It is sometimes seen as simply a way of getting 'official' (predetermined, prescriptive) health agendas and messages more efficiently to groups of the population who are otherwise 'hard-to-reach': the 'community out-reach' stance. This is perhaps characteristic of some recent 'Community approaches' in coronary prevention, drug abuse and AIDS work. Or it may be seen as merely a way in which individuals may benefit from the helping process within peer groups: aspiring to no more than individual change by self-empowerment, along the line of PCH. This is perhaps the feature that distinguishes CDH from the health self-help movement – related but different. Or CDH may be viewed principally as a device for ensuring that there is more thorough 'co-ordination' of the complex mix of health and welfare services at local level, so that fewer of the most needy 'fall through the net' of provision – which is more akin to the 'legislative action' strategy, and the CDH specialist who is assimilated to this model will be acting as an 'interface' worker, seeking to foster better interagency co-operation. There are, however, increasing numbers of accounts of local-community health-action projects which make it clear that this is a distinctive approach, which can mobilize groups, get their voice heard in relevant places and contribute to the process of enfranchisement or emancipation of the groups concerned (Community Health Initiatives Resource Unit/London Community Health Resources 1987).

The high profile that CDH has achieved in the last decade in Britain is quite striking. Ten years ago there were scarcely a handful of projects taking forward this style of work (Hubley 1980): in 1981 the London Community Health Resource (LCHR) was set up within the London Voluntary Services Council to support the proliferating CDH initiatives in the London area; in 1983 CHIRU (the Community Health Initiatives Resource Unit) was established at the National Council for Voluntary Organisations to do the same job for the expanding numbers of projects around Britain as a whole. In April 1988, these two combined and became independent as a new membership organization, NCHR (National Community Health Resource). This has had major funding from the DHSS and the HEA, and two of its major developmental programmes are perhaps characteristic – the Women's Health Network and the Black Health Forum (National Community Health Resource 1988). The HEA itself in 1988 established a new Division (one of the six that make up the HEA) for 'Professional and Community Development'; and several of the recently appointed staff there have been recruited from backgrounds in prominent CDH projects. The

177

HEC/HEA have helped to sponsor much of the rapidly growing literature on CDH, and it is interesting to see how the 'health focus' is now attracting considerable interest within the wider world of 'generic' community work and community development (Saunders 1988).

However, the rise to prominence of CDH strategies is not without its problematic aspects. The difficulties created by the assimilation of CDH – conceptually and in practice – to quite different schools of thought within health promotion have been mentioned. Governmental disapproval of the term 'community development for health' has prompted a widely publicized controversy within the HEA during 1989. At its meeting in April that year, one senior member of the HEA Board identified the terms of reference of the debate quite unambiguously, observing that: 'the phrase community development carries echoes of an earlier and outdated social philosophy that is inappropriate for present Government policies.[1] The face of the newly established 'Professional and Community Development' Division as the HEA currently hangs in the balance, while a high-level and high-speed audit exercise is carried out.

Indeed, the emerging mainstream of CDH projects encounters several critiques. Perhaps the most obvious is that it is sometimes unforgivably naive in its claim to be able to transform the lives and social prospects of deprived groups. CDH initiatives in practice often find themselves recapitulating the experiences of that earlier generation of community-development projects in Britain in the early 70s, sponsored by the Home Office, which focused on housing and social-planning issues (Community Development Projects 1977); as well as of related experiences in the USA in the late 60s and early 70s (Marris and Rein 1975). These reveal quite fundamental problems in a mode of work which sets out to give a voice to the underprivileged, yet which is paid for from state funds. Trouble starts as soon as the communities who are the focus of this attention start to get mobilized, and (inevitably) start to challenge, confront and criticize existing services or policies – to 'bite the hand that feeds them' (Loney 1983). Related to this is the persistent doubt whether local action can ever achieve more than marginal and token victories in the face of the larger social inequalities and social injustices which, of course, reflect policies at national level (Craig *et al.* 1982).

The changing shape of health promotion

The analysis presented in the last few pages reveals considerable growth of activity within the last decade in all directions on my fourfold map: continuing paradoxes in the deployment of persuasion techniques; hesitant and often beleaguered efforts to revive legislative action; an astonishing efflorescence of personal counselling for health; and a marked advance (from a meagre base) of community-development initiatives. But this analysis also highlights, and I hope begins to explain the deep divisions of view that surround the development of health-promotion policies – swinging, as I have tried to show, between the most fundamental poles of social theory and political action: between individualistic and collectivist modes of intervention, and between paternalist, 'imposed' and consultative 'participatory' forms of authority.

Another line of enquiry beckons invitingly at this point, namely to try to map the changing overall shape of health-promotion policies in different sectors and at different levels: to show how alternative strategies have been mixed and combined, which ones have been favoured at different times in different places, and why I would like to offer a few glimpses of the sort of analysis that promises to be interesting, with apologies for the brief and preliminary nature of the material I can present in this chapter – in some respects this is little more than a fast re-run of an already sketchy vignette of contemporary history.

Health services

The HEC between 1968 and 1987 pushed, and was pulled, in several directions simultaneously in ways that often appear contradictory. It devoted the largest amounts of its money to health propaganda campaigns, sometimes evidently against the better judgement of its own officers and expert advisors (Sutherland 1987). At the same time it invested heavily in pioneering a whole series of new programmes for personal – social – health education in schools; and in doing so became not only the most prominent agency of support for the so-called 'pastoral curriculum' in schools, but also (through that support) the single biggest resource for curriculum innovation in the school system, after the demise of the Schools Council (Hyde 1983; Reid 1981). It also provided substantial amounts of pump-priming support to a cohort of local demonstration projects in community development for health (Grigg pers. comm.). And in some publications, at least, the HEC addressed, albeit tentatively, the legislative and fiscal changes essential 'to make the healthier choices the easier choices', as in the case of coronary prevention (Health Education Council/Coronary Prevention Group/Department of Health and Social Security 1984). Given the HEC's awareness of the whole matrix of strategies, the political considerations that determined the favouring of high-profile mass-media work deserve careful analysis, as do the repeated reflexes of recoil and suppression in reaction to modest exercises in thinking about social change strategies. Such an analysis would provide bench-marks to examine the way policy is shaped at the HEA, where the early signs are that they will be constrained even more tightly by short planning cycles, by budgets earmarked for specific high profile campaigns and by disapproval of projects that stray too far towards the collectivist pole.

The DHSS 'Care in Action' guidelines (Department of Health and Social Security 1981) include a section on 'Health Promotion/Disease Prevention' and the DHSS organized a series of seminars on 'Prevention' for Regional Health Authorities (Department of Health and Social Security 1983–5). The RHAs have without exception responded by incorporating into their 10-year strategic plans a section on 'Health promotion/disease prevention' (Castle and Jacobson 1987). Some are more detailed than others; many consist mainly of 'targets' for the reduction of 'avoidable mortality and morbidity'; some go further and spell out a major new area of co-operation between health authorities and local voluntary organizations in health promotion and/or community care. It is fair to say, however, that the majority of RHA plans draw on an unreconstructed 'health persuasion' model, and systematic appraisal of strategic options for health promotion is conspicuous by its absence.

At District Health Authority level, the HEC itself ran some seminars on health promotion for DHA Chairmen (Health Education Council 1983). In the absence of any survey of DHA plans, I can do no more than comment briefly on two to which I have access. In Victoria Health Authority in London in 1984 (before a further reorganization) an impressively systematic 'Strategy for prevention and health promotion' was prepared by a member of the Community Medicine staff (St George 1984), which adopted my own fourfold map as a 'conceptual framework . . . to clarify the options that are available to the Authority' . . . and to establish 'a comprehensive and integrated programme of activities'. In this case, the framework was explicitly used to argue the case for extending health-promotion policy away from the traditional 'medical model' and towards all three alternatives in Paddington and North Kensington Health Authority (also in London; also further reorganized within the last year) the Health Education Department established a coherent policy within which CDH played a prominent part, and which became the context for a long and cumulative series of projects and research studies exploring the practicalities of CDH within a health education unit (Drennan 1985, 1986). It is an outstanding example of a deliberate, sustained drive to establish the feasibility of CDH as a centrepiece within a DHA's health-promotion policy.

The place that community health councils might play in health-promotion-policy formation has also received attention. The HEC ran a seminar for CHC Chairs (Health Education Council *et al.* 1983). And some CHCs have sponsored innovative experiments in community participation, for example the Children's Health Club in St Thomas'/West Lambeth CHC in Kennington, South London (Levine *et al.* 1981) and the Catford Community Development Project at Lewisham CHC in SE London (Lewisham Community Health Council 1986). A national survey by Piette indicated, however, that most CHCs gave a low priority to health promotion and typically had a limited and traditional view of it (Piette 1985). She suggested that CHCs needed to be much better informed about the strategic repertoire of health promotion and that their most useful contribution would lie in pressing DHAs to develop more systematic wide-ranging policies for health promotion.

Other sectors

Because the focus of this book is on the health service, it would be inappropriate to examine in depth the shape of policies for health promotion in the several other settings in which it occurs. But a brief mention seems essential if only as a reminder of the complex policy issues that arise because of this multiplicity of locations.

For example, much of the momentum of the spread of PCH work has been carried by the school system. The HEC started these waves of curriculum innovation in partnership with the Schools Council in the mid-70s, then carried on alone; but with increasingly firm support in DES and HMI reports and guidelines. But very recently much of that momentum has been abruptly arrested. The whole field of sex education and education for personal relationships (which overlaps very extensively with health education especially in its recent form of personal-social development and pastoral (tutoring) is now heavily curtailed by the new and far-reaching legal framework established by the 1986 Education Act (Department of Education and Science 1987). This gives responsibility for deciding whether sex education should occur at all in a school to the school governors.; if it does, whether parents should be able to withdraw their child from such lessons; and (again if it does) what form it should take, subject to the requirement (enshrined in the Act) that it should be provided 'within a moral framework', that is, must 'have due regard to moral considerations and the value of family life'. On top of this, the 1988 Education Reform Act, in its plans for a National Curriculum makes no mention whatsoever, at any point, of health education or personal-social education – in spite of their striking rise to prominence in schools in recent years (National Association for Pastoral Care in Education 1988). There was just a hint of what might be government thinking on this in the 1987 White paper on the proposals for a National Curriculum (Department of Education and Science/ Welsh Office 1987). This did mention health education (but not personal-social education, of which it forms the largest part) – but only to suggest that it should be linked to biology teaching – a view that has been insupportable for many years, and which even appears to contradict the 1986 Act so far as sex education is concerned. The National

Curriculum Council is expected to report in 1990 on the possible place of personal–social education, health education and other 'cross-curriculum' topics; but at present the whole future of the personal-development strategy for HE in schools is fraught with new uncertainties.

Several of the individual voluntary organizations who have been prominent in the health field over many years have shown a characteristic pattern of 'diversification' from an original narrow focus on campaigning and lobbying for legal action of specific health issues (e.g. FPA on Abortion Law Reform; MIND on reform of the Mental Health Acts; Age Concern on benefits for older people, etc). The have typically extended their work more broadly across the strategic map of HP. The FPA moved into counselling, groupwork, and personal–social–health education; and also intermittently into community work (The Grapevine Project; the FPA 'outpost' at the Albany Community Centre, Deptford) MIND developed extensive programmes of information, education and group support work, with extensive networks in local communities. Age Concern has compiled directories of community-based initiatives and extended its personal education work in several directions. These examples perhaps indicate that constructive exploration of the repertoire of health-promotion stragegies, and the interweaving of different approaches is an important developmental pathway for such agencies in their serarch for an effective 'strategic mix'. Current cuts in state funding for these agencies are now forcing rather stark choices on them, however, prompting full internal review, and strong pressure to 'trim'; and there are obvious tensions between returning to a narrow, more medically defined focus and moving forward with a firm commitment to participative, consumer-centred work (Cooper and Lybrand 1988).

It is local authorities that have been the most prominent supporters of legislative action for health in the past few years, and the revival of the 'public health tradition' has been closely associated with the reconstitution of health departments within a number of authorities (Moran 1985). A marker of this was a two-day conference in July 1987 organized by Health Rights, entitled 'rethinking public health: an agenda for local government' (Health Rights 1987). This was, amongst other activities, the occasion for the launch of new 'Public Health Alliance' which brings together several bodies with a stake in legal and environmental action for health, including a consortium of LAs. However, the axis of development in HP policies is beset with difficulties. Several of the LAs who pioneered new intitiatives in this direction were in fact metropolitan authorities, and were dismantled in 1986 (for example, Greater London Council 1985); several others appear to be among those hardest hit by the community charge-capping of LAs – the LAs involved in the public health revival appear to be exclusively those with Labour Party majorities. The WHO 'Healthy Cities' network mentioned earlier (p. 172) may be extending the lives of some of these intitiatives.

Health promotion as a challenge in social administration

I claimed earlier that my 'structural map' of health-promotion strategies offers a basis for an analysis of recent policy debates that can usefully make connections with wider theoretical discussions. An initial move in this direction is to relate policy debates in health promotion to the broader arguments that are common in the field of social administration. Three current issues will serve to illustrate the possibilities: they concern disputes about political philosophy, claims to professionalism and competing notions of accountabilty.

Conflicting political philosophies in health promotion

It must be clear from the analysis I have offered so far that different HP/HE strategies tend to correspond with broadly different political orientations. For example, the call to revive legislative and environmental action for public health has in the main come from 'old-left' groupings, frequently located in LA contexts and demanding more systematic planning by the state, both centrally and locally. The CDH strategy has emerged most visibly from broadly 'new-left' groupings, heterogeneous and often associated with the pattern since the 1960s of 'single issue' political activism. The persistent invocation of persuasion tactics I cannot avoid seeing as commonly bound-up with a traditionalist broadly 'conservative' political ideology, which perhaps finds in campaigns directed at individual behaviour modification an acceptable 'minimal' role for the state: giving people information 'for their own good', so that, if they don't act upon it, that's 'their bad luck'. The political philosophies behind PCH activities are more elusive. They are often claimed indeed to be 'apolitical'; it appears to be a strategy that lends itself both to being annexed and co-opted by the 'new right' – who see in its anti-collective stance the promise of privatization and individual self-help; and simultaneously to being colonized by moderates, liberals, democrats and some fractions of the new left who approve of its anti-authoritarian and humanistic style.

In Figure 7.2; I have attempted to portray these connections, and to summarize a framework for delibration on questions of political conflict in health promotion.[2] I have no doubt that the clarity and cogency of decision making in this field would be greatly enhanced by systematic use of recent work on the analysis of political ideologies in the welfare

PATERNALIST

HEALTH PERSUASION TECHNIQUES 'CONSERVATIVE'	*LEGISLATIVE ACTION FOR HEALTH* 'REFORMIST'
– reluctant collectivists, minimalists, segregators	– Marxists, Fabians, centrists, dirigistes
– *deficit* model	– *deprivation* model
– individual inadequacies require correction	– social injustices require techno-bureaucratic recuperation
– individual risks require control, – elite privileges are protected	– unequal life–chances require resource redistribution
– sponsored mobility for select individuals	

INDIVIDUALIST ——————————— **COLLECTIVIST**

PERSONAL COUNSELLING FOR HEALTH 'LIBERTARIAN'	*COMMUNITY DEVELOPMENT FOR HEALTH* 'RADICAL PLURALIST'
– anti-collectivists, privatizers	– post-Marxists, Utopians
– *opportunity* model	– *emancipation* model
– personal troubles require review	– social discontents require sharing and articulation
– active reshaping of own biography	– popular movements for community mobilization and direct action
– individual mobility on basis of free competition	

PARTICIPATORY

Figure 7.2 Conflicting political philosophies in health promotion

state, of the sort that I have drawn on in this representation. Policy making in health promotion needs to become much more familiar and more comfortable with the range of antagonistic value positions within a pluralist society, so as to openly acknowledge and work with such conflicts in the way that other welfare sectors have done – such as social services planning (Walker 1984) and educational planning (Lawton 1973).

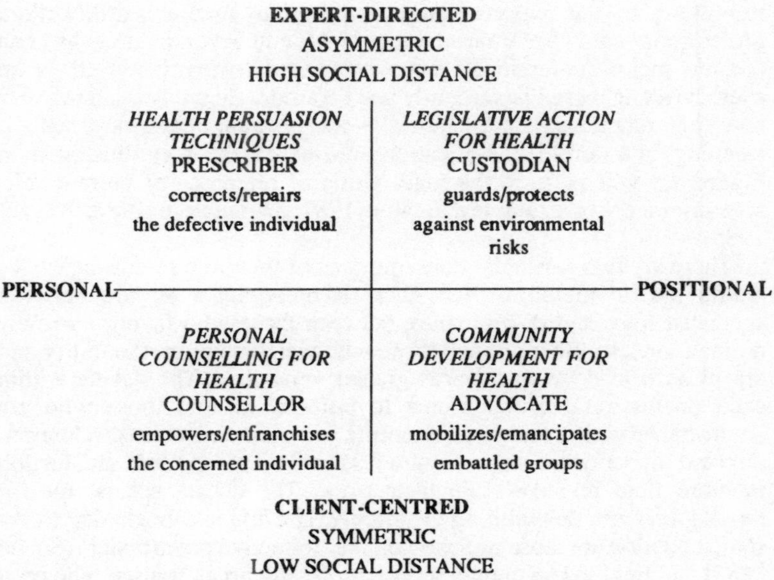

EXPERT-DIRECTED
ASYMMETRIC
HIGH SOCIAL DISTANCE

HEALTH PERSUASION TECHNIQUES PRESCRIBER corrects/repairs the defective individual	*LEGISLATIVE ACTION FOR HEALTH* CUSTODIAN guards/protects against environmental risks

PERSONAL ──────────────────── POSITIONAL

PERSONAL COUNSELLING FOR HEALTH COUNSELLOR empowers/enfranchises the concerned individual	*COMMUNITY DEVELOPMENT FOR HEALTH* ADVOCATE mobilizes/emancipates embattled groups

CLIENT-CENTRED
SYMMETRIC
LOW SOCIAL DISTANCE

Figure 7.3 Shifting professional boundaries in health promotion
Source: Beattie 1984a.

Shifting professional boundaries in health promotion

The opening-up of new strategic directions for health promotion has profound links with shifts in the ways in which health-related professionals actually work. Within each of the different strategies for health promotion is embedded a distinctive paradigm for the professional/client relationship, such that what the professional does in practice is quite different in each strategy Figure 7.3 is an attempt to summarize the current repertoire of different roles that practitioners of health promotion may play, in terms of differently ordered social relationships with clients.[3]

The established and mainstream professions have become increasingly interested and involved in health promotion at a time when independently of one another, each of the professions has been vigorously examining and seeking to consolidate their own knowledge base, their definitions of professional competence, etc. It is striking that within each major profession in turn there are increasing claims that health promotion lies at the foundations of their work; and the widening repertoire of roles in health promotion is clearly becoming a central element in the recasting of professional/client relationships and the rethinking of the experts that is appropriate to the health/welfare professions as they look ahead to the 1990s and beyond. As far as I can see, no major professional group has failed to involve itself in an exercise along these lines recently and I confidently predict that in every case (e.g. medicine, nursing, social work, hospital chaplaincy, school-teaching) a fourfold classification scheme of the sort illustrated in Figure 7.3 will pick up the main terms of reference of current self-scrutiny (see, for examples, Beattie 1987; Durguerian 1982; Keyzer 1985).

There are two particular consequences of this 'role re-casting' that I would like to mention. First, there is emerging a tension between specialist roles and diffuse roles, between those who favour narrowly defined job specifications and those who welcome more flexibility and are pleased to develop towards greater versatility. The debate within each professional group seems to polarize around those who are comfortable with a technical-scientific view of their role (the 'expert-directed' upper quadrants in Figure 7.3); and those who find satisfaction in more fluid boundaries in their work. The debate seems ripe for moving on from this limiting dichotomy. Useful ideas beginning to get some attention are those of Schon on the 'reflective practitioner' (Schon 1983) and England on human service professionals as 'artists' who need to improvise creatively to put together an appropriate mix of practice on the basis of 'theoretical pluralism' (England 1986). Much discussion and innovation in professional training will lie ahead if this sort of rethink is to go forward.

A second consequences of the parallel trends towards 'extended professional roles' in health promotion concerns new ambiguities in the demarcations between different professional groups. There is the irony, for instance, that almost every professional in health promotion (it sometimes seems) wants to become a counsellor. The attractions – logical, personal, maybe even financial, etc. – of this newer role have the effect of leaving the other quadrants of the role map rather thinly occupied and leading to overcrowding in the section to which everyone wants to migrate and in which different groups are surprised to find themselves in such numerous and diverse professional company (Campbell 1985). This raises new issues for inter-professional education, shared learning, collaborative work and team development – issues which are widely recognized but on which it proves very difficult to make practical progress (Lonsdale *et al.* 1980).

Competing structures of accountability in health promotion

This theme is closely connected with the re-casting of professional roles. In the very period when some fractions within health promotion

PRESCRIPTIVE

HEALTH PERSUASION TECHNIQUES 'PROFESSIONALIST'	LEGISLATIVE ACTION FOR HEALTH 'MANAGERIALIST'
– agenda determined by expert	– agenda determined by bureaucratic rules
– validated by colleagues (peers in the craft)	– validated by scientific–legal authority

PRIVATE ———————————————————————— PUBLIC

PERSONAL COUNSELLING FOR HEALTH 'CONSUMERIST'	COMMUNITY DEVELOPMENT FOR HEALTH 'SYNDICALIST'
– agenda determined by the enterprising patron/customer	– agenda determined by collective negotiation among allies

PARTICIPATIVE

Figure 7.4 Competing structures of accountability in health promotion
Source: Beattie 1979b.

have been actively seeking 'occupational closure' by setting-up a register of recognized/qualified practitioners (to tread the time-honoured avenue to professionalization), others have begun to realize that the extending repertoire of roles leads to severe conditions within the professionalizing tendency. Some of those favouring the PCH role and strategy recognize that this is in fact a challenge to traditional professional modes of regulation; while those favouring CDH often actively and explicitly link this to a belief in deprofessionalization. These debates can usefully be seen as worked examples of broader discussions around professional power, managerialism and the representation of consumer interests in social welfare systems.

Figure 7.4 is an attempt to summarize the wider terms of reference that it would be helpful to bring to bear on such questions within the health promotion.

With this structural map to hand, I will draw out just two implications. The first is that much of the acrimony and ferocity of the disputes over alternative strategies of health promotion recently are a clear expression of concepts of accountability. There has been in recent health promotion simultaneously a marked 'tightening of the grip' by powerful professionals and bureaucracies, especially in the DHSS/ Health Education Authority spheres of activity; and a vigorous opening up of consumer power and voluntary action – domains which typically view the professionas as 'disabling' (Wilding 1982) and the bureaucracies as 'insensitive' (Clode *et al.* 1987). A second implication of this line of thought is that the appeals widely made (by the WHO, the Public Health Alliance and others) for 'inter-agency action' in health promotion need careful examination. As the 1987 Audit Commission Report on Community Care showed with surprising clarity (Audit Commission 1987), there are major and often insuperable obstacles to co-operation between agencies at local level that spring directly from the different administrative structures of local authority, health district and voluntary organizations. Not merely may the 'professional self-image' and standpoint of health-promotion practitioners differ according to where they have chosen to work, the lines of authority and accountability they operate within will force them into quite different postures in relation to the public (Beattie 1988). Attempts at interagency co-operation for health promotion will prove an intriguing testing ground for theory and practice in this area.

Health promotion as a frontier of contemporary cultural change

The lines of analysis that can be opened up around the administrative challenges raised by contemporary health promotion are, I think, vitally important for coherent reflection on practice and on policymaking. But this is essentially middle-range theory; and for me, one of the major attractions of the fourfold mapping that I have presented in this chapter is the links that it makes possible with some longer-range theoretical arguments. I am convinced that the development, use and contestation of health-promotion strategies at all levels of modern society (by whatever agencies and sections of society) is centrally bound up with some very deep currents of cultural change. We need theoretical frameworks that can give us some purchase on these processes; and I would now like to present three brief illustrations of some promising possibilities, which (in turn) conceptualize health promotion as a moral economy, as a mode of socialization and as a system of rhetoric.

Health promotion as a moral economy

The scheme devised by Mary Douglas (1970; 1978) for examining the boundaries of the moral economy, and the way these are patrolled, defended, fought over and sometimes moved around, its defined in terms of the two dimensions of grid and group. 'Grid' refers to the total system of rules and constraints which a culture imposes on its people; and 'group' refers to the extent to which an individual is pressured or coerced through being a member of a bounded face-to-face unit; it is a measure of the strength of association. In Figure 7.5 I have aligned the

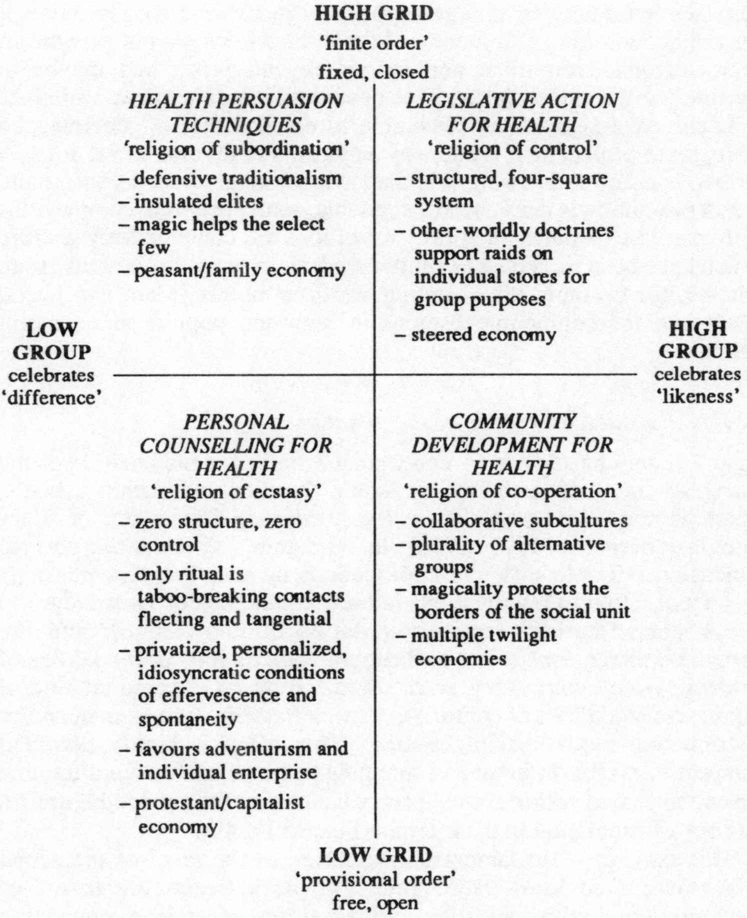

HIGH GRID
'finite order'
fixed, closed

HEALTH PERSUASION
TECHNIQUES
'religion of subordination'
 	
– defensive traditionalism
– insulated elites
– magic helps the select
  few
– peasant/family economy
	LEGISLATIVE ACTION
	FOR HEALTH
	'religion of control'
	
	– structured, four-square
	  system
	– other-worldly doctrines
	  support raids on
	  individual stores for
	  group purposes
	
	– steered economy

LOW GROUP celebrates 'difference'

HIGH GROUP celebrates 'likeness'

PERSONAL
COUNSELLING FOR
HEALTH
'religion of ecstasy'
 	
– zero structure, zero
  control
– only ritual is
  taboo-breaking contacts
  fleeting and tangential
– privatized, personalized,
  idiosyncratic conditions
  of effervescence and
  spontaneity
– favours adventurism and
  individual enterprise
– protestant/capitalist
  economy
	COMMUNITY
	DEVELOPMENT FOR
	HEALTH
	'religion of co-operation'
	
	– collaborative subcultures
	– plurality of alternative
	  groups
	– magicality protects the
	  borders of the social unit
	– multiple twilight
	  economies

LOW GRID
'provisional order'
free, open

Figure 7.5 Health promotion as a moral economy

fourfold map of health-promotion strategies with Douglas's grid/group scheme, and I suggest that a wealth of socio-anthropological insights are immediately yielded.

I wonder if I am alone in experiencing a rare intellectual frisson in contemplating major, government-inspired health campaigns as rituals in a religion of subordination, as a form of magic which is only ever expected to help the select few; or in seeing the activities of local authorities engaged in 'Health for All' programmes as manifestations of other-worldly doctrines that support raids on individual stores for group purposes (until they are charge-capped); or in viewing the rapid rise of personal counselling as a marker of the seductive charms of privatized, personalized adventurism and individual enterprise; and maybe in considering the mixed fortunes of community-development initiatives in health as a sign of the inevitable turbulence that is generated by struggles to protect their borders by a plurality of diverse social units. A further benefit of throwing this net of theoretical speculation around health promotion is that it makes available some intriguing comparisons with parallel disputes in other institutions of contemporary culture which have been subjected to similar analysis in terms of the grid/group scheme, for example the changing world of hotels (Mars and Nicod 1984) and the competing fashions in high and popular arts (Martin 1981).

Health education as a mode of socialization

Basil Berstein has devised a conceptual scheme for the analysis of the changing codes of socialization within families and within schools, which is very closely related to the grid/group framework of Mary Douglas (Bernstein 1971, 1975). In Bernstein's scheme, the vertical dimension refers to different codifications of knowledge, which may vary from 'strong classification' (closed boundaries of knowledge) to 'weak classification' (open boundaries of knowledge); and the horizontal dimensions refers to different codifications or modalities of control, which may vary from 'weak framing' (personal and/or expressive modalities of control) to 'strong framing' (impersonal and/or instrumental modalities of control). This offers a highly pertinent perspective on the different and changing forms of health education that are encompassed within contemporary health promotion, and Figure 7.6 sets out a formulation in these terms (Beattie 1984b).

This highlights fundamental similarities, at the level of the social relationships of knowledge and control, between the forms of contemporary health education and the forms of wider socialization processes that Bernstein identifies. For example 'education for bodily regulation' may be seen as an 'indoctrination system', in which learning is effected through subordination within dominance hierarchies: 'education for social/environmental understanding' may be seen as an 'instruction system', in which learning is effected through assigned duties within homogeneous groups: 'education for personal growth' may be seem as an 'interpretation system', in which learning is effected through personalized active participation; and 'education for community development' may be seen as an 'interruptor system', in which learning is effected through co-operative activities within groups whose commonality lies in their emphasis on finding their own solutions.

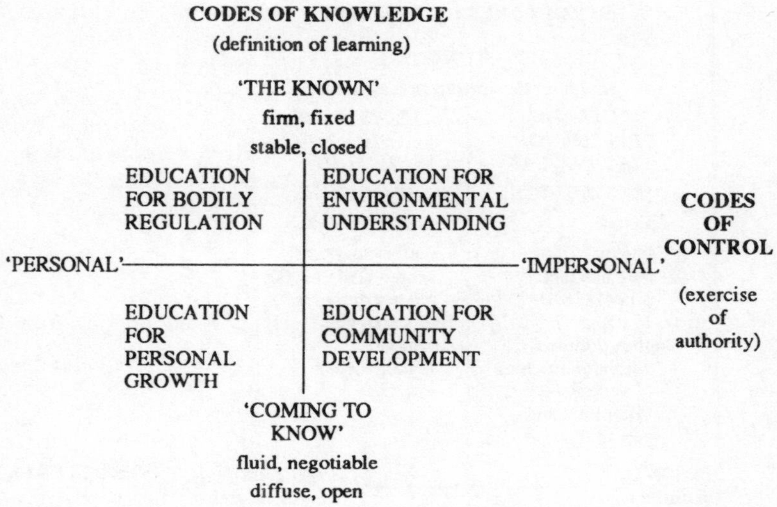

CODES OF KNOWLEDGE
(definition of learning)

'THE KNOWN'
firm, fixed
stable, closed

EDUCATION FOR BODILY REGULATION	EDUCATION FOR ENVIRONMENTAL UNDERSTANDING
EDUCATION FOR PERSONAL GROWTH	EDUCATION FOR COMMUNITY DEVELOPMENT

'PERSONAL'————————————————'IMPERSONAL'

CODES OF CONTROL
(exercise of authority)

'COMING TO KNOW'
fluid, negotiable
diffuse, open

Figure 7.6 Health education as a mode of socialization
Source: Beattie 1984b.

Valuable insights flow from this analysis, for example, concerning the biasses and exclusions that are built into formal systems of schooling, which favour strong classification and 'the known', and against which innovative projects in school health education regularly come to grief (Jenks 1978; McCallum 1984).

Health promotion as a system of rhetoric

The line of argument adopted in this chapter insists that the way in which health promotion strategies are deployed in the modern state both reflects and helps to reproduce fundamental features of the distribution of social power; and that current policy debates need to be examined as a matter of cultural politics rather than (as health promotion debates are so often presented) as matters of technical rationality. It may be especially helpful therefore to draw on the ideas of Foucault and others (Foucault 1972) and to consider past and present developments in health promotion as 'discursive formations', as part of a system of rhetoric. It is fairly obvious that 'health persuasion techniques' could appropriately be examined in the light of work on propaganda and rhetoric in modern literary and historical studies (see, for examples, Foulkes 1983; Hawthorn 1987; MacKenzie 1984). As I see it, however, a much more fundamental enlargement of our understanding of the significance of

191

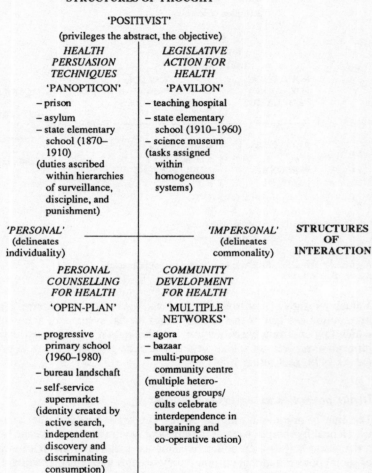

STRUCTURES OF THOUGHT

'POSITIVIST'
(privileges the abstract, the objective)

HEALTH PERSUASION TECHNIQUES	*LEGISLATIVE ACTION FOR HEALTH*
'PANOPTICON'	'PAVILION'
– prison	– teaching hospital
– asylum	– state elementary
– state elementary school (1870–1910)	school (1910–1960)
(duties ascribed within hierarchies of surveillance, discipline, and punishment)	– science museum (tasks assigned within homogeneous systems)

'PERSONAL'
(delineates
individuality)

'IMPERSONAL'
(delineates
commonality)

STRUCTURES OF INTERACTION

PERSONAL COUNSELLING FOR HEALTH	*COMMUNITY DEVELOPMENT FOR HEALTH*
'OPEN-PLAN'	'MULTIPLE NETWORKS'
– progressive primary school (1960–1980)	– agora
– bureau landschaft	– bazaar
– self-service supermarket	– multi-purpose community centre
(identity created by active search, independent discovery and discriminating consumption)	(multiple hetero-geneous groups/cults celebrate interdependence in bargaining and co-operative action)

'PHENOMENOLOGICAL'
(privileges the experiential, the subjective)

Figure 7.7 Health promotion strategies as a system of rhetoric

contemporary health promotion would come from a consideration of the whole repertoire of health promotion as elements in a system of rhetoric. On this view, each different strategy of health promotion 'interpellates' (hails) the public, and recruits us, transforms us, 'socializes' us by reconstituting us within particular modes of subjectivity and social meaning. Foucault's insight into the way in which the modern state has come into existence and maintains itself through the construction of 'the human sciences' and through their associated social practices of power and technologies of governance, permits us to see the far-reaching cultural interconnections of strategies of health promotion – and why they are a point of convergence for many professions and bodies of expertise, a focus of profound disagreement and an arena of great political turbulence.

In Figure 7.7 I have attempted to depict contemporary health-promotion strategies as four distinct rhetorical modes, each of which (following Foucault's arguments) may be characterized in terms of its own specific 'genealogy'. Each of them celebrates a particular structure of thought and a particular structure of interaction, among the 'deep structures' of the modern state; and each of them emerges as a technology for 'spatializing' a particular version of social order.

This is a rather packed diagram, summarizing some elusive ideas. I present it here in the belief that the insights it offers may be more useful than any others discussed in this chapter, as a means of getting hold of the deep structures of society and of social policy that are at stake and being contested in contemporary health promotion. This perspective has been used in an extremely illuminating way to 'de-construct' the rhetoric of 'social and life skills' programmes in schools (Bennet 1987) and the rhetoric of 'care and concern' in nurse education (Glen 1988). These analyses show how current discourses in both these two areas co-opt and appear to celebrate liberal–individualistic values, while simultaneously masking their own authoritarian roots, and excluding public/collective action from the realms of the possible (the thinkable).

Directions for social research in health promotion

One of the things that writing this chapter has reminded me is that sociology has contributed to the shaping of current health-promotion discourse in 'unconscious' as well as in conscious ways (in Foucault's sense). And in searching for an understanding that can unmask the structures of knowledge and control that health-promotion initiatives are bound up with, it is clear to me that the perspectives from critical sociology and cultural analysis are essential. I am inclined to wonder, though, whether perhaps we do not already have a clear-enough picture of the exclusions, prohibitions and limits through which contemporary health promotion has been (and is) shaped, to give partisan action a higher priority than disinterested study. I would certainly want to enter a plea for much more action research and practitioner research in health promotion, informed by large theoretical ideas, but bringing such ideas directly to bear on current policy and practice through case-studies using ethnographic methods. There are many, very many, areas of health promotion, past, present and future, in which practice might be illuminated and transformed by work of this kind.

Alongside such work, there is perhaps a place for more basic and theoretically oriented enquiry, most obviously into cross-classification matrices as a tool of analysis. These exemplify the concept of a 'parameter space', which has been used quite widely in the social sciences to prompt the enumeration of a range of logical possibilities in a domain under scrutiny (Barton 1962). Apart from the conceptual and empirical refinement that could be achieved through other related work (on cultural analysis), there are also intriguing ways in which the use of the fourfold matrix might be extended. One is exemplified in the work of Spiro, who – as long ago as 1962 – made detailed analytical use of a fourfold matrix to plot tensions, conflicts and systems changes in a systematic approach to the study of politics, and in particular, to chart phases and cycles in the 'flow of policy' (Spiro 1962). A second direction for extension of the 'morphological manifold' as an analytical tool is to move it into three dimensions by using the topological geometry of 'catastrophe theory'. This has been used by Zeeman (Zeeman 1979) to develop a model of 'the dynamic aspects of governmental change envisaged by different ideologies', in terms of 'opinion spaces' and 'conflict lines' (he derives this basic parameters from Eysenck's 'Psychology of Politics'). Exactly the same 'cusp catastrophe' has been employed by Thompson (1976, 1979) as a way of representing major cycles of innovation and reaction in higher education and in high fashion. He recommends this as a way of deciphering when and why certain 'fashionable' ideas come to be 'rubbished' (and vice versa); drawing on the work of Bernstein and Douglas, he argues that this delineates a 'geometry of credibility'.

I find this line of theoretical enquiry enormously thought-provoking for the way in which it helps to get hold of the idea of 'critical limits' and boundaries of credibility in social ideologies, the rates of attack and defence on which determine the conditions for system stability and crisis, and for system transformation. I see here a glimpse of a way of dealing analytically with the complex 'pushes and pulls' around the key axes of power/knowledge in health promotion – as an unstable dynamic equilibrium. If we could understand this, of course, we might be able to intervene in and transform the babel of competing rhetorics, by offering a basis for principled debate on the areas of legitimate disagreement – the 'essentially contested concepts' (Gallie 1956) of contemporary health promotion. I would take this as the hallmark of an open society.

Faced with what I see as a frightening rise in authoritarianism and the ascendancy of contemptuous new economies with the truth, my commitment is to try to ensure that the debate about health choices is kept open. What balance between social research and social action that will require is a question that practitioners and social scientists need to address together.

Notes

1. This is based on personal attendance at the meeting of the Board of the HEA on April 11 1989; events at that meeting were subsequently publicized in the *Guardian*, Tuesday 16 May 1989 (Leader) and the *Independent*, Tuesday 16 May 1989 (page 2).
2. This was first presented in Beattie (1980) 'Health education policy and theory: issues for the future', paper for TACADE Conference, Nottingham University. It drew heavily on: George and Wilding (1976) *Ideology and Social Welfare*, London: Routledge & Kegan Paul.

   I have subsequently added to it in the light of the following: Lawton (1988) 'Ideologies of Education', in D. Lawton and C. Chitty (eds) *The National Curriculum*, Beford Way Paper no. 33.
3. This was first presented in Beattie (1984a) 'The price of political awareness', paper for 'The Challenge of Choice' Conference, St Bartholomew's Hospital, May.
4. This was first presented in Beattie (1979) 'Social policy and health education: the prospects for a radical practice', paper for National Deviancy Conference, Edgehill College, September. The analysis draws heavily on Johnson (1972) *Professions and Power*, London: Macmillan.

Acknowledgement

I would like to thank my discussant, Sally MacIntyre, for her comments on an earlier version of this chapter.

References

Anderson, D. (1980) 'Blind alleys in "health education" ', in A. Seldon (ed.) *The Litmus Papers A National Dis-Service*, London: Centre for Policy Studies.
—— (1982) 'State health education: three cases for contraction', in A. Flaew (ed.) *The Pied Pipers of Education*, London: The Social Affairs Unit.
Anionwu, E. (1988) 'Health education and community development for sickle cell disorders in Brent', PhD thesis, University of London Institute of Education.
Armstrong, D. (1979) 'The emancipation of biographical medicine, *Social Science and Medicine* 13A: 1–8.
Ashton, J. and Seymour, H. (1988) *The New Public Health*, Milton Keynes: Open University Press.
Ashton, J., Grey, P. and Barnard, K. (1986) 'Healthy cities – WHO's New Public Health Initiative', *Health Promotion* (3): 319–23.
Audit Commission (1987) *Making a Reality of Community Care*, London: Audit Commission.

Baric, L. (1982) 'A new ecological perspective emerging for health
education', *International Journal of Health Education* 20 (4).

Barton, A.H. (1962) 'The property space concept', in P. Lazarsfeld and M.
Rosenberg (eds) *The Language of Social Research*, Free Press.

Beattie, A. (1979a) *Styles of Communication in Health Education: a review of
HEC policy*, Report to the Health Education Council.

——(1979b) 'Social policy and health education: the prospects for a radical
practice', paper for National Deviancy Conference, Edgehill College,
September.

——(1980) 'Health education policy and theory: issues for the future', paper
TACADE Conference, Nottingham University.

——(1982) *Changing Codes of Health*, Seminar Notes, University of
London, Institute of Education.

——(1984a) 'The price of political awareness', paper for 'The Challenge of
Choice' Conference, St Bartholomew's Hospital, May.

——(1984b) 'Health education and the science teacher: invitation to a
debate', *Education and Health* 9–16, January.

——(1986) 'Community development for health: from practice to theory',
Radical Health Promotion (4):12–18.

——(1987) 'Making a curriculum work', in P. Allen and M. Jolley (eds) *The
Curriculum in Nursing Education*, London: Croom Helm.

——(1988) *The Pandora's Box of Informal Care: A Report on a Local
Development Project to Improve Multi-disciplinary Support for Carers*,
Report for Informal Carers Support Unit, London: King's Fund, March.

Becker, M.H. (ed.) (1985) *The Health Belief Model and Personal Health
Behaviour*, C.B. Slack.

Bennett, S. (1987) 'An analysis of "lifeskills" teaching programmes', MA
dissertation, University of London Institute of Education, September.

Bernstein, B. (1971) 'On the classification and framing of educational knowledge',
in *Class Codes and Control*, vol. 1, London: Routledge & Kegan Paul.

——(1975) 'Class and pedagogies visibles and invisible', in *Class Codes and
Control*, vol. 3, London: Routledge & Kegan Paul.

Bernstein, B. and Henderson, E. (1974) 'Social class differences in the
relevance of language and socialization', ch. 2, in *Class Codes and
Control*, vol. 2, London: Routledge & Kegan Paul.

Black Report (1980) *Inequalities in Health: Report of a Research Working
Group*, London: DHSS.

Blackham, H.J. (ed.) (1987) *Education for Personal Autonomy*, London:
Bedford Square Press.

Botvin, G.J. (1984) 'The life skills training model: a broad-spectrum approach
to the prevention of smoking', in G. Campbell (ed.) *Health Education and
Youth*, Brighton: Falmer Press.

Burkitt, A. (1983) 'Models of health', in J. Clarke (ed.) *Readings in
Community Health*, Edinburgh: Livingstone.

Campbell, A.V. (1984) *Moderated Love: A Theology of Professional Care*,
London: SPCK.

——(1985) *Paid to Care? – The Limits of Pofessionalism in Pastoral Care*,
London: SPCK.

Canadian Public Health Association (1974) 'Policy statements on health promotion', *Canadian Journal of Public Health* 65:140.

Castle, P. and Jacobson, B. (1987) *The Health of our Regions*, London: HEC.

Chaplin, J. and Adams, D. (1986) *London Health Action Network*, London: National Community Health Resource.

Clode, D., Parker, C. and Etherington, S (eds) (1987) *Towards the Sensitive Bureaucracy: Consumers, Welfare and the New Pluralism*, London: Gower.

Cohen Committee (1964) *Health Education*, Report of Joint Committee, London: HMSO.

Collins, L. (1984) 'Concepts of health education: a study of four professional groups', *International Journal of Health Education* 23 (3).

Community Development Projects (1977) *Gilding the Ghetto: the State and Poverty Experiments*, London: CDP.

Community Health Initiatives Resource Unity/London Community Health Resource (1987) *Guide to Community Health Projects*, London: National Community Health Resource.

Cooper, S. and Lybrand (1988) *A Strategy and Structure for the 1990s: a Report to the FPA*, London: Family Planning Association, October.

Craig, G., Derricourt, N. and Loney, M. (eds) (1982) *Community Work and the State*, London: Routledge & Kegan Paul.

Crawford, R. (1977) 'You are dangerous to your health: the ideology and politics of victim blaming', *International Journal of Health Services* 7: 663–80.

Cust, G. (1979) 'A preventive medicine viewpoint', in I. Sutherland (ed.) *Health Education Perspectives and Choices*, London: Allen & Unwin.

Dallas, D. (1972) *Sex Education in School and Society*, Slough: NFER.

Dennis, J., Draper, P., Holland, S., Snipster, P., Speller, V. and Sunter, J. (1982) 'Health promotion in the reorganised NHS', *The Health Services*, 26 November.

DES (Department of Education and Science) (1977) *Health Education in Schools*, London: HMSO.

——(1987) *Sex Education at School*, Circular 11/87, London: DES.

DES/WO (Department of Education and Science/Welsh Office) (1987) *The National Curriculum 5–16 A consultation Document*, London: DES, July.

DHSS/WO (Department of Health and Social Security/Welsh Office) (1987) *AIDS: Monitoring Response to The Public Education Campaign*, London: DHSS.

DHSS (Department of Health and Social Security) (1981) *Care in Action: a Handbook of Policies and Priorities*, London: HMSO.

——(1983–85) *Seminars on Health Promotion and Disease Prevention*, vols 1–4, London: DHSS.

Douglas, M. (1970) *Natural Symbols, Explorations in Cosmology*, London: Penguin.

——(1978) *Cultural Bias*, London: Royal Anthropology Insititute, occasional paper no. 35.

Doyal, L. (1981) *The Political Economy of Health*, London: Pluto Press.

Draper, P. (1983) 'Tackling the disease of ignorance', *Self-Health* 1: 23–5.
Draper, P., Best, G. and Dennis, J. 'Health and wealth', *Royal Society of Health Journal* 97:121–7.
Draper, P., Griffiths, J., Dennis, J. and Popay, J. (1980) 'Three types of health education', *British Medical Journal* 281: 493–5.
Drennan, V. (1985) *Working in a Different Way*, London: Community Nursing Service Paddington and N. Kensington Health Authority.
——(1986) *Effective Health Education in the Inner City*, Report of a Feasibility Study, London: Health Education Department, Paddington and N. Kensington Health Authority, June.
Durguerian, S. (1982) 'The role and training of family planning nurses', PhD thesis, University of London Insitute of Education.
Engel, E. (1978) 'Health education in schools: a philosophical dilemma', *Health Education Journal* 37: 231–3.
England, B. (1986) *Social Work as Art*, London: Allen & Unwin.
Eskin, F. (1983) *District Food Policies: Issues, Problems and Opportunities*, Unit for Continuing Education, Manchester: Manchester University Medical School, July.
Ewles, L. and Simnett, I. (1984) *Promoting Health: A Practical Guide to Health Education*, London: Wiley.
Farrant, W. and Russel, J. (1985) *HEC Publications: A Case Study in the Production, Distribution and Use of Health Information*, London: Final Report to Health Education Council, January.
——(1986) *The Politics of Health Information*, London: Bedford Way Paper no. 28.
Fishbein, M. (1976) 'Persuasive communication', in A.E. Bennet (ed.) *Communication Between Doctors and Patients*, Oxford: Oxford University Press.
Foucault, M. (1972) *The Archaeology of Knowledge*, London: Tavistock.
Foulkes, A.P. (1983) *Literature and Propaganda*, London: Methuen.
French. J. and Adams, L. (1986) 'From analysis to synthesis: theories of health education', *Health Education Journal* 45(2): 71–4.
Freudenberg, N. (1989) 'Shaping the future of health education: from behaviour change to social change', *Health Education Monographs* 6 (4).
Gallie, W.B. (1956) 'Essentially contested concepts', *Proceedings Aristotelian Society* 56:167–98.
Garside, P. (1987) 'History of public health', Paper/Audiotape for Conference 'Rethinking Public Health', Birmingham, July.
Gatherer, A., Parfit, J., Partner, E. and Vessey, M. (1979) *Is Health Education Effective?*, London: Health Education Council Monograph no. 2.
George, V. and Wilding, P. (1976) *Ideology and Social Welfare*, London: Routledge & Kegan Paul.
GLC (Greater London Council) (1985) 'Health care', ch.8 in *The London Industrial Strategy*, London: GLC.
Glen, S. (1988) 'Nursing and moral education', MA dissertation, University of London Institute of Education, September.
Grigg, C. (pers. comm.) Formerly Officer responsible for Review of Health Education Council Policy on Community Development.

Halmos, P. (1965) *The Faith of the Counsellors*, London: Constable.
Hardy, J. (1981) *Values in Social Policy: Nine Contradictions*, London: Routlege & Kegan Paul.
Hawthorn, J. (1987) *Propaganda, Persuasion and Polemic*, London: Edward Arnold.
Health Education Council (1983) *Prevention and Health Education*, Report of Conference for Chairmen of District Health Authorities, London: HEC/King's Fund.
Health Education Council/Coronary Prevention Group/Department of Health and Social Services (1984) *Coronary Heart Disease Prevention: Plans for Action*, London: Pitman.
Health Rights (1987) *Rethinking Public Health. An Agenda for Local Government*, Conference, Birmingham, July.
Henderson, P. and Thomas, D.N (1980) *Skills in Neighbourhood Work*, London: Allen & Unwin.
HMI (1978) *Curriculum 11–16: Health Education in the Secondary School*, London: DES.
Hubley, J. (1980) 'Community development and health education', *International Journal of Health Education* 18.
Hyde, H. (1983) *'The Role of the Health Education Council in School Education'*, *Monitor* (TACADE) 64: 8–9.
Ingleby, D. (n.d) 'Professionals as socializers: the Psy-complex' unpublished paper.
Jenks, J. (1978) 'The management of health knowledge in schools', MSc dissertation, Chelsea College, London University, September.
Johnson, T. (1972) *Professions and Power*, London: Macmillan.
Jones, W.T. and Grahame, H. (1973) *Health Education in Britain*, TUC Centenary Insitute of Occupational Health, London: School of Hygiene.
Kanfer, F. J. and Goldstein, A.P. (1975) *Helping People Change*, Oxford: Pergamon.
Kennedy, I. (1983) *The Unmasking of Medicine*, London: Paladin.
Keyzer, D. (1985) 'Learning contracts, the trained nurse and the implementation of the nursing process', PhD thesis, University of London Institute of Education.
King's Fund (1983) *Health Promotion: the Challenge for CHCs*, Conference Report (Kings's Fund Report KFC 83/152), London: King's Fund, September.
——(1988) *The Nation's Health: A Strategy for the 1990s*, London: King's Fund.
Lawton, D. (1973) *Social Change, Educational Theory and Curriculum Planning*, London: Hodder & Stoughton.
——(1988) 'Ideologies of education', in D. Lawton and C. Chitty (eds) *The National Curriculum*, London: Bedford Way Paper no.33.
Leathard, A. (1980) *The Fight for Family Planning*, London: Macmillan.
Levine, S., Beattie, A., Plamping, D. and Thorne, S. (1981) *St Thomas' Children's Health Club: An Experiment in Peer Teaching*, London: King's Fund.

Lewisham Community Health Council (1986) *Catford Community Health Project: Evaluation Report.*

London Food Commission (1986) *Tightening Belts: A Report on Food and Low Income,* London: London Food Commission.

Loney, M. (1983) *Community Against Government: the British Community Development Projects 1968–78,* London: Heinemann.

Lonsdale, S. Webb, A. and Briggs, T.L. (eds) (1980) *Teamwork in the Personal Social Services and Health Care,* London: Croom Helm.

McCallum, B. (1984) 'Perceptions of health and health education in the primary school', MA dissertation, University of London Institute of Education, September.

MacKenzie, J.M. (1984) *Propaganda and Empire: The manipulation of British Public opinion 1880–1960,* Manchester: Manchester University Press.

McKeown, T. (1976) *The Role of Medicine,* Oxford: NPHT/Oxford University Press.

McKinlay, J.B. (1979) 'A case for refocussing upstream – the political economy of illness', in E. G. Jaco (ed.) *Patients, Physicians and Illness,* Glencoe, Illinois: Free Press.

McNaught, A. (1988) *Health Action and Ethnic Minorities,* London: National Council for Voluntary Organisations.

McPhail, P. (1977) *Living Well: HEC Project 12–18,* Cambridge: Cambridge University Press.

Marris, P. and Rein, M. (1975) *Dilemmas of Social Reform,* London: Penguin.

Mars, G. and Nicod, M. (1984) *The World of Waiters,* London: Allen & Unwin.

Martin, B. (1981) *A Sociology of Contemporary Cultural Change,* Oxford: Blackwell.

Mills, C. Wright (1959) *The Sociological Imagination,* Oxford: Oxford University Press.

Moran, G. (1985) 'Local authorities and the prevention of ill-health', *Radical Health Promotion* (1).

Murray-Parkes, C. (1979) 'The use of community care in prevention', in M. Meacher (ed.) *New Methods of Mental Health Care,* Oxford: Pergamon.

National Association for Pastoral Care in Education (1988) *Personal and Social Education: After the Act,* London: NAPCE.

National Community Health Resource (1988) *A New Voice for Health,* London: NCHR, October.

Nutbeam, D. (1984) 'Health education in the NHS: the differing perspectives of community physicians and health education officers', *Health Education Journal* 43 (4): 115–19.

Olsen, N., Roberts, J. and Castle, P. (1981) *Smoking Prevention: An Action Guide for the NHS,* London: ASH.

Open University (1982) *Health Choices* and *The Good Health Guide,* Milton Keynes: Open University Press.

Pattison, S. (1988) *A Critique of Pastoral Care,* London: ASCM Press.

Pearson, G. (1973) 'Social work as the privatized solution of public ills', *British Journal of Social Work* 3 (2): 209–27.

Piette, D. (1985) 'A study of the contribution of Community Health Councils in health education for children', MPhil thesis, London School of Hygiene.

Politics of Health Group (1979) *Food and Profit*, London: POHG.

Powles, J. (1973) 'On the limitations of modern medicine', *Science, Medicine and Man* 11–30.

Priestly, P. and McGuire, J. (1983) *Learning to Help*, London: Tavistock.

Radical Therapy Collective (1974) *The Radical Therapist*, London: Penguin.

Rawson, D. (1985) *Purpose and Practice in Health Education*, London: Report to Health Education Council, March.

Reid, D. (1981) 'Health education into the mainstream: a survey of progress and prospects', *Times Education Supplement*, 17 April.

Rogers, C.R. (1969) *Freedom to Learn*, New York: Merrill.

Room, G. (1979) *The Sociology of Welfare: Social Policy, Stratification, and Social Order*, Oxford: Blackwell/Robertson.

Rosenthal, H. (1980) *Health and Community Work: Some New Approaches*, London: King's Fund Centre.

——(1981) 'Neighbourhood health projects', *CHC News*, March.

Saunders, L. (ed.) (1988) *Action for Health: Initiatives in Local Communities*, London: Community Projects Foundation.

Scarrow, H.A (1972) 'The impact of British Domestic Air Pollution Legislation, *British Journal of Political Science* 2: 2.

Schon, D. (1983) *The Reflective Practioner*, London: Temple Smith.

Schools Council/Health Education Council (1977) *Health Education 5–13*, London: Nelson.

Smith, C. (1981) *Community Health Initiatives*, London: NCVO.

Spiro, H.J. (1962) 'Comparative politics: a comprehensive approach', *American Political Science Review* 56: 577–95.

St George, D. (1981) 'Who pulls the strings at the HEC?', *World Medicine* 28 November, pp. 51–5.

——(1984) *A Strategy for Prevention and Health Promotion*, London Victoria Health Authority, April.

Sutherland, I. (1987) *Health Education: Half a Policy. The Rise and Fall of the Health Education Council*, London: National Extension College.

Taylor-Gooby, P. and Dale, J. (1981) *Social Theory and Social Welfare*, London: Arnold.

Thompson, M. (1976) 'Class, caste, the curriculum cycle and the cusp catastrophe', *Studies in Higher Education* 1: 31–46.

——(1979) *Rubbish Theory*, Oxford: Oxford Universtiy Press.

Tones, B.K. (1981a) 'Health education: prevention or subversion', *Royal Society of Health Journal* 101: 114–17.

——(1981b) 'The use and abuse of mass media in health promotion', in D. Leathar, G.B. Hastings and J.K. Davies (eds) *Health Education and the Media*, Oxford: Pergamon.

——(1984) 'Health promotion – a new panacea', *International Journal of Health Education*.

Tuckett, D. (1979) 'Choices for health education: a framework for decision-making' in I. Sutherland (ed.) *Health Education Perspectives and Choices*, London: Allen & Unwin.

Tuckett, D., Boulton, M., Olson, C. and Williams, A. (1985) *Meetings Between Experts: An Approach to Sharing Ideas in Medical Consultations*, London: Tavistock.

US Department of Health and Human Services (1982) *Health Promotion and Education Services in HMOs*, Washington: USD HHS.

US Department of Health, Education and Welfare (1978) *Disease Prevention and Health Promotion*, Washington: USD HEW.

Van Parijs, L. (1980) 'Reflections on the medical model and the objectives of health education', *International Journal of Health Education* 23:205.

Walker, A. (1984) *Social Planning: A Strategy for Socialist Welfare*, Oxford: Blackwell.

Walkerdine, V. (1984) 'Developmental psychology and the child-centred pedagogy', in J. Henriques, W. Holloway and V. Walkerdine (eds) *Changing the Subject*, London: Methuen.

Watt, A. (1985) 'Addressing the confusions', in G. Somerville (ed.) *Community Development for Health*, London: King's Fund Centre.

Whitehead, M. (1987) *The Health Divide*, London: Health Education Council.

Wilding, P. (1982) *Professional Power and Social Welfare*, London: Routledge & Kegan Paul.

Winter, J. (1985) *The Great War and the British People*, London: Macmillan.

World Health Organization (1978) *Primary Health Care*, Report of Alma Ata Conference, Geneva: WHO.

——(1981) *Health Edcation and Lifestyles*, Copenhagen: WHO.

——(1985) *Targets for Health for All by the Year 2000*, Copenhagen: WHO.

Zeeman, E.C. (1979) 'Geometrical model of ideologies', in C. Renfrew and K.L. Cooke (eds) *Transformations: Mathematical Approaches to Culture Change*, London: Academic Press.

Chapter eight

The confused boundaries of community care
Hilary Land

Community care means providing services and support which
people who are affected by problems of ageing, mental illness,
mental handicap or physical or sensory disability need to be able to
live as independently as possible in their own homes, or in
'homely' settings in the community. The Government is firmly
committed to a policy of community care which enables such
people to achieve their full potential.
(Department of Health/Department of Social Security 1989:3)

This is how the government defined community care in The White
Paper, *Caring for People*, which attempts to set out the legislative
framework for the community care services in the 1990s.

This chapter will explore some of the issues confronting the policy
makers and practitioners who are attempting to plan the future of community care services. It will first look at the history of the fragmented
and confused way in which we have funded, allocated and administered
our systems of health care, personal social services and social security
which make up the formal system of community care. Second, it will examine the current debate about the boundaries, both between and within
formal and informal systems of community care and raises the question
of whether the issues associated with these systems are the same as those
of thirty years ago when community care began to appear on the
political agenda. Finally, the questions these issues pose for policy
makers, practitioners, administrators and researchers are identified.

The structure of formal community care

The fragmented nature of the services which contribute to what we call
'community care' has a long history. Between 1971 and 1988, the
health, personal social services and social security systems were the
responsibility of a single government department, the Department of
Health and Social Security (DHSS), although the Department of

Environment had overall responsibility for the financing of local government. This was not the case in the immediate post-war years for local government had kept its responsibilities for public and mental health and welfare as well as for some aspects of maternity care. The tripartite structure of the National Health Service meant that both the hospital and general practitioner services were each separately and differently administered. In addition under Part III of the 1948 National Assistance Act, local government had responsibility for providing residential accommodation (henceforth known as Part III accommodation) for the elderly and infirm who needed care but not constant medical care, as well as for the homeless. Local authorities also had to establish children's departments under the 1948 Children Act, but until 1965 had no powers to do preventive work with children still living with their families. This included giving financial assistance.

Under the 1946 National Health Act, local authorities were empowered to provide 'domestic help for householders where such help is required owing to the presence of any person who is ill, lying-in, an expectant mother, mentally defective, aged or a child not over compulsory school age' (section 29). It was another twenty years before there was a statutory obligation to provide a home-help service although by 1957 all local authorities were making some provision.

Local authorities had first acquired the power to provide domestic help under the Maternity and Child Welfare Act 1918, which required them to appoint maternity and child welfare committees. Home helps could only be provided for maternity cases, and during the inter-war years the service developed mainly in conjunction with health visitors. It was not until the Second World War, in 1944, that home helps could be used to assist a broader range of clients, including sick or elderly people. The massive mobilization of women during the war meant that they were less able to provide family care at times of illness or other emergencies. The home-help service therefore had to be expanded and by 1945, two-thirds of local authorities had a scheme compared with only half in 1939. Many worked closely with the Women's Voluntary Service. Use of the private sector was encouraged by extending the tax relief for resident housekeepers to non-resident housekeepers and by dropping the restriction that the housekeeper must be a female relative.

After 1946, home helps remained very much associated with health care. Looking back over the first ten years of the post-war home-help service in London, David Donnison wrote that it was 'an essential ancillary to the hospitals, the domiciliary health services, the old people's welfare services and the child-care services' (Donnison and Chapman 1965: 89). In areas like London where hospital beds were in short supply, home helps were used to keep the chronically sick in the community. The proportion of elderly people among home-help clients increased from 58 per cent of clients in England and Wales in 1953 to 75 per cent in 1960. By this time there were 55,000 home helps compared with 30,000 in 1953 (Dexter and Harbart 1983: 13). This change occurred for a number of reasons. Apart from pressure on expensive and scarce hospital beds and insufficient residential provision for the elderly (much of which was in any case old and grim and, rightly, associated with the workhouse (see, for example, Townsend 1962)), the growing numbers of old people preferred to stay in their own homes. At the same time there was a shift from home confinements to hospital confinements, so domestic help for maternity care was less pressing. In any case, charging policies meant that those with a wage earner in the family paid relatively more than those on benefit, i.e. the old and chronically sick. There was therefore an incentive for families to make their own arrangements when a new baby arrived.

In the reorganization of the NHS in the early 1970s, local authorities lost most of their health service responsibilities. They did, however, keep their responsibilities for providing residential care for the elderly and infirm and they also kept the home-help service. This moved into the newly created social services departments thus shifting it from association with health care to being part of a social-work service. It was argued at the time that the home-help service was important in keeping children out of care. However, most of their work continued to be with the elderly. Indeed, by 1980, 88 per cent of their clients were elderly people (Dexter and Harbart 1983). The newly created area health authorities (AHAs) were then co-terminous with local authority boundaries but in the subsequent changes of the 1980s which abolished AHAs, co-terminosity at the local level was lost.

Throughout this period the social security system has been administered directly by central government through a system of local offices. The offices dealing with contributory and means-test benefits remained separate until the Ministry of Social Security was created in 1966 when a system of integrated local offices began to be established. The extent to which the social security system had been involved with the Ministry of Labour (subsequently the Department of Employment) in the administration of employment benefit had varied during this period, as had its relationship with local authorities over the payment of various benefits to help claimants meet the costs of housing and rates.

It is too early to tell what impact splitting the DHSS will have. It may well make it more difficult to discuss trade-offs between cash benefits or services, for example. However, putting responsibility for all these services (with the exception of housing) within the remit of one central government department, the DHSS, had not reduced fragmentation at the local level. Neither had it produced less confused policies. Indeed, some of the changes, particularly in the 1980s, made matters worse, not better.

On one hand, there is now no co-terminosity between the health and welfare services. As Griffiths says in the introduction to his report *Community Care: Agenda for Action*, joint planning, joint finance and increased accountability 'would be helped by restructuring at the local level with health authorities, social service authorities and family practitioner committees enjoying co-terminosity or even being brought within a common structure' (Griffiths 1988: vi). He does not recommend that this be done because of the turmoil it would create, coming so soon after the last NHS reorganization. However, it is a pity that in their determination to reduce the power of local authorities, this government took no notice of the Royal Commission on the NHS which ten years ago argued for building on the existing co-terminosity, albeit limited, that the NHS and local authorities already had.

On the other hand, we now have what is probably the most centralized social security system in Europe – if not the world. The Social Security Advisory Committee (SSAC) is one of the remaining channels whereby outsiders can speak directly to the minister responsible for the social security system. Many other social security systems allow for far more participation and accountablity at the local as well as the central level. In France, for example, there is a local structure which gives room for far more experimentation and flexibility in responding to local needs over and above the nationally established benefits. For this, and other historical reasons, France does not have the divisions we do between those providing help in the form of social work services, health care, cash and housing services. I doubt whether the resources allocated for community care in the new Social Fund, which have to be used in conjunction with local authorities and therefore require some cooperation between social security staff and local social services departments will make for a great deal of improvement. There will be some room for experimentation at the local level for the first time, although the amount of money involved is small (£60 million in 1988–89). However, the accountability of the social security system as a whole to the local community has not increased one iota. Indeed, one of the truly shocking aspects of the Social Security Act 1986 is the extent to which the system is now barely accountable even to Parliament.

The funding of each of these services has remained different. Social security benefits are paid for out of taxes and contributions. The cost of the NHS is almost entirely borne by the tax system with only a small proportion coming from contributions. Local authority services are paid for by a mix of taxes and rates (or commuity charge after April 1990). Their charging policies have always been different. Recipients of services provided by the NHS, including health visiting and district nursing services are not charged. Neither are patients in hospitals or nursing homes, although after six weeks in hospital (reduced from eight weeks in April 1988) those receiving state contributory benefits have their benefits reduced by 40 per cent and after a year reduced to an amount sufficient for personal expenses (£10.55 in a nursing home and £11.75 in a hospital in 1990). Those receiving Supplementary Benefit (now Income Support) received the amount for personal expenses only, from the time they entered hospital, although necessary housing commitments were paid for.

Local authorities have always had to charge for residential care, the minimum amount being the national insurance pension less a small amount (£9.40 in 1990) for personal expenses – excluding clothing and footwear, which the local authority is supposed to provide. The rates used by local authorities for assessing the income and assets of an old person entering one of their residential homes have always been different from those used by the DHSS when paying for the residential care of a claimant in the private or voluntary sector. An old person entering a local authority home is expected to sell their house, if they have one, within a matter of a few months, and more probably weeks, once it is clear that they are unlikely to be able to return to it. Their need for residential care is assessed by the social services department before they enter. The proceeds of the sale of the house together with any capital over a minimum amount (£1,200 in 1987) will then be used to pay the fees for the home. The local authority also has first call on the old person's estate when they die. There is no upper limit of capital which disqualifies an old person from entering a local authority home or being sponsored in a voluntary home, but it is assumed that any capital over the minimum earns a weekly tariff income (25p for every £50 capital).

Local authorities have also charged for home helps. In 1965 local authorities had been urged in a Ministry of Health circular not to charge National Assistance claimants. Ten years later, 80 per cent of all home-help clients were receiving a free service. However, after 1976, local authorities were forced to cut their budgets and at the same time were under pressure to support people in the community who had previously been in long-stay hospitals. Charges for home helps where therefore increased and growing numbers of Supplementary Benefit claimants were charged. As a result the Supplementary Benefit system began to pick up a heavier bill for home helps just as, five years later, it was to pick up a heavier bill for residential care. In 1980, the Supplementary Benefit Commission declared: 'Any authority making charges for this service to people – usually elderly and frail – so poor that they live on supplementary benefit, ought to be ashamed of itself' (Dexter and Harbart 1983 : 137).

The 1980 Social Security Act abolished additional payments with respect to local authority home helps. It remained possible to claim an additional payment to cover the cost of private domestic help. The average payment made in the last year of operation was £48 a week. However, unlike the private residential-care market, the private domestic-help market did not respond by expanding rapidly at the expense of the social security system. The provision remained little known and therefore not widely used, and there were no entrepreneurs waiting on the side lines to take advantage. In any case, the profits to be made were, and are, unlikely to be so great. Nevertheless in the 1986 Social Security Act, this, together with all other special payments, has been abolished.

The Independent Living Fund (ILF)

The abolition of assistance with the cost of domestic help, although not widely used did raise problems for a number of severely disabled claimants whose needs could not be met even after the government had conceded the need for a two-tier disability premium for those on Income Support. Instead of incorporating an additional benefit into the social security system, the government chose instead to create a charitable fund – The Independent Living Fund (ILF) – which operates in a similar fashion to the Family Fund which was established in the early 1970s as a method of meeting the needs of families with disabled children. The ILF is administered by the Department of Social Security together with the Disablement Income Group. In its first year it was allocated £5 million.

The ILF is a discretionary trust and helps applicants living alone or with someone (not necessarily a relative) who is unable to provide all the personal care or domestic assistance required. They are either receiving Attendance Allowance, or can satisfy the criteria for it and are in receipt of Income Support or have insufficient income to pay for the care needed. They must also have capital of less than £6,000. In the first six months of its operation The Fund received 12,567 applications, of which 3,067 were successful. The average payment granted was a little over £62, although a quarter received more than £200. The government would appear to seen an increasing role for the ILF as its fund has been increased to £20 million for the year 1990–91. However, the White Paper mentions it only briefly and then to point out that: 'There would clearly be an overlap between the ILF and the responsibilities of the local authorities which will need to be reviewed' (para 9.10).

The meaning of 'community care' policies

If the structure and organization of the services is fragmented and con-fusing, so too is the meaning attributed to 'community care'. This has changed. Some of the debate about community care in the 1950s and

1960s was informed by an understandable desire to get rid of large, remote institutions which provided low standards of impersonal care. As far as children were concerned, in 1946 the Curtis Committee had recommended that children should be fostered with families or placed in *small* homes and indeed this was the policy adopted in the 1950s. Interestingly, when these smaller children's homes became the responsibility of the social services departments created as a result of the Seebohm Report, they were renamed 'community homes'. Meanwhile the policy in the sixties had shifted from removing children from their families to undertaking preventive work with them so that most could remain in their own homes. The policy in the eighties has been to close all children's homes.

Similar consideration informed the debate around policies for the elderly. In 1958 the Minister of Health stated that the 'underlying principle of our services for the old should be this: that the best place for old people is in their own homes, with help from home services if need be' (Townsend 1962: 196).

Five years later the Ministry of Health's report 'Health and Welfare' emphasized the need for elderly people to have access to a range of domiciliary services, social clubs and if necessary home nursing, etc. However, they forecast a rise in home helps of only 45 per cent in the next ten years compared with an 87 per cent rise in residential staff. The Royal Commission in the Law Relating to Mental Illness and Mental Deficiency in 1957 likewise recommended a shift from hospital care to community care and they defined this to mean 'all forms of care (including residential care) which it is appropriate for local health or welfare authorities to provide' (p. 208). Already, then, there was some confusion about whether or not community care is an alternative to institutional care.

In the 1970s a further strand was woven into the debate and this is one which has become more rather than less important in government thinking. Janet Finch and Dulcie Groves argue that 'the Skeffington (1969) and Seebohm Reports introduced the idea of citizen participation in local social services and the Aves Report (1969) underlined the possibilities for the use of volunteers in the social services' (Finch and Groves 1985: 221). Thus the emphasis in community care had broadened to include not only care *in* the community but care *by* the community. In the context of concern to cut public expenditure from 1976 onwards, care by family, friends, neighbours and volunteers became more heavily emphasized. Thus, in their White Paper *Growing Older*, the government in 1981 stated:

Whatever level of public expenditure proves practicable and however it is distributed, the primary sources of support and care

209

for elderly people are informal and voluntary. These spring from
personal ties of kinship, friendship and neighbourhood. They are
irreplaceable. It is the role of public authorities to sustain and
where necessary develop – but never to displace – such support and
care. Care *in* the community must increasingly mean care *by* the
community.

(Department of Health and Social Security 1981: 3)

In the 1980s, the philosophy of enhancing 'consumer choice' also
emphasized the need to develop a variety of sources of care and support.

In the light of this philosophy, the role of the state has become one of
co-ordinating social care whether provided in the private market, the
voluntary sector or by statutory authorities rather than *providing* it.
However, in looking at what this actually means in practice, and
examining the gap between the rhetoric and reality, it is important to
look at some of the other changes which have led to the issues of
community care becoming so high on the political agenda. For while
both Labour and Conservative governments in the 1960s and 1970s
failed to develop fully the domiciliary services identified as necessary,
and after 1976 both subsequently cut back on local government
spending, they failed to curb the expenditure on residential care. Quite
unexpectedly, the open-ended commitment to support claimants in
residential accommodation, which had existed in the social security
system throughout the post-war years, became a problem in the 1980s.
Initially the concern focused on young people, but rapidly the focus of
attention became elderly people. Why?

Board and lodging payments

Until the end of the 1970s, board and lodging payments were an insig-
nificant part of the budget of the Supplementary Benefit system. In
1978–79 the cost was £6 million (£12 million in 1986 prices). Two years
later this had doubled and it doubled again during the next two years.
During 1983 the cost rose even faster increasing by over £100 million in
that year alone (Audit Commission 1986). By 1987 the figure had
reached £489 million and by May 1989, £1 billion (including nursing-
home care). What had brought this about?

First, pressure was being exerted by demographic changes. The birth
rate in the UK had peaked in 1964 when there were nearly a million
births, compared with nearer three-quarters of a million a year throughout the 1970s. This large cohort of young people were entering the
labour market during the early 1980s at a time when unemployment was
rapidly rising. Those who left home in search of work claimed board and

lodging from the Supplementary Benefit system. At the end of 1984, 70 per cent of the 163,000 claimants in ordinary board and lodging were claiming because they were unemployed. Half of them were aged between 16 and 25 years (Audit Commission 1986).

There was also an increase in the numbers of elderly people, in particular those aged over 75 years. In 1974 there were just under 2.5 million in England and Wales. These numbers increased by a quarter of a million over the following five years; by 1984 there were nearly 3.2 million. By the end of 1984 in England and Wales there were over 190,000 elderly people in residential homes compared with just over 140,000 ten years earlier (Audit Commission 1986). Nearly all the increased provision was in the private sector.

A second reason for the increased pressure on the social security budget arose from the impact of the cuts in local authority spending which had started in 1976. Capital programmes are easier to cut in the first instance than revenue-costly programmes, hence local authority provision of new residential places slowed down. If necessary, old people were sponsored in the voluntary or private sectors. However, after the 1980 changes in the regulations governing the payment of board and lodging allowances in the Supplementary Benefit system, local authorities began encouraging the direct use of the private sector because the social security system would meet the bill. They were then able to shift the cost of residential care for elderly people from their budgets to the DHSS. Between 1980 and 1984 the number of local authority sponsored residents in private homes fell by 57 per cent and the numbers sponsored in voluntary homes by 30 per cent (Audit Commission 1986). This increased use of residential care occurred without any professional assessment of the old person's need for it.

The third reason a shift in responsibility between health service and local authority provisions. As already outlined, the policy of successive governments over a number of years had been to promote community-based services and to reduce long-stay hospital provision. But as the Audit Commission (1986) points out, not only was the mechanism for achieving the necessary shift in funding from the health budget to local authority budgets inadequate, but in some cases local authorities found themselves penalized by the Department of Environment through the grant system for developing the community services the government was supposed to be encouraging. The whole development of these services became caught up in the general onslaught on local government expenditure and staffing levels. Not surprisingly, provision in the private sector supported from the social security budget seemed an easy way out after 1980. Numbers of local authority sponsored residents in private and voluntary homes for the physically or mentally handicapped fell at the same time as the number of places in these homes was increasing (Audit Commission 1986).

Finally, there were what appeared to be minor changes in the regulations concerning board and lodging payments, made in November 1980 when the Supplementary Benefit scheme was revised. Board and lodging allowances had been paid to a small number of elderly people in private or voluntary homes since 1948. However, prior to 1980 the level of the allowance was set with reference to the prevailing local charges that an independent adult would have to pay for board and lodging. Higher rates would be paid at the discretion of the local office but a decision was unlikely to be known before the old person became a resident. After 1980 it was made clear that the level of allowance was to be set by reference to charges in an 'equivalent establishment' and that 'the needs of residents' could be taken into account. This meant that local board and lodging charges could be set on a par with charges in the private and voluntary residential sectors. Also the discretionary addition in effect became an automatic payment to elderly people in residential homes whose incomes were low. The new regulations allowed extra to be paid for 13 weeks to give a resident time to move to cheaper accommodation, if the allowances based on the new guidelines did not meet the fees and leave them sufficient for personal expenses. However, if 'there were special factors which make it unreasonable for the resident to move, supplementary benefit will continue to meet the shortfall indefinitely or until a charitable source of income intervenes' (Parker 1988: 87). In practice, this meant that the old person stayed put because local officers were reluctant to insist that they moved somewhere cheaper.

Ministers became alarmed and after consulting SSAC (Social Security Advisory Committee) in 1983, new regulations were introduced. These were based on a three-tier system of local limits which distinguished between residential homes, nursing homes and ordinary board and lodgings. Because local discretion was removed, the allowances were higher, being set with reference to the highest reasonable charge in the area. Consequently, the cost of board and lodging payments in 1983 escalated from £203 million to £380 million while the proportion of Supplementary Benefit claimants among residents in the private sector increased from 20 per cent to 30 per cent. Much public concern was focused on young people in board and lodgings, for it was alleged many were having seaside holidays at the tax payer's expense. Further controls were introduced in 1985 and fixed national limits were set. Young people's rights to claim board and lodging allowance in a particular locality were limited to a few weeks: if they could not find a job, they were expected to move elsewhere or, preferably, to return home. However, as far as elderly people were concerned, there was continuing pressure to make the allowances more sensitive to local variations again, not only from the private sector, but also from the voluntary sector and pressure groups representing the elderly. At the end of 1985 the national limits were increased again and the following summer there was another round of increases. By this time, Normal Fowler was reviewing the whole social security system and the 1986 Social Security Act contained rather different strategies for curbing the cost of residential care.

The Social Security Act 1986 gives powers to social security officials to assess whether or not a claimant needs residential care. In other words, since 11 Apil 1988 the social security system no longer has to pick up the bill when an elderly person with limited resources enters residential care if the Social Fund officer decides that the claimant's needs could be better and more cheaply met in the community. To facilitate this, the Social Fund, which largely replaces the special-needs payments of the old Supplementary Benefit system with loans, has a small part of its budget (£60 million in the first year) to spend on community care grants. It is envisaged that decisions about how to spend this money will be made in consultation with local authority social services departments. How well this is working it is too early to tell, but even before this was implemented, the Griffiths Report (1988) recommended that this money for community care should not be claimed via the Social Fund at all, but allocated directly to local authorities.

Under the new rules of Income Support, an old person wanting to move into residential care was expected immediately to raise a loan on the house they were vacating, prior to selling it, unless a member of the family aged 60 or more was living there. If the loan they could raise was more than £6,000, they would render themselves ineligible for Income Support. They would remain ineligible once the house was sold as long as the amount realized in the sale exceeded £6,000. Such a rule would have been likely to have delayed entry to residential care until it was absolutely necessary as, having entered it, it would be far harder to move out again. Even if this happened, the DHSS would have recouped more quickly a larger part of the cost of residential care than was formerly the case. However, such was the public and political outrage at the impact of these rules on old people, especially those living in parts of the country where it is difficult to sell a house quickly, that the rules were changed within a fortnight. In future, an old person will be given up to six months to sell their home after entry to residential care.

Unresolved boundaries

The 1988 Social Security Act contains provisions for at least curbing what seemed to be an exponential rate of growth in the cost of residential care falling on the social security budget. However, many issues remain unresolved and community care still has a high political profile. The government waited until 1989 to produce a White Paper on the Griffiths Report. One of its key recommendations is that local authority departments be made responsible for arranging and managing the appropriate package of care for each person needing it. This closely follows Griffiths, who did not envisage that local authorities necessarily *provide* the care. However, he did propose that the local authorities be given earmarked funds to *manage* it. (Hence his proposal, that the community care element of the Social Fund should be administered by them. Clearly, there is the possiblity of yet another boundary dispute if the responsibility of local authorities and the ILF, with respect to disabled individuals needing considerable personal care, are not carefully spelt out.)

To a government committed to taking responsibilities and funds *away* from local authorities, this did not find favour. The White Paper is remarkably reticent about the magnitude of the resources the government believes will be necessary to fund community care in the next decade. There are *no* estimates of what local authorities, health authorities, the voluntary, the private and the informal sectors may be expected to spend on community care. We are only told what *has* been spent in the past and that demographic trends will increase the need for community care at the same time that they are likely to reduce the future availabily of informal carers.

The White Paper does, however, indicate how the social security budget from April 1991 will cease to meet the cost of care, whether domiciliary or residential:

> The Government proposes to introduce a single unified budget to
> cover the costs of social care, whether in a person's home or in
> residential care or nursing home. The new budget will include the
> care element of social security payments to people in private and
> voluntary residential care and nursing homes.
>
> (DHSS 1989, para. 8.17)

This means that people needing care whilst in their own homes or in an institutional setting will claim help from the Income Support system of personal allowances and premiums and from Housing Benefit. In this way, the government hopes that:

> The financial incentive towards residential care under present
> Income Support rules will therefore be eliminated. Other than any

necessary adjustments to the Housing Benefit entitlement, the sources of income from the benefit system will remain the same when a person enters or leaves a private or voluntary residential setting.

(ibid, para 8.18)

As Griffiths recommended, local authorities will have responsibility for managing their care budget but they will not be allocated a specific fund. The White Paper asserts that:

The Government gave careful consideration to Sir Roy Griffiths' case for a specific grant but concluded that a large scale specific grant is not necessary to secure community care objectives. Support for community care expenditure, as with other important local authority functions would be best provided principally through the Revenue Support Grant.

(ibid, para 8.25)

This will be done by taking into account 'the amount of expenditure appropriate for local authorities to incur on supported community care services' in the Standard Spending Assessment formula for the personal social services. The details of this have yet to be worked out with the local authority associations.

Health authorities will not be given specific grants either as recommended by Griffiths because:

attempting to do so would carry too great a risk of distorting future spending in this area. The growth of community care will depend crucially on the availability and growth of community-based alternatives to care in long-stay institutions. Setting aside a fixed sum for this purpose will not provide the flexibility which will be needed to respond to this diversity of opportunity.

(Ibid para 8.29)

Community care services, then, are going to have to compete for scarce resources from budgets which both in the local authority sector and health care sector are under growing pressure from other legitimate demands. Such uncertainty that budgets will be adequate is hardly likely to lead to the collaboration between medical, nursing and social service agencies which the White Paper recognizes will be essential. Inevitably, there will be a temptation to draw the boundary both around local authority services and around the health services as tightly as possible.

Domiciliary care services, for example, have unresolved boundary disputes. While the boundary between the local authority home-help service and the social security system has been firmly drawn (although as discussed on p. 208 the Independent Living Fund adds another boundary), there are still unresolved issues in relation to the health service. Home helps are now often called home care assistants, which reflects a shift in their work from domestic to personal care, i.e. housework has been dropped from their job description. Increasingly, they are working with clients who in the past would have been in institutional care. (Whether or not that is the most cost-effective way of allocating their time is another question: their time might be better spent giving less help to larger numbers of families and enabling them to continue caring for a slightly less dependent relative.) It certainly raises questions concerning the relationship between the health service, in particular family practitioners and their ancillary workers,. and local authority social services departments. It also does not resolve the issue of charges, because it is still the case that community nursing services are free however wealthy the patient, while home helps are not. Griffiths argued, 'It seems right that those able to pay the full cost of community care services should be expected to do so' (Griffiths 1988: 18). If that is accepted, where does personal care end and medical care begin?

Yet another boundary dispute affects those, such as people with mental disabilities, who in the recent past would have been living in hospitals. There have been some innovative and exciting projects piloted in the Care in the Community programme which have been funded jointly by central DH and DHS funds (£19 million), NHS Resources, social services funds and imaginative use of social security benefits. The Audit Commission's Report (1986) highlighted some of the difficulties and anomalies. One of these involved determining how much 'care' is provided in assisted lodging and family placement schemes because after April 1989 only the *basic* board and lodging payment has been available to boarders to cover 'normal' living expenses. Before that, they could qualify for the higher residential care rate (although since 1987 people in homes with less than four residents have only done so if the carer employed experienced staff and provided day and night cover). The Minister of Social Security explained in 1988 that:

> Whilst we accept that placements of this type described . . . are a very good way of keeping or reintegrating dependent people within the community, it is not and never has been the role of supplementary benefits to meet the costs by providing intensive individual care, however high.
>
> (*Community Care*, 3 March 1988, p.8)

This extra care, in future, may be paid for by the Independent Living Fund, the social services departments or in the case of mentally ill people from an earmarked grant payable to the social services authorities via the regional health authorities.

Only in the case of services for those with a mental illness is it believed that proper collaboration and joint planning will be facilitated by a specific grant. This is because the White Paper explains: 'In the face of other calls on resources local authorities generally have not been able to give as much priority to providing services to those with a mental illness as other vulnerable groups' (DHSS 1989 para 7.14).

Meanwhile, whoever is responsible for assessing a person's 'need' for domiciliary or residential care will have to balance health against social factors. Also, how will the *preference* of that person and their family be taken into account, if at all? Local authority social services departments have already had experience of this of course, because, as mentioned, they do not accept anyone into one of their homes without making such an assessment. But how will financial considerations in future influence their decisions? With the growth of owner occupation (already 52 per cent of 60 to 69-year-old people and 46 per cent of those aged over 80 years are owner occupiers (CSO 1990: 138)), many elderly people will therefore have a valuable asset in the shape of their house, although how valuable will depend on the area in which they happen to live. The old person's family, as well as the local authority social services department and the Department of Social Security (DHSS) will have an interest in the resources tied up in that house. The *Economist* suggested in a recent article called 'Paying for granny':

> To encourage more of these children to care for their parents, governments could offer granny a deal: rely on your family for help, and you can bequeath your house almost tax-free; leave the job to us, and we will recoup the cost from your estate.
>
> (*Economist* 8 July 1988, p.16)

Griffiths, too, is in favour of using the equity in any property owned by an elderly person to pay for their care but are such 'deals' consistent with the attitude and expectations of elderly people and their families? If not, will their willingness to provide such care be adversely affected or not?

Informal care

Both Labour and Conservative governments have taken family care for granted. For example, in 1978, Mr. Callagham said: 'Caring families are the basis of a society that cares' and shortly after, Mrs Thatcher said: 'Not only is the family the most important means through which we show care for others, it is the place where each generation learns its responsibilities towards the rest of society.' Feminists over the past ten years have persistently pointed out that 'community care' means 'family care', which in turn means 'women care'. Politicians and policy makers are beginning to recognize this, but often only because they represent a cost-effective option. The Audit Commission calculated in 1985 that carers saved the government over £3,000 a year per elderly person cared for and therefore concluded that: 'Carers have needs and rights – since their work is important to the economy of the health and social services' (Audit Commission 1985: 43). However, recognizing their needs and rights would cost money and the problem for the government is, as the DHSS recognized in their review of research studies on community care services: 'The cost-effectiveness of these packages often depends on *not* putting a financial value on the contribution of the informal carer' (Tinker 1984, my emphasis). The unwillingness of the government to make *any* resources available to carers was demonstrated by the failure to include a premium for carers in the new Income Support system introduced in 1988 and defining the eligibility rules for the severe disability premium so that those with a carer receiving the Invalid Care Allowance are excluded. Under pressure, the government have agreed to introduce a new carers' premium from October 1990 (worth £10 a week).

The amount of care provided by the family has recently been documented in the General Household Survey. In a recent report, based on an analysis of the 18,500 adults living in private households included in the sample for the annual General Household Survey, it is estimated that one adult in seven are providing informal care and that one household in five contains a carer. Altogether, there are 6 million carers in Britain, 3.5 million women (15 per cent of adult women) and 2.5 million men (12 per cent of adult men). Four out of five were caring for a relative, one in five were caring for more than one person and nearly one in four were spending at least 20 hours a week. (This last figure is an underestimate of the time spent caring, for the survey *excluded* time spent 'on call' while sleeping.) Lewis and Meredith's study of daughters caring for mothers at home illustrates how wearing sleeping in can be for the carer (Lewis and Meredith 1988). Middle age (45 to 64 years) is the peak age for caring: nearly a quarter of all women of this age and 16 per cent of men were carers.

Interestingly, caring affected the employment status of men of working age far less than that of women. Of those in this age group providing at least 20 hours of care a week, 45 per cent of men were working full-time compared with 16 per cent of women. In contrast, only 3 per cent of men worked part-time compared with 25 per cent of women. These figures may explain why relatively few men claim the Invalid Care Allowance (which is restricted to those under retirement age). Men and women also differed in the amount of responsibility they carried – two-thirds of women and half of men carried the main responsibility for care; women were more likely than men to care for someone outside the household. Not surprisingly, the amount of care provided for someone outside the carer's household was less: three-quarters spent less than 20 hours. Conversely, 45 per cent of carers living in the same household spent more than 50 hours a week and among those aged over 65 years the proportion was even higher – 50 per cent. Men and women are just as likely to be looking after a spouse, but women are far more likely than men to be looking after a parent or child.

There is not the space to discuss all of the fascinating details in this report, but there are two very important findings of which health services should take notice. First is the amount of ill health reported among the *carers*, Among the 30 – 44-year-old carers giving at least 20 hours a week of care, a quarter had a limiting long-standing illness, nearly two-fifths a long-standing illness and a fifth reported that their health had not been good in the past 12 months. The proportions for the older people of working age were higher: over a third, nearly one half and just under a quarter, respectively. These proportions were similar to those aged 65 or over. Second, although the majority of those being cared for did *not* receive regular visits from voluntary or statutory agencies, the doctor and community nurse were the most frequently mentioned.

We are therefore becoming better informed about the volume of care provided by the informal carers and better informed about *who* is doing the caring. However, appropriate support will not be forthcoming unless the nature of caring is better understood and more highly valued. We also need to recognize that because care has been assumed to be women's work, that men faced with caring may need support of a different kind in some respects. Caring confirms a woman's gender but may be felt to undermine a man's. The person being cared for may need different support if the carer is a man, especially as for so many, care is taking place within a marriage relationship predicated on the reverse pattern of care.

But most important, whatever the gender of the carer, it must be recognized that caring involves more than a set of tasks. It involves a relationship which takes up more time than that needed to complete specific tasks. The daughter in the Lewis and Meredith study understood this very clearly, for example, when she said: 'Caring is not just washing and dressing them. It's time to talk to them, unpick their knitting that's gone wrong' (Lewis and Meredith 1988: 48). Moreover, the most 'efficient' way of meeting an old person's needs may not be the most satisfactory from their point of view or that of their carer. Anthea Tinker gives an example of this in her study of caring schemes for elderly people in which she reported that some wanted to keep coal fires. She comments: 'while it would be more sensible to replace coal with gas or electricity, carers did acknowledge that the regular popping in they had to do kept them in contact with the elderly person' (Tinker 1981: 122).

Such considerations also hold in the formal sector. Ursula Huws wrote recently, criticizing the emphasis on:

> the need for efficiency in services and the need for public services to learn from the private sector in this regard. It seems to me that this is the wrong way to approach the problem of developing services to meet the real needs of users.
>
> (Huws 1988)

All the studies that have been made of paid carers in the formal sector have emphasized that the amount of unofficial help they give should not be underestimated (Tinker 1984: 120, for example), but the search for efficiency and increasingly, profit, goes against that.

How then, do we ensure that caring is more highly valued? The answer clearly is not just to value carers and their time in money terms, although the Social Security system should ensure that poverty is not the price people pay for either needing care or providing it, as is too often the case today. Nearly twenty-five years ago, Richard Titmuss, recognizing that the rhetoric surrounding community care could so easily be used to mask real reductions in public expenditure, warned against 'pontificating about the philosophy of community care . . . but unless we are prepared to examine at this level of concrete reality what we mean by community care, we are simply indulging in wishful thinking (Titmuss 1968: 106). He was right: there is still a large agenda for politicians, policy makers, administrators and researchers.

Part of this chapter draws on 'Social security and community care: perverse incentives' in S. Baldwin, C. Glendinning and R. Walker (eds) (1988) *Social Security and Community Care*, Aldershot: Gower.

Acknowledgement

I would like to thank my discussant, Gillian Dalley, and the editors for their comments on an earlier version of this chapter.

References

Audit Commission (1985) *Managing Social Services for the Elderly More Effectively*, London: HMSO.
——(1986) *Making a Reality of Community Care*, London: HMSO.
Baldwin, S., Glendinning, C. and Walker, R. (eds) *Social Security and Community Care*, Aldershot: Gower.

CSO (1990) *Social Trends* 20: 138.

Dexter, M. and Harbart, W. (1983) *The Home Help Service*, London: Tavistock.

DHSS (Department of Health and Social Security) (1981) *Growing Older*, London: HMSO, Cmnd 8173.

Department of Health/Department of Social Security, Wales and Scotland (1989) *Caring for People – Community Care in the Next Decade and Beyond*, London: HMSO Cm 849.

Donnison, D. and Chapman, V. (1965) 'The first ten years of a home help service', in *Social Policy and Administration*, London: Allen & Unwin.

Finch, J. and Groves, D. (1985) 'Community care a case for equal opportunities?' in G. Ungerson (ed.) *Women and Social Policy*, London: Macmillan.

Griffiths, Sir R. (1988) *Community Care: Agenda for Action*, London: HMSO.

Huw, U. (1988) 'Consuming passions', *New Society*, 19 August.

Lewis, J. and Meredith, M. (1988) *Daughters Who Care*, London: Routledge.

Parker, R.A. (1988) *The Elderly and Residential Care, Some Australian Lessons*, Aldershot: Gower.

Royal Commission on the Law Relating to Mental Illness and Mental Deficiency (1957) *Report*, London: HMSO, Cmnd 169.

Tinker, A. (1984) *Staying at Home, Helping Elderly People*, London: HMSO.

Titmuss, R. (1968) 'Community care: fact or fiction', in *Commitment to Welfare*, London: Allen & Unwin.

Townsend, P. (1962) *The Last Refuge*, London: Routledge & Kegan Paul.

Chapter nine

The agenda for sociological health-policy research for the 1990s

Margot Jefferys

Previous Chapters in this volume have considered the contribution which sociological analysis, in one or other form, made to understanding various aspects of the National Health Service and British health policy issues more generally during the 1980s. *Pace* Bryan Turner (1989), it is an impressive record of intellectual achievement which reflects the growing confidence of those who have helped to develop a specialized branch of the main discipline of sociology. Furthermore, as Stacey argues in Chapter 1 of this volume, its applied value for health service practice is acknowledged in the requirement that more than a nodding acquaintance with the sociology of health and healing is now a part of the essential educational preparation of most health-care professionals, including medical practitioners.[1]

What now needs to be considered is the future. In this Chapter, I propose first to outline briefly the main changes likely to occur in the British National Health Service during the 1990s. I then consider the probable agenda for health policy research which will be set by the Department of Health, and the role which sociologists of health and health policy can expect to play in the official research programme. In doing so, I suggest that unless sociologists are willing to participate in multidisciplinary research institutions, often initially in subordinate positions and on problems not of their own choosing, they will not have the opportunity to contribute to a greater understanding of the processes and structures of health care. I finish with some comments on the independent part which sociological theorists can play in more fundamental health-care research.

To give adequate treatment in this Chapter to all the issues I have designated as likely to be of significance in the development of health services in the 1990s is clearly impossible. Moreover, there will undoubtedly be many matters of great sociological importance in relation to health, illness and suffering, which merit research by sociologists but which I have not mentioned specifically. This Chapter, therefore, must not be regarded as setting out a definitive framework for the work of

222

medical sociologists. That work clearly can and should legitimately encompass many issues relevant to health other than those maintained here. In view of the nature of this book, I have concentrated on those which involve political actions and collectivities rather than clinical practices and individuals.

The National Health Service of the future

Previous chapters have traced briefly the evolution of the NHS since its inception in the immediate post-Second World War years, and analysed in greater detail the health policy issues during the Conservative Party's first two terms of office from 1979 to 1987. Given that that party's explicit policy was to reduce public-sector enterprise and expenditure by various means, including privatization, the departures from the consensus policies on health matters of previous Labour and Conservative governments were low-key rather than spectacular. Rectifying other aspects of the economy were given greater government priority, and radical NHS reform was put on the back burner.

Early on in the 1980s, an administrative tier (the area health authority) was abolished; the legislative reins which had held the physical development of private medical facilities in check were relaxed; management structures at hospital and district health authority levels were simplified; managers were given more decision-making power and encouraged to buy hospital domestic and hotel maintenance services from private firms providing low tenders; general practitioners' freedom to prescribe was slightly restricted with the introduction of the limited list of approved drugs.

None of these measures was seen by those with vested interests in any part of the NHS to be serious enough in themselves to threaten the underlying and nearly universal belief that, whatever the deficiencies in the operation of the NHS or its failure to meet overt and escalating demand, the system devised in the aftermath of the Second World War on a wave of popular emotion was basically as sound if not sounder than any viable alternative. The government was still popularly credited with being true to its repeated election pledges that the 'NHS is safe in our hands'. Exchequer expenditure on the NHS has been increased steadily, at least in line with general inflation, if not in line with medical-care costs.

Nevertheless, according to most health professionals, the extra moneys were insufficient to meet the additional pressures generated by the increases in both the relative numbers of very elderly people and the technical capacity successfully to treat the previously untreatable. In the eyes of health service workers, as well as in those of the Labour Party Opposition in Parliament, what was chiefly required to remedy defects

223

was massive new investment and greater expenditure – at least to bring it nearer to the level attained by nearly all equally developed industrial countries.

The Conservative Party's Manifesto for the 1987 general election, which gave them an even greater parliamentary majority and a third term of office, set out no specific plans for the future of the NHS. In a few months of its victory, however, the government was confronted with a demand from nurses for a substantial increase in salaries – an increase for which the government had not budgeted. The demand was received by the public with great sympathy. So much so, that the government found it expedient to yield to some extent to the pressure. At the same time, it parried the growing dissatisfaction with the services from both health workers and the public, by promising a fundamental review to be followed by proposals for internal health service reform. These latter, it claimed, would improve the quality of the NHS while maintaining or increasing its capacity to deal with the growing volume of demand. Unlike earlier reviews of the NHS, which had involved consultation with most of the interested bodies representing the professions and health and local government authorities, the government conducted its own review, aided simply by its Conservative Party advisers.

At about the same time, the government had invited Sir Roy Griffiths, who had earlier advised it on the management structure of NHS authorities, to review arrangements for the community care of frail elderly, mentally and physically disabled people. Responsibility for the welfare of such people was divided, by no means clearly or unambiguously, among a number of agencies, including the hospital and community services of the NHS, the social services and housing departments of local authorities, housing associations, voluntary organizations, and private-sector housing. Costs were escalating as increasing numbers of elderly people were surviving into extreme old age and as perceptions of what should be the minimum tolerable standards of care for those of them who became greatly dependent on others rose. An increasing proportion of the costs of meeting dependency needs fell on central government's social security budget. In assigning Sir Roy Griffiths to the task of investigating the problem and making proposals, the government undoubtedly considered that much of the cost escalation was due to administrative muddle and inefficiency, which could be eliminated by better management.

In the event, Griffiths (DHSS 1988) reported nearly a year before the government revealed its own proposals for the acute sector of the NHS; his recommendations, for the future development of community care, were not to the government's taste. They were to give the responsibility for care management to the local authorities, with many of whom the government had been fighting running battles and whose resources and authority it had little by little reduced. It was not until mid-1989, and after publication of its own White Paper on the NHS, that Griffiths' main proposals for community care were reluctantly accepted and embodied in a White Paper (DH 1989a).

Perhaps predictably, the government's own proposals for the future of the NHS (DH 1989b), and its accompanying proposals for a new contract for general practitioners, were met by a storm of indignation and rejection from all the bodies representing doctors and other health service workers. Dismay was also expressed by the lay appointed bodies responsible for the administration of the NHS – the regional and district health authorities – and even by many of the salaried NHS managers, whose power was likely to be enhanced by the proposals.

Despite the unpopularity of the proposals, the government embodied them as well as its proposals for community care in a bill (the NHS and Community Care Bill) which has been enacted and will provide the basis for the NHS's structure and *modus operandi* during the last decade of the twentieth century. A new General Practitioner Contract has already been imposed and is fully operational from April 1990 (DH 1989c).

How far do these government policies for the future mark a departure from the structural provisions for health care which have evolved without major changes since the inception of the NHS in 1948?

The answer is quite a lot, although perhaps not as much as Margaret Thatcher's particular brand of conservatism would have liked to see. Mrs Thatcher is an unashamed ideologue. She believes that the free play of market forces is both the most effective and the most efficient means of securing national prosperity, including its health. For a while, indeed, she and a former Secretary of State for Health, John Moore, habitually referred to the NHS as the health industry and not the health service. However, she is also a pragmatist. Having discovered that it would be expensive as well as unpopular to provide the finance for health services for the population as a whole through a voluntary or compulsory health insurance scheme, she decided to continue to fund the NHS from general taxation, and to make its primary and specialist care services available to all mainly without payment. To this extent, the British health service continues to differ from those of almost every other western capitalist country.

At the same time, conservative thought has it that any state monopoly – and the NHS is held to be one – is likely to be inherently inefficient in the management of its resources because its managers and professionals have none of the usual private business incentives needed to promote efficiency. In particular, they are not subjected to competition nor rewarded for improving their performance. Since it is politically inexpedient to disband the NHS, therefore, steps have to be taken to introduce elements of free enterprise into it, that is, to create an 'internal market' within it. Steps to achieve this at both hospital and community level are to be accompanied by measures which the state, as purchaser of services on behalf of all its citizens, can make to ensure that those with whom it makes contracts reach and maintain acceptable standards of performance.

Before considering what research issues will confront sociologists of medicine and health care as a result of the government's proposals, I will give a bare outline of the proposed changes in hospital, general practice and community-health management structures and procedures. I do not propose to deal in this paper with the criticisms which have been levied against them.

Hospitals

From 1991, some hospitals will be able to acquire 'Hospital Trust' status. Those which do will have a much greater degree of self-government and of freedom from the district health authority than hospital units at present possess. They will be able to plan what services to provide and to sell them to purchasers of health care who will include not only health authorities but general practitioners who are budget holders (see below) and private medical-care entrepreneurs. Efficient hospitals, which provide what such customers want (so the theory goes), will increase their revenue and be able to attract more high-powered managerial and professional staff and reward them accordingly. Less efficient hospitals will have an incentive to improve their services or risk going out of business. Some provisions, we are assured, will be embodied in the regulations to ensure that hospital trusts take a proportion of the high-cost patients requiring prolonged and/or intensive care, who might otherwise be rejected by them as economically unrewarding care recipients.

General practice

The major innovatory proposal here is that general practitioners with 11,000 or more patients registered with their group practice will be able, if they wish, to become budget holders. Their budget allocation will depend on the size and demographic composition of their patient list. The budget will cover, not only the expenses which, as independent contractors they incur in providing primary care services for their patients, but also the specialist care which they deem necessary to obtain for these patients. They will be able and expected to shop around for such care in order to achieve the best buy from hospitals or other specialist centres. Their budget will include a notional or indicative allowance for drugs.

At the same time, all general practitioners who wish to provide services under the NHS will be subject to a new contract which involves them in a range of duties which are specified for the first time. For example, they will have to inform their patients and the family practitioner committee which holds their contract when they will be available for consultation; they must provide the FPC with an annual report and practice-development proposals; to obtain the maximum financial reward, they must achieve a certain level of immunization among their pre-school age patients, and must visit annually all patients aged 75 or over. A greater proportion of their income will come from per capita payments for patients registered with them, so providing an incentive for them to attract more patients. Patients will find it easier to change doctors under the new regulations; but doctors will retain the right to refuse patients who wish to register with them.

Community care

From 1991, local authority social services departments will be given a budget from which they must purchase the personal social service care required by all elderly, mentally or physically disabled people in need of long-term personal support.[2] These departments will be responsible for appointing a care manager for every such individual. After consultation with the individual, his/her informal carer(s) and professional adviser(s), the care manager will devise a plan and arrange for its implementation. The individual's position will be reassessed at intervals and services adapted to changing circumstances as necessary – or so the theory goes.

Care managers will be expected to secure the most suitable packages of care for individuals at the least cost. The inadequately tested assumption is that the most satisfactory solutions from both cost and quality-of-life viewpoints for most individuals are likely to be continued domiciliary care in their own home or that of a relative. Care services of all kinds will be able to be purchased from the voluntary and/or private sector as well as being provided directly by the local authority. Indeed, the local authority is likely to be discouraged from providing its own residential accommodation, because central government will not pay local authority housing costs, whereas it will make a substantial contribution to such costs if an individual is admitted to a private profit or a voluntary sector home.

Sociological research issues in health: the 'clients' priorities

It is in the nature of the research enterprise today that the piper's paymaster calls the tune. Of course, ever since social science research was officially recognized as a useful preliminary to policy formulation by government and significantly supported financially – I date this as a mid-1960s phenomenon – the central government agency responsible for health services has formulated its own research requirements and assigned them certain levels of priority. However, until the early 1980s, tacit acceptance of the principles which Lord Rothschild (1971) had suggested should govern the relationships between government departments, in the role of clients, and research workers, in the role of contractors, still allowed health care researchers some latitude and, more important, some resources to initiate and pursue issues which they considered researchable.

Little by little since then, opportunities for social scientists to obtain funding to undertake research on matters which they see as sociologically relevant have been eroded. The major 'client' for health-care research – the Department of Health – has set its research priorities more rigidly on short-, rather than intermediate- or long-term policy issues.[3] The Department no longer sets aside funds to finance small-scale, non-priority projects for which researchers used to be able to apply. Theoretically, the Medical Research Council performs the function of supporting research on longer term health policy issues with money allocated to it from the Department's funding; but its record suggests that it has been largely indifferent, if not hostile, to research which does not conform to a strict, epidemiological, positivist formula.

The Economic and Social Research Council (ESRC),[4] which is charged with financing more fundamental disciplinary research, has also been compelled to take more account of officially voiced policy needs in the decisions it takes on specific research proposals. Furthermore, in order to secure its own survival, it has decided to pursue a more proactive policy, that is, to set out its own research agenda and seek out suitable contractors for it, rather than depend reactively on judging and financing projects submitted to it spontaneously by investigators.

Given what we know of the government's plans for health and community care, as well as its ideological stance, it is possible to forecast with some confidence the kind of research which the Department of Health will want from social scientists as long as the Conservatives are in power. If they want to have continuing remunerative employment in this field, sociologists will be put under pressure to participate in research bearing directly on resource and patient management. This much is clear from the paper giving the Department of Health's (1989d) response to a House of Lords Select Committee's Report on Science and Technology.

I foresee favoured projects relating to five, overlapping, interconnected themes, as follows:

1. Audit and outcome measures.
2. 'Consumer' preference and/or choice.
3. Opportunity and social costs involved in policy and practice options.
4. Health care implications of increasing numbers of survivors into extreme old age.
5. Health care implications of the prevalence of AIDS and HIV-positive status.

There is no doubt in my mind that sociology is a discipline whose proponents have potentially a legitimate and valuable contribution to make to knowledge on issues subsumed under all five headings. A sociological perspective, for example, is particularly important in identifying the meanings which participants in health-care organizations (whether as planners, practitioners or patients, potential and actual) attach to the behaviour of others, which in turn act as a guide to their own. It is equally important in identifying latent values which help to determine reactions to policies as well as the tensions and ripple effects occasioned by change in actual and perceived circumstances. Sociologists, because they have developed an impressive body of knowledge about the structural relationships in which individuals are embedded, are also likely to make more penetrating analyses of institutions and individuals in the process of change than are exponents of other social science disciplines with narrower foci.

The clients for resource and patient management research, however, are not likely, in framing their research agenda, to consider the specifically sociological. Indeed, there will be contenders from other social science and allied disciplines for scarce research contracts, and it is likely that sociologists will only be able to make a contribution if they ally themselves with epidemiologists, statisticians, health economists, geographers, social psychologists and business-study analysts, all of whom can claim some expertise and a unique perspective on the research issues. The Department of Health's (1989d) paper on *Priorities in Medical Research* places more emphasis on epidemiology as a guide to management decision-making than on any other discipline.

Multi- or inter-disciplinary research is not a prospect which is generally welcomed by sociologists. Past experience has taught some of those who have tried it that the maintenance of any specifically sociological perspective is often impossible. Genuine dialogue on an equal footing between scientists drawn from different disciplines rarely exists in situations where one occupational group – in this case, the medically qualified practitioner – dominates.

Nevertheless, if we are to be realistic, the continuation of any serious health policy research undertaken from a sociological perspective may only be feasible in institutional settings dominated by health service managers, medical practitioners or proponents of other disciplines, for example, health economics. Rather than waste time resenting this situation, I believe that sociologists should accept it and use their energies in trying to ensure that their own contribution makes a significant impact on the research undertaken, even if it cannot permeate it to any great extent.

I would argue, moreover, that this kind of response does not amount to betrayal, nor deserve the calumny which may be heaped upon it from those purist defenders of the sociological faith who deplore any tinge of eclecticism. The grounds for so arguing are to be found in the previous chapters in this volume. They seem to me to provide a vindication for the softly–softly approach to health policy research on the part of sociologists of health and healing which I am advocating.

In the first place, it should be noted that most of them have been written by authors working from multidisciplinary institutional settings. In the second place, they are informed by acquaintance with other disciplines besides sociology. And third, it is perhaps significant that several of the authors are post-graduate converts to medical sociology from other social science disciplines. In short, in my view, the chapters demonstrate the considerable pay-off for the sociological enterprise itself which can be obtained from work in multidisciplinary settings. They are by no means devoid of contributions to sociological theory as well as illustrating its use to applied issues.

An unauthorized sociological research agenda

Nothing in the previous paragraphs should be taken to imply, however, that I am not in favour of health policy research which deals with the major concerns of classic sociological theory and is fed primarily by a lively sociological imagination. On the contrary, I feel that there is an urgent need to undertake such research. It should run parallel to that which the Department of Health is likely to promote, feeding from it but asking a different set of questions from the data generated. Research of this kind does not necessarily call for substantial funding. The ESRC, currently headed by a sociologist, is a possible funder. Unquestionably, such research could benefit from inputs on the part of main-stream theoreticians, who, with a few notable exceptions, have hitherto tended to neglect the sociological significance of health and health care institutions.

Sociology, at its most profound level, is concerned with the determinants of social structures and social processes, and with the causes of change in them, whether great or small. It is also concerned with the consequences of secular turbulence for social institutions and social behaviour. If I am right, the changes now in progress in the National Health Service are not merely cosmetic or historically trivial. They are the outcome, at least in part, of more fundamental changes in the nature of the capitalist system in Britain, themselves occasioned by its destabilization in the network of world economies.

At the same time, the health status and demographic characteristics of nation states have gradually acquired greater socio-economic salience, and therefore forced themselves onto the political agenda. Up for renegotiation at the societal level, therefore, are such fundamental issues as the nature of the contract between the individual and the state, between the doctors and the state and between the doctors and their patients.

What is required is a sociological appraisal of the historical development of the interrelationships between the organs of state authority and the providers and utilizers of health care. Only against such a background can contemporary events and trends be seen in their proper perspective.

Notes

1. Stacey (1988) *The Sociology of Health and Healing*, makes out a powerful case for renaming medical sociology 'the sociology of health and healing'.
2. In July 1990 the Government announced a postponement of the full implementation of the provisions of the 1990 Act.
3. In 1988, the Department of Health and Social Security was split to form two departments, the Department of Health and the Department of Social Security.
4. The erstwhile Social Science Research Council.

References

DH (Department of Health) (1989a) *Caring for People*, London: HMSO.
—— (1989b) *Working for Patients: the Health Service Caring for the 1990s*, London: HMSO.
—— (1989c) *General Practice Contract*, London: HMSO.
—— (1989d) *Priorities in Medical Research*, London: HMSO, Cm 902.
DHSS (Department of Health and Social Security) (1988) Community Care: Agenda for Action, a Report by Sir Roy Griffiths, London: HMSO.

Rothschild, Lord (1971) *Report on the Organisation and Management of Government Research and Development*, London: HMSO, Cmnd 4814.
Stacey, M. (1988) *The Sociology of Health and Healing*, London: Unwin Hyman.
Turner, B.S. (1989) 'The body in sociology', *Medical Sociology News* 15 (1): 9–16.

Name index

Subject index